Exploring History 1

for Bilingual Classes

Moderated by
Dr. Christa Lohmann

Written by
Rolf J. Kröger
Dr. Deanna Nebert
Barbara Nerlich
Thomas Söhrnsen

westermann

Eine kommentierte Linkliste befindet sich unter:
www.westermann.de/geschichte-linkliste

Westermann Schroedel Diesterweg Schöningh Winklers GmbH, Braunschweig
www.westermann.de

Druck A^3 / Jahr 2010
Alle Drucke der Serie A sind im Unterricht parallel verwendbar.

Redaktion: Christoph Meyer, Dorle Bennöhr
Herstellung: Udo Sauter
Typografie: Thomas Schröder
Satz: pva, Druck und Medien-Dienstleistungen GmbH, Landau
Druck und Bindung: westermann druck GmbH, Braunschweig

ISBN 978-3-14-**111048**-7

1. Absolutism and Enlightenment 6

Louis XIV 8
The Three Estates 10
Mercantilism 12
Louis's Wars 14
History Workshop: Analysing Paintings 16
Revolution in England / The Bill of Rights 18
The Age of Enlightenment 20

2. The American Revolution 22

A New Beginning in a Foreign Land 24
The Road to Independence 26
The USA – A New State 28
History Workshop: Analysing Maps 30
All Men are Created Equal – Indians 32
All Men are Created Equal – Blacks and Women 34

3. The French Revolution 36

The Outbreak of the Revolution 38
The Rights of Men and Women 40
France Becomes a Republic 42
The Reign of Terror 44
History Workshop: Analysing Sources 46
Napoleon 48
The Revolution and Europe 50
The Wars of Liberation 52

4. Industrialization 54

The Industrial Revolution 56
Driving Force – Textile Industry 60
Industrialization in Germany 62
The Take-off Period 66
History Workshop: Analysing Statistics 70
Living Conditions 72
Attempts to Solve Social Problems 74
Church and Government React 76

5. The Struggle for Unity and Liberty 78

The Congress of Vienna 1815 80
European Unrest 1815–1848 82
Examples of Unrest in Germany 1815–1847 84
The Revolution of 1848 86
Problems of the National Assembly 88
History Workshop: Analysing Cartoons 90
The End of the 1848 Revolution 92

6. Imperial Germany 94

Prussia – Leading Power 96
The Road to German Unity 98
The Franco-Prussian War 1870–1871 100
Politics in the New Germany 102
Domestic Problems in the New Germany 104
Social Structure in the New Germany 106
Liberty – for Women, Too? 108
Principles of Bismarck's Alliance System 110
History Workshop: Analysing Historical Monuments 112

7. New Imperialism and the Scramble for Africa 114

The "New Imperialism" 116
Europeans in Africa 118
German Rule in Southwest Africa 120
International Tensions 122
The Effects of Imperialism 124
History Workshop: Research on the Internet 126

8. The First World War 128

The Road to War 130
The Modern War Begins 132
The War at Home 136
Towards Allied Victory – The USA Enters the War 138
The End of the War 140

Glossary 142

Vocabulary 145

Index 149

Picture Credits 152

Absolutism and Enlightenment

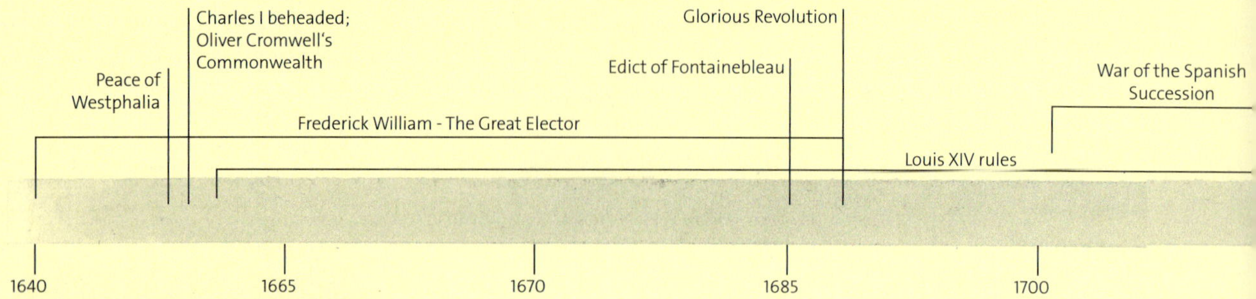

Louis XIV
Painting by Hyacinthe Rigaud,
about 1700

The Demasking
Caricature by W.Thackeray, about 1840

The Palace of Versailles
Painting by Pierre-Denis Martin, 1722

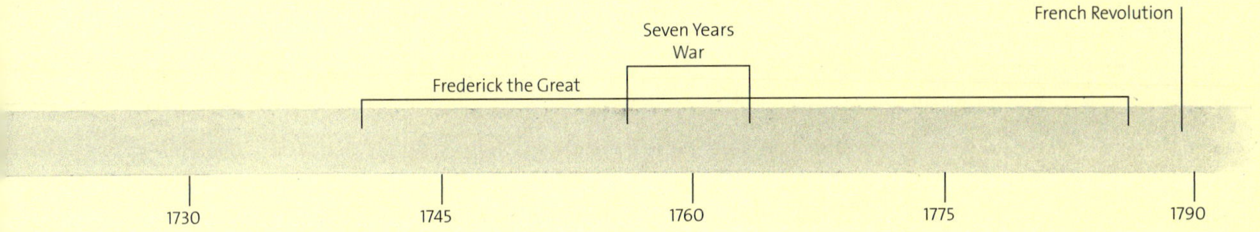

The Execution of King Charles I in 1649
Copper etching from 1649

Frederick II – The Fluteplayer
Painting by Adolph von Menzel, 1852

M 1 Le "Roi Soleil"

M 2 Lettre de Cachet

Louis XIV sold arrest warrants which meant imprisonment for people. Some were even sold blank:

"On request of the closest relatives of Jean-Philippe de Villeneuve des Languedoc We have given orders to take him to the island of Sainte-Marguerite in order to prevent any embarrassing consequences of his loose conduct from taking place. We are writing you this letter to inform you that it is Our will that he may be put there until further notice. Food and expenses will be taken care of by the family."

Renaissance-Glaubenskämpfe-Absolutismus, edited by Franz Dickmann, München 1982, p. 441,transl. and edited by RJK.

to succumb: to submit, to surrender
benediction of God: blessing, approval of God
interest: money you have to pay when you have borrowed money

Louis XIV

More Power to the King

As a consequence of the horrors and the unrest of the wars of religion many thought the monarch had to be more powerful. In France this development had begun when Francis I had successfully strengthened his position at the expense of the nobility and the clergy. At the end of the 16th century Henry IV brought peace to France with the Edict of Nantes, which gave the Protestants (the "Huguenots") security and relative religious freedom after a long time of being persecuted. Because of financial problems Louis XIII had to call the Estates-General in 1614, for the last time before the great revolution and to hardly any result. His new Prime Minister, Cardinal Richelieu, whose motto was "the end justifies the means", proved to be more successful. His successor Cardinal Mazarin, Prime Minister since 1642, educated the new king, Louis XIV, and put down rebellions started by different groups of society. After he had crushed the "Fronde", an aristocratic uprising against further centralization of government, there was nobody to stop him from forming the new type of state.

Louis XIV

When Mazarin died in 1661 Louis XIV took over himself. His idea of government did not allow for people to speak out against him, so he crushed all kinds of opposition. Even the parliaments, which had been important strongholds of aristocratic power, had to *succumb* to the king's will.

A new system of administration was introduced, in which the noble governors of the provinces lost nearly all their power to the new "intendants", who were responsible for executing the orders of the king directly. This system resulted in a standardization of the laws, the police and the civil service. The "intendants" belonged to the Third Estate; they were all appointed by the king for a certain time, so that they were entirely dependent on him and supported him without reservation – just like the rich merchants and landowners who bought aristocratic titles from the king.

But Louis did not want to change the French society in general, he just wanted to be in control of it. So he invited the high nobility to live at his court, giving them profitable jobs and high-sounding titles in order to neutralize them politically.

Above all he was certain that he had the *benediction* of God and that he symbolized the nation. Any private person was only an individual facing his king.

Financial Difficulties

But all these measures did not solve Louis's financial problems. The king had to borrow money from the rich, who in return were given privileges and monopolies apart from the high *interest* rates they charged. Even worse was the fact that he offered people the chance to buy their way into office. He rented out the collection of customs and taxes. He even leased the state's income from agricultural activities, markets, and mining. Rich people could buy "lettres de cachet", blank arrest warrants from the king which the owner of the document could fill in himself.

With the help of his minister Colbert he also set up an economic system designed to raise more money for the state.

M 3 Louis's Lever

Louis XIV's bedroom was the central room in the palace of Versailles. Saint-Simon, a nobleman who lived at the court, wrote a report about his getting up at eight o'clock sharp, which was enacted like a ceremonial:

"He was woken up by his valet de chambre, who had slept in the bedchamber. The chief physician, the chief surgeon and Louis's childhood nurse all entered the room at the same time. The nurse kissed him and the night chamberpot was removed. At a quarter past eight the grande entrée began. The privilege to be a part of it was restricted to nobles and could be bought. The king stayed in bed in his nightshirt. The Grand Chamberlain of France presented holy water to the king and his morning clothes were laid out. Then the Master of the Bedchamber and the First Servant, both high nobles, pulled the king's nightshirt over his head. The Grand Chamberlain presented the day shirt, which was changed only sometimes. At this stage the nobles could try to have a brief private word with the king, which they would have rehearsed beforehand. Then they withdrew and the king held a short private prayer. Then the première entrée began, which included persons of lesser privilege. They watched the king getting dressed and getting shaved. He was given a dressing gown and a mirror was held for him while he dressed underneath the gown. Other privileged courtiers entered while the king was putting on his stockings and his shoes. During this entrée de la chambre the king's readers and his director of festivities also entered. The fourth group to arrive in the king's bedroom were his ministers and secretaries, who were allowed in at the entrée du chambre. A fifth entrée admitted ladies for the first time, and a sixth entrée admitted the king's children, legitimate and illegitimate, who entered through a special backdoor."

Adapted by RJK from: wikipedia|org

M 4 Louis's Memoirs

In his memoirs Louis XIV revealed his motives:

"As my emblem I have chosen the sun, which according to the rules of *heraldry* is the noblest sign. It is without any doubt the liveliest and the most beautiful emblem of a great prince, because it is *entirely unique*, because of the light it gives to the other stars, which almost form its court, because of the fair distribution of its light to all the different parts of the sky, because of the many favours it does everywhere, because of the life, the joy and the activity it arouses, because of its *perpetual* motion and its radiation of a sense of calm at the same time, because of its constant and unchangeable way.
God, who has set the kings over their subjects, wanted them to be acknowledged as his representatives. He has reserved the right to himself to judge on them. It is his will that those who have been born as subjects, have to totally submit."

L. Steinfeld, Basel, Leipzig 1931, S. 187 und 271, translated by RJK.

heraldry: the study of the coats of arms and of old families
entirely: totally, completely
unique: there is only one of it
perpetual: never-ending

Tasks

1. Describe the problems France had before Louis XIV took over government.
2. Analyse what Louis's way of starting the day says about him and his view of himself (M3).
3. Explain how Louis defined his role in society and what he thought a good king should do (M4).

The Three Estates

A New Type of Administration

Unlike his father Louis XIV did not call the Estates-General even once. He denied them any right to political participation. They consisted of the clergy, the nobility and the Third Estate and had originally had the right to approve taxes and to tell the king about any social injustice in the country. But as Louis saw himself as God's right hand on earth he was not *answerable* to anybody. He did not even have to obey the laws he made himself, he had only to follow divine laws. But would anybody have objected if he had broken them? So in effect he had unlimited power.

By centralizing and standardizing public administration he took power away from the nobles and gave it to well-trained and loyal civil servants. The old provinces were replaced by newly cut districts, for which Louis selected administration specialists, who were not from the area and did not belong to the nobility, but owed their careers to the king. To get even more control he transferred them to other districts from time to time. Nevertheless, the old order of the three estates still existed.

to be answerable to: to be responsible for
to befit sth.: to be suitable for sth.
alms: charity, gifts
to feel obliged: to think sth. is necessary or must be done

The Clergy

Being the protector of the Roman Catholic Church, Louis followed the principle of one king, one law, one belief ("un Roi, une loi, une foi"). So from 1680 onwards the persecution of the Protestants (the Huguenots) set in again. After he cancelled the Edict of Nantes nearly 300,000 of them left France, which caused a major loss to the French economy.

M 1 **People in the City.** Market day in Paris. Painting, 17th century

The clergy took over parts of the administration for the state with their church register. They hardly had to pay taxes, although a voluntary contribution was welcome. Every five years an elected delegation discussed issues of the Catholic Church with the king. It consisted of the high clergy appointed by the king and the low clergy, whose members were mostly poor and also badly trained for the job. Together less than 1 per cent of the people belonged to the clergy.

M 2 **The Three Estates**

Doves and rabbits the farmer wasn't allowed to hunt eat the harvest. On the sabre it says "red from blood", on the stick "drained in tears". Caricature, 1789

The Nobility

The members of the Second Estate (2 per cent) had either inherited their titles, were appointed by the king or had received a title because of a special job they had done. They hardly had to pay taxes, either. Their income came from the land they owned. Taking part in business and trade were not regarded as *befitting* their status. They could not take any of the well-paid jobs in administration because they had no legal training. The high nobility lost a lot of influence but tried to compensate by living at the royal court at Versailles. The low nobility was dependent on the development of the economy and on the harvests. Even though their financial situation was difficult at times, they kept their privileges.

The Third Estate

Banker or farmhand – whoever did not belong to the first two estates belonged to the third, which represented 97 per cent of the population. So there were huge differences between the individual members of this group. Most of them lived in the country and depended on agriculture. But only the rich farmers could earn a living easily. For most farmers life was hard because of taxes, duties, the hunting and fishing rights of the noblemen, and the various wars.

M 3 Memorandum to Louis XIV, 1698

Louis's architect and builder of his fortresses, Vauban, wrote in a memorandum to his king in 1698:

"I have come to the conclusion that almost a tenth of the people have become beggars in recent years. Of the remaining nine out of ten, five are not able to support them by *alms* because they have only just been lucky enough to escape their fate. Three of the remaining four are rather poor and there is only one out of ten that I count as well off to rich. Fewer than 100,000 families in France belong to this group. However, it is the other part of the population that make king and country rich through hard work, trade and taxes. They are the most important part of the population, but they have never been regarded as such.
I *feel obliged* to inform His Majesty about this. These people carry all the burden; they have suffered in the past and they suffer even as I write."

Adapted from: Lautemann / Schlenke, Geschichte in Quellen, Vol. 3, p. 462, translated and edited by RJK.

Tasks

1. Explain the structure of French society and find out what the chances of upward mobility were.
2. Describe the activities that can be seen in the painting (M1).
3. Work out the changes in society during Louis XIV's time.
4. Talk about the situation of the poor people (M3).

M 1 **Jean Baptiste Colbert (1619-1683)** served his king faithfully for 22 years. Everybody at the court treated him with respect although he wasn't a nobleman. Their "sweet life" depended on the success of his system of mercantilism.

intervention: getting involved in order to help
blueprint: draft, model
subsidies: money the state gives people for investment

Mercantilism

In Need of Money

In the middle of the 17th century about twenty million people lived in France, 90 per cent of whom led a miserable life full of hard work. On the other hand there was the court of Versailles, which was a symbol of luxury and thoughtless spending of money.

When Louis XIV took over the government in 1661, the state income of the following three years had already been spent. So something had to be done. Louis's minister of finance, Jean Colbert, developed an economic system for France which was not really new. The Dutch and the English had been using it for quite some time. But because Colbert wrote many articles about the system of mercantilism which gave a boost to the French economy, he is regarded as its inventor.

State *Intervention*

The king needed more money for his army, his luxurious lifestyle, his palaces, his civil servants and his wars. Taxes could not be raised as most of the people already had major problems paying them. Colbert supported the new factories financially and freed them from taxes, so that they produced goods more cheaply. Besides, work was completely reorganized – split up, so that workers became specialists. The goods were sold abroad in order to get more money into France. Colbert's aim was a positive balance of trade, which he achieved by the following measures:

- most raw material for the production of goods came from the French colonies where it was cheap
- export of raw material was forbidden or made extremely expensive
- high customs duties were put on imported goods
- transport in France was improved and became cheaper
- units of measure and weight were standardized
- rich Frenchmen were "persuaded" to invest in the new factories.

M 2 **The Production of Playing Cards in a Factory**
Painting, 17th century

Winners and Losers

Colbert's system worked quite well and production increased. Trading boomed and merchants earned a lot. A part of the profit, especially the money the state had invested and some consumption taxes, had to be returned. But the owners of small workshops did not benefit from the system. They suffered from the competition of the factories and went bankrupt. Also, many farmers became poorer, because they had to sell their produce at fixed low prices. As Louis XIV did not care about the state of his finances the country lost out as well. When he died in 1715 he left behind a country that was regarded as the *blueprint* of a successful state by many other leaders in Europe. But behind the façade it stood on the brink of financial collapse.

M 3 Memorandum

In 1664 Jean Baptiste Colbert wrote the following memorandum:

"If we had factories in France then we would not have to buy goods from Holland for our own use – but we would produce enough goods ourselves to have some left over for our own export, which would in turn give us more money. This alone is the only goal of trade. An annual sum should be spent each year for the founding of factories and improvement of trade. In addition *subsidies* should be paid to everyone who buys or builds ships. The country roads should be improved, new bridges should be built, the customs barriers on the rivers removed, […] the rivers should be made navigable and the idea of a canal should be considered carefully."

J. B. Colbert, Lettres II, Paris 1863, p. 226f., adapted and translated by RJK.

M 4

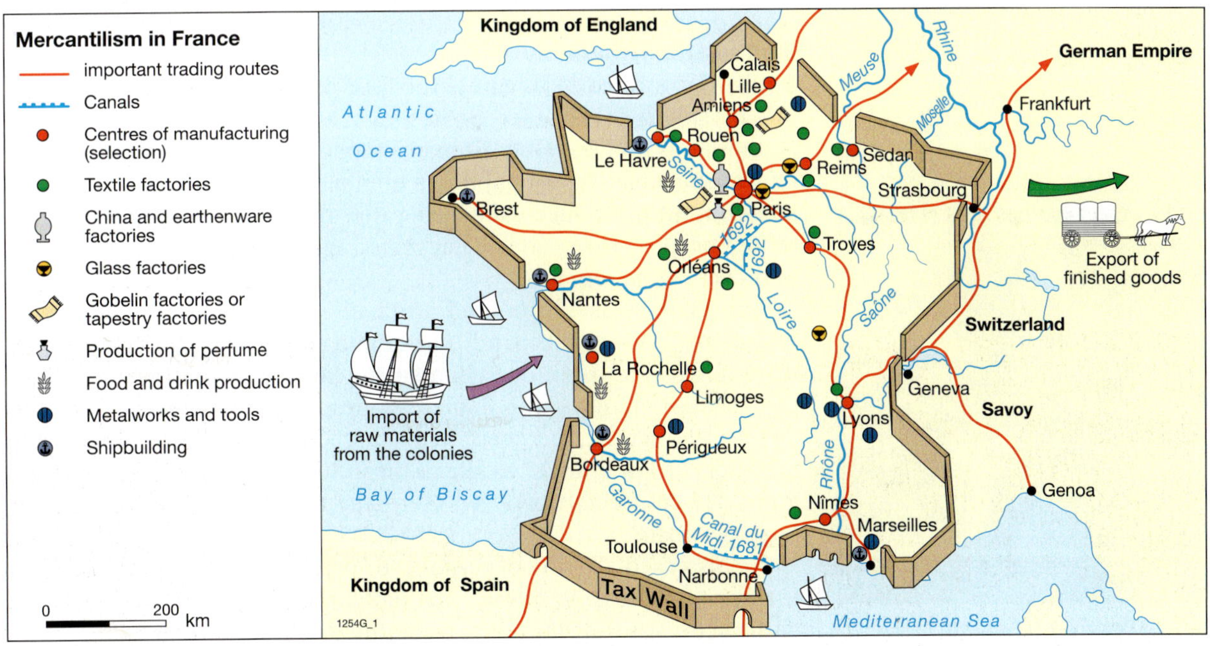

Tasks

1. Describe the different kinds of work done in the playing card factory (M2).
2. Find out how many women worked in the playing card factory (M2).
3. Complete the list of measures introduced to improve trade and commerce (M3).
4. Assess Colbert's economic system (M3, M4).

hegemony: being the first among countries, domination of others
encirclement: being surrounded
mercenary: a soldier who will fight for anybody for money
shelling: shooting by big guns
to raze sth.: to destroy, to flatten
bone of contention: reason for a conflict
animosity: hostility, hatred
war of succession: war over who will be the next king
deliberately: willingly, according to a plan
arsonist: sb. who sets things on fire

Louis's Wars

Preparing War

Louis XIV applied a policy of *hegemony* in Europe that led to a long series of wars, because he could not stand the idea that anybody was more important than him. His ambition to make France the leading power in Europe corresponded with his idea that war was the best means to demonstrate the power and the reputation of a sovereign. Moreover, he feared *encirclement* by the House of Habsburg. However, the other European states were not willing to give in to his aggression.

The formation of a standing army with a strict hierarchy was his first move. As commander-in-chief he gained control over the nobility who served in the military by tradition. All soldiers had the same uniforms. They exercised together and trained in manoeuvres, so that they were prepared for war in a much better way than *mercenaries*. As the economic situation was bad for many people there was no need to recruit soldiers – they joined the army simply to earn money.

At the same time Louis secured the northern and eastern borders. A line of 300 fortresses and fortifications of a new type was developed by his engineer Vauban, who designed them to resist even *shelling*. After their completion Louis had the last medieval city walls and fortified places in France *razed*, so that resistance inside France became impossible.

M 1 **The French General Melac**
A leaflet showing the French General Melac in front of the burning palace at Heidelberg. The text introduces him as a murderer and an *arsonist*. Some people in the Palatinate still call dangerous dogs "Melac". Engraving, 1689.

Fighting for Hegemony

Louis XIV wanted to integrate the land on the left bank of the Rhine into his sphere of influence. So he fought against the Habsburg Spanish Netherlands and the Holy Roman Empire as well as Holland. At first he was successful in conquering a number of towns and large areas of land. But the more successful he became, the more opposition from the other European states grew. They united against France for the "balance of power" in Europe.

But Louis was clever and used all kinds of tricks. He made diplomats and jurists find out about ancient claims based on documents in "reunion chambers". Taking advantage of their investigations and of the emperor's desperate situation in his fight against the Turks, he "reunited" large parts of Alsace including Strasbourg with France. As late as the 20th century this area remained a *bone of contention* between Germany and France, leading to long term *animosity*.

He also used all sorts of reasons for wars when he needed them. In the *war of succession* in the Palatinate he attacked the country in the name of his sister-in-law Liselotte of the Palatinate and tried to occupy the southeast of Germany. French troops destroyed many towns and vast areas *deliberately*, because Louis had been advised to leave the land bordering France so weak that it could never again become dangerous. Liselotte was very unhappy as she felt that people held her responsible for the horrors of the war.

Trying to gain hegemony over Europe, Louis went too far in the War of the Spanish Succession (1701–1713). France was beaten by the

M 2

allied European countries, but remained a strong state because Britain wanted to keep the "balance of power". When Louis died in 1715 he had made France bigger, but thirty-five years of war had also ruined the finances of his country.

M 3 War in the Palatinate

The war in the Palatinate left its scars. On 19 October 1688 a part of Louis XIV's army occupied the town of Oberwesel and stayed until March 1689. The official town chronicles contain the following account by a man called Schwarz:

"The commander-in-chief General Marquis de Bretèche took quarters at the Schönburg. The abbeys and the monasteries had to hand over nearly all of their treasures for his court. In the town were 1400 foot soldiers, 200 knights, most of higher rank, and 416 horses. The people had to give them their pay and food. Three thousand tons of grain and 1575 tons of oats, the last bale of hay and straw, the last cow and the last pig, everything was requisitioned. When the troops left they destroyed gates, towers and Schönburg castle. Then they set the town on fire, thus destroying both town halls, two nobles' mansions and 115 town houses as well as most of the hospital church."

Town Records of Oberwesel: http://www.regionalgeschichte.net/mittelrhein/region/orte/orte-o/oberwesel.html, adapted and translated by RJK.

Tasks

1. Analyse the role of the military in Louis's France.
2. Explain what reasons Louis had to start so many wars.
3. List all the measures of protection Louis introduced for his country.
4. Assess the final outcome of the wars for France.
5. A well-off director of a bank from a town in the Palatinate complains to countess Liselotte. Write his letter (M1, M3).
6. Compare the European borders of 1715 to the borders today (M2).

M 1 **Louis XIV**

Painting by Hyacinthe Rigaud, about 1700. Rigaud received orders to paint a life-size picture of the king. The painting was meant to be sent to Spain, where Louis XIV's grandson was about to become king. However, the king liked the painting (2,77 m high and 1,94 m wide) so much that he only sent a copy to the Spanish court.

Analysing Paintings

Historical paintings provide information about the past. As with all other sources some critical questions must be asked when you want to use a painting as a source of information. In addition you must know that paintings do not show reality but a painter's view of it. There have been times when painters were simply not interested in what reality looked like, so they painted what they liked to see or what their customer told them he wanted to see. Another obstacle is that the fashion of painting changed.

What is the advantage of paintings as historical sources then? In former times fewer people could read. But they were very well-trained in *deciphering* signs, codes and symbols. The language of images was widespread. That is why a painting hardly ever contains elements which do not *convey* a message. So the ruler of a state had himself painted in order to show people what he wanted them to see and to believe. And that is why paintings can be so valuable as historical sources, if only you have the means to find out.

to decipher: to succeed in finding the meaning of sth. that is hidden
to convey: to make ideas or feelings known to sb.
significance: the importance of sth.
to take into account: to consider particular facts when making a decision

Portraits of Louis XIV

From early childhood Louis XIV stood in the limelight. So he saw the opportunity to create his own image. Not only did he use the ceremonies at court, but he also had all sorts of paintings, tapestries, statues, poems and other works of art done for him that presented him as an antique god, as Apollo or even as the sun. His aim was to inform people about his political activities, but also about his personality. His subjects were to see that he was an outstanding person who was at the same time dangerous and powerful, always close but nevertheless unreachable.

When Louis XIV invited a group of painters (among them Rigaud) to his court in 1655, he practically founded his own public relations agency. These painters developed a new style of representational portrait and created a new fashion, which quickly spread to other parts of Europe.

Painting Analysis Worksheet

1. Describing the painting

a. Describe the painting as exactly as you can.
b. Name the painter.
c. Find out when it was painted.
d. Find out about its original size.
e. Find out according to whose orders it was painted and who paid for it.

2. Finding information

a. Analyse the way the main person looks and how he is positioned.
b. Explain all the elements of his dress (with the help of an encyclopaedia or the Internet).
c. Look for the symbols of the king's power and explain their *significance.*
d. Examine from what position the observer of this painting looks at the king.
e. Investigate why the painting was made.

3. Interpreting the painting

a. *Taking into account* all the information you have collected, assess the painting as a work of art but also as a historical source.
b. Give reasons why you think this painting is worth investigating or not.
c. Show what message Louis XIV wanted to convey with this painting.

M 1 **James I of England (1603-1625)**

considerable: great in importance
modest: not talking much about your abilities
gentry: the high social class in the country
petition: an official document asking for sth. to be done
to summon: to arrange an official meeting
to ally (with): to join forces with

Revolution in England / Bill of Rights

In the 17th century England was the only country in Europe with a parliament that had *considerable* influence on the king. The right to decide on finances and to give advice to the king in legislation dated from 1215 when King John had granted the barons special rights in the Magna Carta. King Charles I (1625–1649), however, wanted to govern the country in the same style as his French colleagues. The conflict arose in two fields: religion and finances.

The Problem of Religion

England had been a Protestant country since 1534 when Henry VIII had founded the Anglican Church. After the Scottish Stuarts inherited the throne in 1603, there was a tendency on the side of the new king to return to Catholicism. Most people did not want to follow the pope again, but wanted to remain Protestants.

One group in particular detested the old belief: the Puritans, who fought for simplicity within the church and a *modest* style of life. Many Puritans belonged to the *gentry* which played an important role in Parliament. They wanted to stop the king appointing Catholics as members of the government.

The Problem of Finances

In peacetime the king was expected to live off his own land and taxes. In times of war he had to ask Parliament to pass a tax which all the country had to pay. In 1628 Parliament only gave the king what he wanted after he had signed a *Petition* of Right, which set out fundamental civil rights as well as the political rights of Parliament. But Charles I dissolved Parliament and ruled the country alone from 1629 to 1640. His policies in this period were very unpopular.

Civil War

When he had to *summon* Parliament again in 1640 because the rejection of the English Book of Common Prayer by the Scots had led to open war, its members accused the king of tyranny instead of granting him money.

In 1642 a civil war broke out which ended with the victory of Parliament led by Oliver Cromwell and the execution of Charles I. In 1649 England had become a republic, but Cromwell dissolved Parliament in 1653 and made himself "Lord Protector", which in effect meant dictator. Parliament wanted to make him king but he turned the offer down. After his death Parliament returned to the old system of government. England became a monarchy once more with the old king's son as Charles II. But soon the old conflicts returned, too.

The "Glorious Revolution"

Only one party in Parliament, the Tories, supported the king, but when the Catholic James II came to the throne in 1685 and joined forces with France they feared absolutism could come to Britain. Even though James granted religious freedom to everybody, they *allied* with William of Orange, James's son-in-law, whom they invited to invade England

M 2 **Meeting of Parliament** without a king whose place has been taken by the speaker. Seal from 1651.

from Holland. After William had driven James out of the country, Parliament made him sign a declaration of the rights of the people of England. This "Bill of Rights" in 1689 made England the first parliamentary monarchy in the world and a model for many states.

M 3 William of Orange (1650–1702) and Mary accept the crown from Parliament. Contemporary painting.

M 4 Extract from the "Bill of Rights"

The Bill of Rights forms one part of the unwritten English constitution (1689):

"4. That *levying* money for or to the use of the crown [...], without grant of parliament, for longer time or in other manner than the same is or shall be granted, is illegal.
5. That it is the right of the subjects to petition the king, and all commitments and prosecutions for such petitioning are illegal.
6. That the raising or keeping a standing army within the kingdom in time of peace, unless it be with consent of parliament, is against the law.
7. That the subjects which are Protestants may have arms for their defense suitable to their conditions, and as allowed by law.
8. That election of members of parliament ought to be free.
9. That the freedom of speech, and debates or proceedings in parliament, ought not to be [...] questioned in any court or place out of parliament.
[...]
13. And that for *redress* of all grievances, and for the amending, strengthening and preserving of the laws, parliament ought to be held frequently."

David C. Douglas (ed.), English Historical Documents Vol. 8, Eyre & Spottiswode London 1955, p. 122 f.

to levy: to use official authority to collect payments

redress: payment for sth. wrong that has happened to people

Tasks

1. The inscription on the seal says: "In the third year of freedom by God's blessing restored". What does it remind you of (M2)?
2. Compare the pictures of the two kings and find out what they show about their attitudes to the job (M1, M3).
3. Explain the change in the role the king played in England.
4. Show what rights the people received in the "Bill of Rights" (M4).

conviction: a strong opinion or belief
superstition: the belief that particular events bring good or bad luck
to modify: to change sth. slightly
renounce: to state formally that you no longer have a particular belief or position
to surrender: to give up sth., when forced to
incompatible: not able to exist together
asserting: behaving in a confident and determined way
immaturity: the state of not being fully developed

The Age of Enlightenment

At about the time of the discovery of America, groundbreaking ideas had been made especially in the natural sciences. The absolute monarchs founded academies whose aim it was to develop the knowledge of mankind. The first "Encyclopaedia" was written by Diderot, a French philosopher. A new way of thinking spread in Europe, which was no longer dominated by the church – the Enlightenment.

The Theory

In the 17th and the 18th centuries some philosophers began to investigate the nature of the state and the nature of power. Their ideas were based on the *conviction* that people were born free. They all had one principle in common to direct people's way of life and the actions of the state alike – reason. They did not accept the old style of ruling based on the "grace of God". Whereas Montesquieu was convinced that a new kind of monarchy was best, one that was limited by laws and by a constitution, Rousseau went further and claimed that the people should be the origin of all power. This form of government is called a "republic".

The Consequences

As a result of the new way of thinking knowledge grew considerably. Large numbers of people learned how to read and write. To possess books became fashionable.

At the universities the sciences gained importance whereas astrology and alchemy disappeared. There was no longer room for *superstition.*

Of course, some monarchs were not amused at first, when they heard about the development that was going on. However, some were interested and wanted to learn more about it. So they invited

M 1 **A Reading in Paris, 1755**
Parisian high society meets in Madame Geoffrins's salon, Montesquieu and Rousseau among the guests. Contemporary painting.

philosophers to live at their courts and teach them. They understood that the new ideas could help them to modernize their states. Some of them, like Catherine II of Russia and Emperor Joseph II of Austria, were even willing and able to *modify* their own role in their states carefully.

M 2 Frederick II, 1764
Contemporary painting

The Reaction in Prussia

Frederick II of Prussia declared himself "the first servant of his state", because he thought that the king should take responsibility for his state and people. He brought about reforms to the system, thus helping the average people to get on. He never thought of handing over power to them, though. On the contrary, by changing things he won the support of his people. He also led a series of wars, because his aim was to make Prussia one of the top European powers. He is very well remembered for his military skills.

M 3 Enlightenment

a) Jean-Jacques Rousseau (1762):

"Man is born free; and everywhere he is in chains [...] Since no man has a natural authority over his fellow, and force creates no right, we must conclude that conventions form the basis of all legitimate authority among men [...] To *renounce* liberty is to renounce being a man, to *surrender* the rights of humanity and even his duties. This is *incompatible* with man's nature."

Jean-Jacques Rousseau, Le Contrat Social (adapted) in: www.fordham.edu/halsall/mod/rousseau-contract2.html

b) John Locke (1690):

"The state is a union of people created for the sole purpose of representing, *asserting* and developing their civil interest."

John Locke (1690), Two Treatises on Government, Cambridge 1960, pp. 286ff.

c) Charles de Montesquieu (1748):

"Every state holds three powers: the power to legislate, the power to carry out what has been legislated, and the power to enforce the law. The second power is called the executive function and the third power, which enables the ruler to punish [...] citizens, is called the judicial function. All would be lost if a single man or authority [...] should succeed in combining the three powers. In a free state, every rational individual would ideally rule himself, but [...] this is impracticable in large states."

Charles de Montesquieu, On the Spirit of the Laws (1748), p. 162ff. (adapted)

M 4 What is Enlightenment?

Immanuel Kant, a German philosopher, became famous for the following definition:

"Enlightenment is man's emergence from his self-imposed *immaturity*. Immaturity is the inability to use one's understanding without guidance from another. This immaturity is self-imposed when its cause lies not in lack of understanding, but in lack of resolve and courage to use it without guidance from another. Sapere Aude! [dare to know] "Have courage to use your own understanding!" – that is the motto of enlightenment."

http://www.english.upenn.edu/~mgamer/Etexts/kant.html

Tasks

1. Explain the new ideas of the three philosophers (M3).
2. Say what would happen if two or even all three of the powers Montesquieu speaks of were in the hands of one person (M3).
3. Analyse Kant's definition of enlightenment as to its message and compare it to the other sources. (M3, M4)
4. Compare the painting of Frederick II with the painting of Louis XIV (page 16). Describe the differences and give your opinion on the reasons for the differences.

The American Revolution

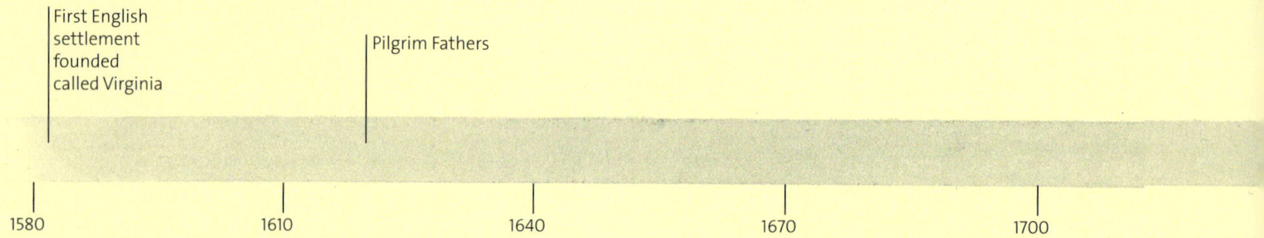

"All Men are Created Equal"

"Life, Liberty, and the Pursuit of Happiness"

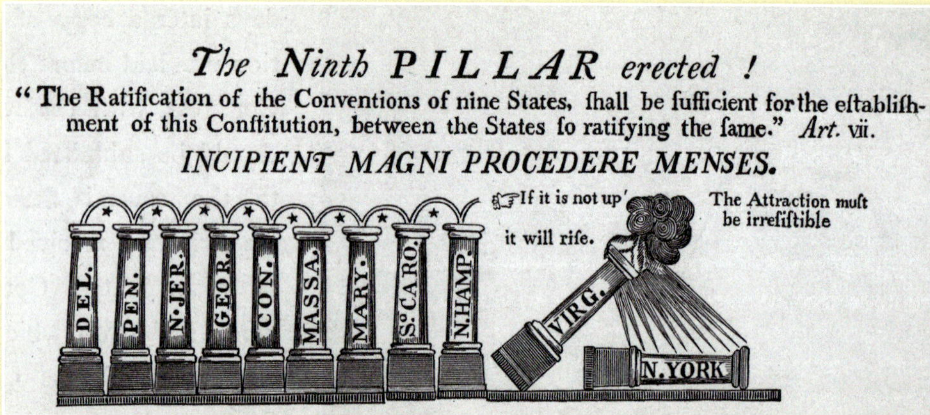

Advertising Unity. Caricature, 1788

Jefferson Hands over the Declaration of Independence. Painting by John Trumbull, 1787–1818

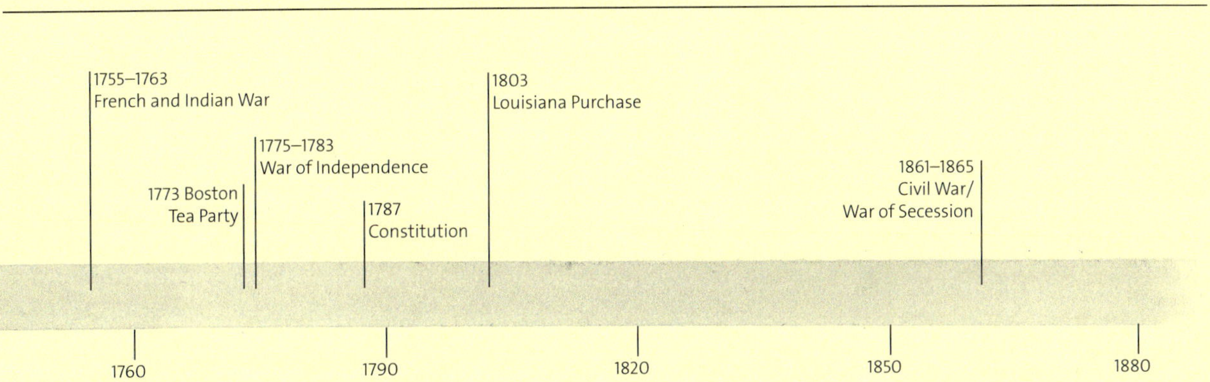

At a Slave Auction about 1850

"Agony" by Charles Deas, 1845

A New Beginning in a Foreign Land

First Encounter

In the second half of the 16th century more and more European adventurers landed on the shores of North America. But it was not until 1584 that Sir Walter Raleigh founded the first English settlement, which he named Virginia after his "Virgin Queen" Elizabeth I. After her death political and religious *persecution* led to more and more Protestants leaving England for America. Among them were a group of twenty-eight women and seventy-four men, all of them Puritans, who reached the coast of what was to be Massachusetts on board the "Mayflower" on 21 November 1620. They had a hard winter ahead of them, which they only survived with the help of the Native Americans.

M 1 **Plymouth 1621**
The fifty survivors thank God and the Indians who helped them with a three-day festival.

The New Inhabitants

As a result of the political and economic turbulence which shook Europe in the course of the Thirty Years War and of the Civil War in England, more and more emigrants left their mother countries hoping for a better future or at least the end of their hardship. Many people had lost their land because it had been destroyed by official troops or mercenaries. Others had been forced to join an army and wanted to get away. A large number of those who left Europe belonged to a religious minority and had been *persecuted* in their country. But there were also shipowners who saw their chance of becoming rich by persuading people to go to America. They used all sorts of tricks and promises to get passengers. Some emigrants went because of a spirit of adventure. Beggars and criminals were *deported*. Those who could not pay for the voyage were allowed to go as "indentured servants", which meant that they had to work for the person who had paid for their voyage for three to seven years after their arrival.

persecution: extremely bad treatment of sb.
to persecute: to treat somebody in a cruel or unfair way
to deport: to send away to a foreign country by force

Getting Organized

Many immigrants worked very hard, not only because they wanted to survive and have a better future but also because they thought God's blessing showed in the success of their work. This Puritan belief became a strong driving force in the economy. The first years were extremely hard as the newcomers had to adjust to differences in the living conditions, especially the climate.

By 1700 colonial government had been established by the British in thirteen colonies. All followed the example set by Connecticut in 1639 and gave themselves constitutions. Free colonists had the same rights as British citizens, but women, slaves, natives, and all those who were not members of the church had no rights.

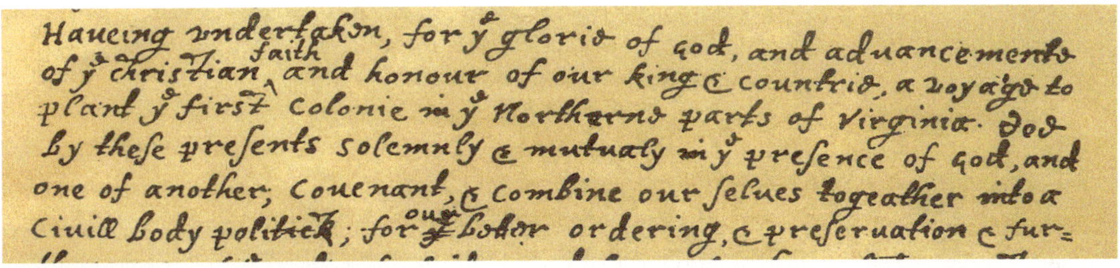
Haueing undertaken, for ye glorie of God, and aduancemente
of ye christian faith, and honour of our king & countrie, a voyage to
plant ye first colonie in ye Northerne parts of Virginia. doe
by these presents solemnly & mutualy in ye presence of God, and
one of another, couenant, & combine our selues togeather into a
ciuill body politick; for our better ordering, & preseruation & fur=

M 2 Mayflower Compact from 1620
Facsimile of the original (excerpt)

M 3 Mayflower Compact

Forty-one men on the Mayflower signed the following compact (1620):

"In the name of God, Amen. We [...] having undertaken for the glory of God, and advancement of the Christian faith, and honor of our King and country, a voyage to plant the first colony in the northern parts of Virginia, do by these presents solemnly and mutually, in the presence of God and one another, covenant and combine ourselves together into a civil body politic, for our better ordering and preservation, and furtherance of the ends aforesaid; and by virtue hereof do enact, constitute and frame such just and equal laws, ordinances, acts, constitutions and offices,
[...] AD 1620."

Thomas V. DiBacco, Lorna C. Mason, Christian G. Appy, History of the United States, Boston 1991, p. 16, adapted by RJK.

M 4 An Account of Pennsylvania

A politician from Pennsylvania described four reasons why people settled in the new territory:

"The true reason why the people of this country buy more and more land is their success in trade. And there is a lot more cheap land to buy. Most of the new Christian land owners are farmers and have large cattle herds. Many of them must now go further up into the country because they can find cheaper and better land there for their cattle. It is also the part of the land where skins, furs, and other animal products are traded in from the Indians. The third advantage of that land is the existence of copper and iron mines. When it was first examined only heathens and very few Christians lived there and hardly anybody wanted to go there because it was wild and dangerous."

Gabriel Thomas, An account of Pennsylvania. Adapted by R.J.K. from: Daniel J. Boorstin (ed.), An American Primer. Meridian, Chicago 1966, p.56f.

Tasks

1. Make a list of the reasons why people went to America.
2. Say what role religion played in the early days of the colonies (M1, M2).
3. Explain how the newcomers saw their new land (M3, M4).

to rage: to continue in a violent way
option: sth. you can choose to have or do
pamphlet: (here) a leaflet containing a political message
skilful: good at doing sth.
obstacle: sth. that hinders you
hath: has
reconciliation: end to a quarrel and start of a good relationship again
to plead: to ask urgently
the slain: the people who were killed
unalienable: sth. that cannot be taken away from you

The Road to Independence

Money Problems

From 1755 to 1763 war *raged* in both America and Europe. The "Seven Years War" in Europe was called the "French and Indian War" in America. Britain won after the surrender of the French in Canada. In the Treaty of Paris, France had to hand over most of Canada and the territory east of the Mississippi River to Britain. But the war had been very expensive for the British so they raised taxes or simply invented new ones. These taxes also applied to the colonists, who found many of them unfair, especially because they had no representatives in the British Parliament to oppose them. They claimed "no taxation without representation" and protested strongly. As a reaction the British cancelled most of the taxes except for the tax on tea, but the protests went on. They culminated in the Boston Massacre in 1770, in which five Americans were killed by British soldiers.

Fighting for Independence

In 1773 Bostonians disguised as Indians threw the cargo of three tea clippers into the harbour, which was closed afterwards by the British. Behind the scenes representatives of the thirteen colonies discussed their *options*. They met at the First Continental Congress in Philadelphia in 1774 and decided not to trade with Britain any longer.

At the same time the colonists founded their own militia, the "Minutemen". The first armed clash in 1775 developed into the War of Independence. Thomas Paine wrote and issued a *pamphlet* with all the arguments the colonists needed for the separation. But it was not before 4 July of the following year that some of the colonists formally declared their independence. One third remained neutral, others stayed loyal to the British king and supported the British troops, as did most of the Indians and about 13,000 mercenaries from Hesse and Brunswick who had been hired out to England by their princes.

M 1 Thomas Jefferson (1743–1826)
the author of the Declaration of Independence. He later became the third president of the USA.

M 2 Yorktown 1781
George Washington discusses the situation with the Duke of Rochambeau and the Marquis de Lafayette.

The army of only 13,000 colonists was trained by the Prussian general Steuben and commanded by George Washington. Their allies were Holland, Spain and France, whose absolute monarch Louis XVI wanted to take revenge on the British for the defeat of France twenty years earlier. George Washington proved to be a very *skilful* commander, but the colonists also had other advantages. All the farmers knew and used their own guns. They were strong believers and nearly all of them were well educated for the time, so communication worked well. They were also encouraged by a free press in the colonies. After several defeats the British surrendered and recognized American independence in the 1783 Treaty of Paris.

It took the Americans another four years until they were able to agree on a federal constitution for the United States of America. The differences among the thirteen former colonies were a main *obstacle* in this process.

M 3 Join or Die
Caricature by Benjamin Franklin, 1754

M 4 "Time to Part"

Thomas Paine, who emigrated to America in 1774, wrote a pamphlet in which he laid out the only solution to the problems between England and the colonies:

"But Britain is the parent country, say some. Then the more shame upon her conduct […]
This new World *hath* been the asylum for the persecuted lovers of civil and religious liberty from EVERY PART of Europe. Hither have they fled, not from the tender embraces of the mother, but from the cruelty of the monster […] I challenge the warmest advocate for *reconciliation* to show a single advantage that this continent can reap by being connected with Great Britain. I repeat the challenge; not a single advantage is derived. Our corn will fetch its price in any market in Europe, and our imported goods must be paid for – buy them where we will […] Because, any […] dependence on Great Britain, tends directly to involve this Continent in European wars and quarrels, and sets us at variance with nations who would otherwise seek our friendship, and against whom we have neither anger nor complaint. As Europe is our market for trade, we ought to form no partial connection with any part of it.
Every thing that is right or reasonable *pleads* for separation. The blood of the *slain,* the weeping voice of nature cries, 'TIS TIME TO PART. Even the distance at which the Almighty hath placed England and America is a strong and natural proof that the authority of the one over the other, was never the design of Heaven."

http://www.ushistory.org/PAINE/commonsense/singlehtml.htm

M 5 The Declaration of Independence

Thomas Jefferson wrote in the Declaration of Independence:

"We hold these truths to be self-evident. That all men are created equal. That they are endowed by their creator with certain *unalienable* rights. That among these are life, liberty and the pursuit of happiness. That to secure these rights governments are instituted among men deriving their just powers from the consent of the governed. That whenever any form of government becomes destructive of these ends it is the right of the people to alter or to abolish it and to institute new government […]."

www.ushistory.org/JEFFERSON/declaration

Tasks

1. Show what arguments Thomas Paine uses to convince his readers (M4).
2. Explain what Benjamin Franklin wanted to point out by his caricature (M3).
3. Make a timeline of the events of the American Revolution.
4. Check the Declaration of Independence for ideas you would support (M5).
5. Find arguments for the view that the War of Independence was more than a mere rebellion.

M 1 The Great Seal of the USA

necessity: the fact that sth. must happen
ambassador: an official who represents his country in a foreign one
to prevail: to be accepted esp. after a struggle

The USA – A New State

A New Type of State

After the war had been won, the thirteen former colonies were only linked by a Congress that had coordinated activities against the English. Even though the political representatives of the individual states saw the *necessity* of some sort of central government there were different opinions on how to organize it so that every single state would be satisfied:

- What rights should the individual states have?
- How should elections be organized and how many representatives should be elected to represent each state?
- How should federalism be set up?
- How could abuse of power be prevented?

Apart from these questions there were practical obstacles like huge distances, the differences in climate and lack of roads, which the British were certain would hinder the states from uniting.

Common Ground

But they also held some principles in common. So they met at a federal convention in 1787 to work out a constitution for the United States. The discussions were influenced by the French philosopher Montesquieu among others. His writings had been sent to America by its *ambassador* to France, Thomas Jefferson, who tried to influence the results of the convention, as he wanted his ideas in the Declaration of Independence to *prevail.* As in the constitution of the Roman Republic power was to be shared so that no one could have complete power. Human rights were to guide all laws. One group of representatives at the convention thought one house in the new Congress, elected by the

M 2

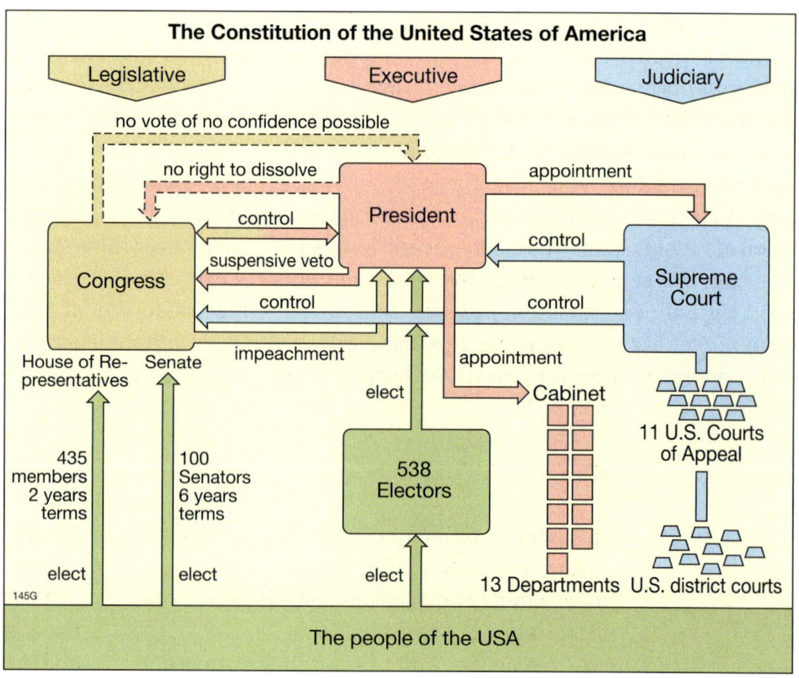

people, was sufficient; another group did not want to hand over too much influence to the mass of the people. However, no one wanted to copy the British system of parliament.

Problems and Results

But all feared that the other states might gain more power and influence than their own, so they chose a system with two chambers. It took the convention more than a year to agree on a solution. Some even left early in disgust. As it was not certain whether the states would ratify the new constitution, a Bill of Rights was added and a campaign was organized to gather support. By June 1788 nine states had ratified. The last two of the original thirteen colonies – North Carolina and Rhode Island, which had not even taken part in the convention – ratified only after the swearing-in-ceremony of the first president, George Washington.

to foment: to create trouble or violence
to abhor: to hate sth.
vassal: servant, sb. who depends on sb. else
providence: God's control of people's lives
disobedient: refusing to obey
to slight: to treat sb. rudely
insolent: extremely rude
intimation: stating sth. in an indirect way
to repeal: if you repeal sth., it is no longer valid
latitude: (here) liberty

M 3 Letters from 1776

a) John Adams, a member of the Continental Congress in Philadelphia, who later on became the fourth president of the USA, received hundreds of letters from his wife, Abigail Adams. She wrote on 31 March 1776:

"I long to hear that you have declared an independency [...] In the new Code of Laws which I suppose it will be necessary for you to make, I desire you would Remember the Ladies, and be more generous and favourable to them than your ancestors. Do not put such unlimited power into the hands of the Husbands. Remember all Men would be tyrants if they could. If particular care and attention is not paid to the Ladies we are determined to *foment* a Rebellion, and will not hold ourselves bounds by any Laws in which we have no voice, or Representation. [...]
Why then, not put it out of the power of the vicious [...] Men of sense in all ages *abhor* those customs which treat us only as the *vassals* of your sex. Regard us then as beings, placed by *providence* under your protection, and in imitation of the Supreme Being make use of that power for our happiness."

b) John Adams to Abigail Adams, 14 April 1776:

"As to your extraordinary Code of Laws I cannot but laugh [...].
We have been told that our Struggle has loosened the bands of Government every where. That Children and Apprentices were *disobedient* – that schools and Colleges were grown turbulent – that Indians *slighted* their Guardians and Negroes grew *insolent* to their Masters. But your Letter was the first *Intimation* that another Tribe more numerous and powerful than all the rest were grown discontented [...].
Depend upon it, We know better than to *repeal* our Masculine systems. Although they are in full Force, you know they are little more than Theory. We dare not exert our Power in its full *Latitude.* We are obliged to go fair, and softly, and in Practice you know We are the subjects. We have only the Name of Masters, and rather than give up this, which would completely subject Us to the Despotism of the Petticoat, I hope General Washington, and all our brave Heroes would fight."

www.masshist.org

Tasks

1. Discuss the necessity for the states to unite. Find at least three arguments for and against unity.
2. Explain why it took the states so long to form the United States.
3. Make a diagram of the checks and balances included in the Constitution (M2).
4. Give an opinion if the way the President is elected is still up-to-date.
5. Show the differences in opinion between John and Abigail Adams (M3).

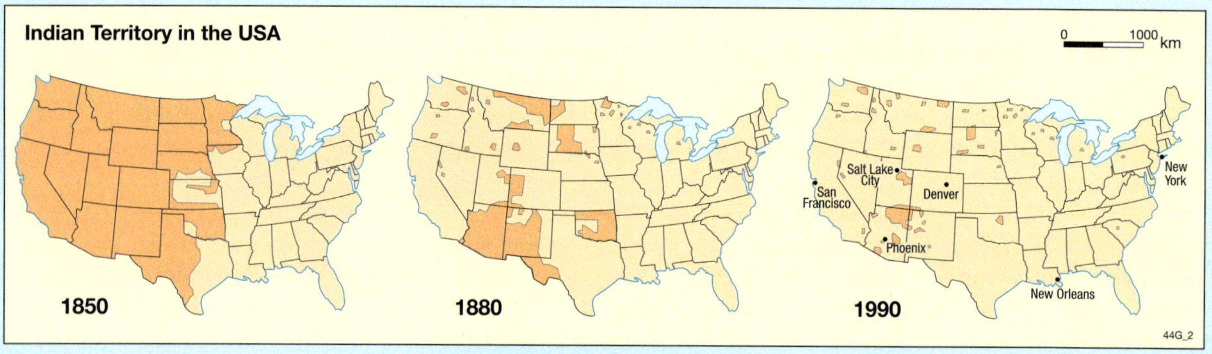

How the West Was Won

Historical maps may not only present a state of affairs at a certain time in history but also show the development of a specific historical process, thus providing information about space and time alike. The more *recent* these maps are the more information has gone into them. But careful: Some makers of maps may try *to deceive* the user by adding or leaving out data which may *blur* the user's understanding of the map or which may not provide the information needed to understand a historic process fully. Sometimes the map makers can only guess about the exact location of a place. They also have to simplify things to make the information clear. But even if a map is made as objectively as possible, it can only hint at why things happened. At best it provides geographical and political facts, gives orientation as to time and space, and stirs up questions that the user can start investigate.

Moving West

After landing in the new world, founding communities, organizing colonies, winning independence and setting up a new state with an *unprecedented* constitution, the Americans set about discovering and conquering their continent. Growth was achieved by different means and in different steps, mainly during the 19th century. Constantly pushing the frontier west and believing that God's own country had been promised them, the settlers, adventurers and engineers needed nearly a hundred years to close the frontier and conquer what is basically the USA today.

recent: only a short time ago
to deceive: to make sb. have a wrong idea about sth.
to blur: sth. that is blurred cannot be seen clearly anymore
unprecedented: what has never existed before
to distinguish: to recognize the difference between two things
to acquire: to buy sth., to get sth.

Map Analysis Worksheet

1. Describing the map

a. What is the title of the map?
b. What area is depicted on the map?
c. What time span is covered?
d. What is the map's scale?
e. Is there a legend and what is to be found in it?
f. Can all the symbols and lines be seen on the map? Can any coloured areas be *distinguished*?
g. Is the map clear?

2. Finding information

a. Does the map show a state of affairs or a development?
b. Is it a political, social, military or an economic map?
c. Find out exactly where the depicted area is located and what the theme of the map is.
d. Is the map complete or can you find missing aspects which should be included?
e. What is the message of the map?

3. Interpreting the map

a. Find out the distance from East to West and compare with distances you know or have already travelled.
b. Make a chronological list of the steps of the development.
c. Compare the different ways of *acquiring* territory. Investigate the matter by looking for other sources.
d. Name the different means of transport you can recognize in the map.
e. Speculate on the shape of most of the states in the West. Then compare the map with a geographical one.
f. Formulate what the main problems of the development.
g. Assess the amount of knowledge you have gained through the map.

curiosity: strong desire to know about sth.
ferocious: very aggressive and violent
to stir up: to make people feel strong emotions
scourge: a thing that causes trouble or suffering

All Men Are Created Equal - Indians

Unbridgeable Differences

The first encounter of the new settlers with the Indians was dominated by *curiosity* and friendliness. Without the Indians' assistance the Pilgrim Fathers would not have survived the first winter. In the New England states things did not change until 1638, but in other colonies the first fights broke out within a few years after the arrival of the whites, usually over land.

The example of Columbus prevailed. In 1622 Indians in the Jamestown area massacred 350 settlers because the Virginia Company had claimed more and more land for tobacco farms. Incidents of this kind helped create the myth of the *ferocious* and uncivilized wild Indian, which was used *to stir up* hatred against these "savages". Not only did Native Americans fight against the armed whites, they also had to deal with other *scourges* like unknown diseases, the bad influence of alcohol and the idea of "possession", which was unfamiliar to them.

The white invaders' greed for land and the way they claimed it were incomprehensible to the natives, as they believed no one could possess any of the four elements water, air, fire and earth. The whites, on the other hand, thought they were justified in taking the land as the Native Americans of the prairie did not cultivate it.

M 1 Painting of the Indian Wars

Relocation

Tribes of Indian "nations" with different languages and different customs resisted the white settlers' expansion into their lands. The American government signed treaty after treaty to *safeguard* the territory, but few settlers took these treaties seriously. In the 18th and the 19th centuries many tribes from the East, the South and the Southwest were relocated to the West by the government; among them were the Cherokees, whose "trail of tears" in 1838 became known as one of the most horrible incidents.

Very often the Indians agreed to move when offered money or new land. Some of the agreements were dishonest and deceived the Indians with offers of poor-quality land. After Congress passed the Indian Removal Act in 1830, the government had the right to force all Indians to move to reservations whether they agreed or not. As the whites had virtually wiped out the buffalo in vast parts of the prairie, some tribes, having lost their whole way of life, went peacefully. But a number of tribes banded together and fought for their right to stay on their ancestors' land. However, the U.S. Army proved too strong and by 1900 all Indians had been resettled.

relocation: moving to a new place
to safeguard: to protect sb. from loss
avarice: greed, extreme desire for wealth
to bequeath (formal): to give sb. property

M 2 Four Indian Chiefs Try to be Heard

a) Wahunsonacock (King Powhatan) in 1609:

"Why should you take by force what you can have by love? Why should you destroy us who have provided you with food? What can you get by war? We can hide our provisions and fly into the woods; and then you must consequently famish by wronging your friends. What is the cause of your jealousy? You see us unarmed, and willing to supply your wants, if you come in a friendly manner, and not with swords and guns as to invade an enemy."

A. LaVonne Brown Ruoff, American Indian Literatures. The Modern Language Association of America, New York 1990, p. 51.

b) Shawnee Chief Tecumseh in 1811:

"Where today are the Pequot? Where are the Narrangansett, the Mohican, the Pocanet, and other powerful tribes of our people? They have vanished before the *avarice* and oppression of the white man, as snow before the summer sun [...] Will we let ourselves be destroyed in our turn, without making an effort worthy of our race? Shall we, without a struggle, give up our homes, our lands, *bequeathed* to us by the Great Spirit? The graves of our dead and everything that is dear and sacred to us? [...] I know you will say with me, Never! Never!"

A.LaVonne Ruoff, p. 51.

c) Chief Joseph of the Nez Perez in 1877:

"Our chiefs are killed. The little children are freezing to death. My people have no blankets, no food. Hear me, my chiefs; I am tired; my heart is sick and sad. From where the sun now stands, I will fight no more."

Elisabeth Wardle, Britain and the American Revolution; London 1993 p. 57.

d) Young Sioux Black Elk in 1890 after surviving Wounded Knee:

"Something else died there [...] A people's dream died there. It was a beautiful dream."

Anne Zeman and Kate Kelly, Everthing you need to know about American Homework, Scholastic Inc. 1997, p. 52.

Tasks

1. Investigate the Cherokees' "trail of tears".
2. Show how the relationship between the whites and the Native Americans developed.
3. Assess the Native Americans' statements (M2).
4. Write two reports of the incidents shown in the painting from the point of view of a Native American woman and of a US Cavalry soldier (M1).

All Men Are Created Equal - Blacks and Women

M 1 **Abraham Lincoln**
President from 1861–1865

Slavery

By the end of the 18th century half a million slaves had been taken to the USA from Africa by means of the "Atlantic Triangle", a system of trade organized by the British and other Europeans. Many slaves, who were handcuffed and chained to each other during the voyage, died before they reached America. The survivors were bought by planters and farmers mainly in the southern states.

In the northern states more and more people rejected the idea of slavery, so it was gradually *prohibited.* But in the South slaves were needed to work on the plantations to guarantee the *prosperity* of the farms and the wealth of their owners.

Even though the slave trade was forbidden in 1808, the number of slaves grew steadily, keeping pace with the production of cotton. After setting the conditions new states had to fulfil to join the Union, Congress compromised in 1820 by drawing a line on the map. North of the line only "free" states (without slavery) could join. This line gave slaves in the South hope, because crossing it meant freedom. When Frederick Douglass escaped in 1837 and became the first "*fugitive* slave" lecturer in America and abroad, the abolitionist movement grew, even organizing civil rights demonstrations.

The Civil War

Abraham Lincoln was elected president in 1860. He wanted to keep the Union together and stop the spread of slavery to new states. Eleven southern states left the Union and elected Jefferson Davis as their president. Slavery was not the only issue at the heart of the division between the North and the South. Almost unnoticed at first because most people still lived and worked on small farms, circumstances had changed completely. In the North many people worked in factories in the cities, whereas the South remained rural. The economic system of the North was based on free labourers who received wages and worked where they wanted to. The South, however, was based on slave labour. Moreover, the southern states argued that it was possible to leave the Union if a state voted to do so. The North denied that states

M 2 **Slaves Picking Cotton on a Southern Plantation.**
Engraving, about 1861.

M 3 **Western View of Manchester,** Engraving, 1861.

had such a right. This situation led to the outbreak of the Civil War from 1861 to 1865, which caused the death of 600,000 Americans.

In the middle of the war Lincoln freed the slaves with the Emancipation Proclamation. Shortly afterwards the Union victory at Gettysburg led to a turning point for the North. A week after the main Confederate army surrendered President Lincoln was *assassinated.* The reconstruction of the Union led to all former slaves becoming US citizens in 1866. In order to overcome strong resistance in the South and to improve the situation of the blacks, a civil rights movement slowly developed which became stronger with the years. But it was not until 1964 that the activities of the *NAACP* and of people like Dr. Martin Luther King, Jr. led to the Civil Rights Act, which granted equality to African-Americans.

to prohibit: to forbid, to ban
prosperity: wealth, success
fugitive: escapee, sb. who flees
to assassinate: to kill (mostly for political reasons)
NAACP: National Association for the Advancement of Coloured People
upstate: in the northern part of a state
suffrage: the right to vote in political elections
significance: the importance of sth., esp. when it has an effect on the future

Women

In 1920 women were given the right to vote in the 19th amendment to the Constitution. Their fight for equal rights had started in 1848 when the first Women's Rights Convention took place in *upstate* New York. After the Civil War women were very disappointed when the right to vote was only given to African-American men, so they launched a *suffrage* movement, which led to women's right to vote in at least some states. After the First World War the right to vote in national elections could no longer be denied to them.

M 4 Extract from "Uncle Tom's Cabin"

In her famous book "Uncle Tom's Cabin" Harriett Beecher-Stowe included a conversation between Mr Shelby and his wife:

"Mr Shelby, you cannot be serious."
"I'm sorry to say that I am," said Mr Shelby. "I've agreed to sell Tom."
"What? Our Tom? – that good faithful creature! – been your faithful servant from a boy! O, Mr Shelby! – and you have promised him his freedom, too, – you and I have spoken to him a hundred times of it. Well, I can believe anything now, – I can believe now that you could sell little Harry, poor Eliza's only child!" said Mrs Shelby, in a tone of grief and indignation.
"Well, since you must know all, it is so..."
"Why sell them, ... if you must sell at all?"
"Because they will bring the highest sum of money – that's why..."

Harriett Beecher Stowe, Uncle Tom's Cabin, New York, 1850.

M 5 Public Punishment 1860

Tasks

1. List all the information you can get from the sources about the living conditions of African-Americans (M4, M5).
2. Assess the *significance* of a book like "Uncle Tom's Cabin" in the situation it was published in.
3. Show why the Civil War broke out.
4. Assess the role Abraham Lincoln played and still plays in his country.

The French Revolution

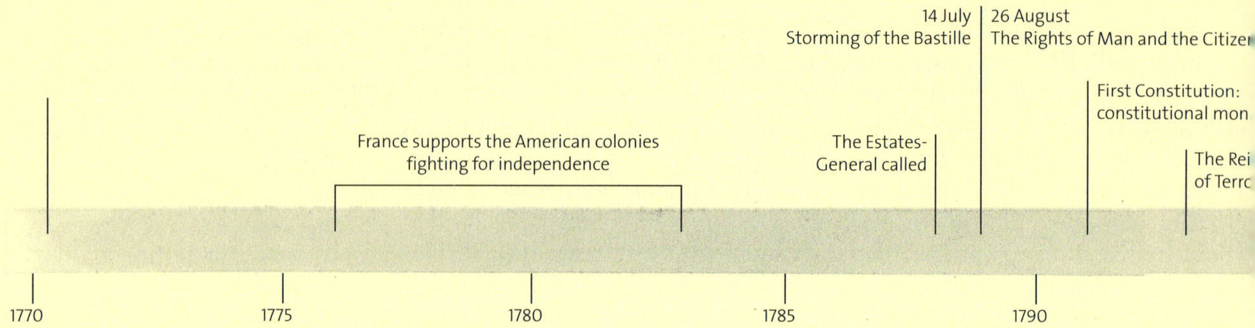

The Execution of Louis XVI
Paris, 1793

Opening the Estates-General
Versailles, 5 May 1789

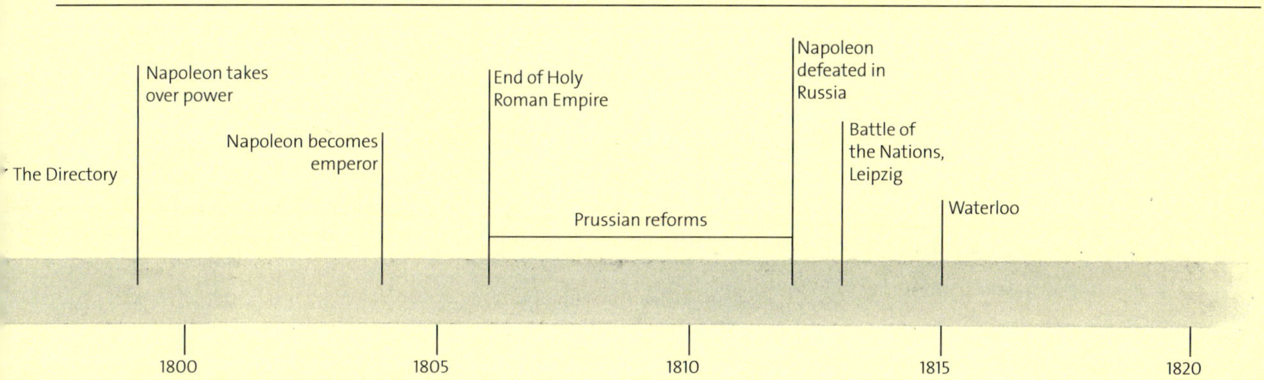

Moscow Burning, 1812

Humboldt University in Berlin

Napoleon's Coronation in Paris, 1804. Painting by Jacques-Louis David

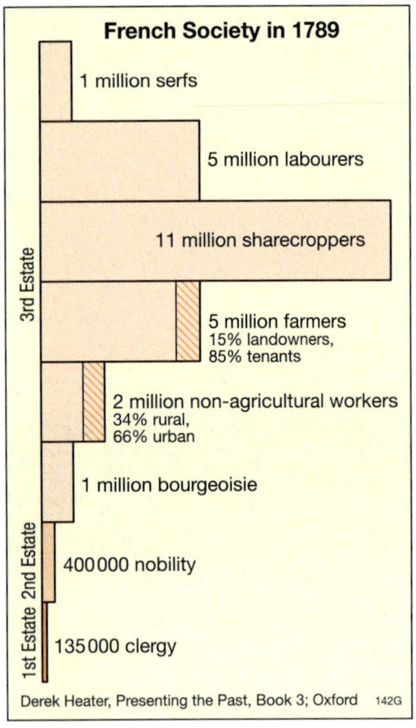

M 1

M 2 **What is the Third Estate?**

Abbé Sieyès, a member of the Third Estate, wrote a pamphlet about the political situation in France:

"The plan of this book is fairly simple. We must ask ourselves three questions:
1. What is the Third Estate? – Everything.
2. What has it been until now in the political order? – Nothing.
3. What does it want to be? – Something. [...]
The Third Estate embraces then all that which belongs to the nation; and all that which is not of the Third Estate, cannot be regarded as being of the nation.
What is the Third Estate? – It is everything."

www.age-of-the-sage.org

The Outbreak of the Revolution

Economic Problems

A long period of economic problems finally led to the start of the revolution in 1789. The state had been bankrupt since the mid-1780s. Ministers made new plans, but things did not improve because the clergy and nobility rejected changes in taxation, while the Third Estate paid most of the taxes. Finally the king summoned the Estates-General, a kind of parliament made up of representatives of the three estates. They were to meet for the first time since 1614.

Political Problems

In many parts of the country people *suffered hardship* when bad harvests led to more unemployment and increased the price of bread. As discontent grew they drew up lists of complaints for their deputies in the Estates-General to discuss with the king. Many of the regional law courts joined their protests but for different reasons. The judges had *become acquainted with* the new ideas of the Enlightenment and the new system established in America after the end of the War of Independence, in which France had supported the colonists. The third group which wanted changes were the rich citizens of the Third Estate who had to pay high taxes but had no influence on government policies.

The Summer of 1789

When Louis XVI welcomed the 291 deputies of the clergy, the 270 of the nobles and the 578 of the Third Estate he had already suffered a defeat because he had been forced to invite twice as many deputies of the Third Estate as he wanted. He tried to play a trick on them by changing the voting *procedures* to one vote for every estate, so that he and his supporters could not be outvoted. This angered the Third Estate so much that they moved out to a nearby empty tennis court on 20 June. Here they swore that they would not leave before they had written a new constitution. By and by deputies from the other estates joined them until Louis gave in on 27 June when he accepted the National Assembly as France's legal parliament.

An Outbreak of Violence

However, the problems of the poor had not been dealt with. They were still hungry and felt disadvantaged. In Paris riots broke out and people tried to get hold of weapons because they were afraid of the reaction of the king. On 14 July an angry crowd stormed the Bastille, Louis's prison and armoury in Paris. They killed the defenders and carried the governor's head through the city on a stake. In order to re-establish order the king gave the rioters permission to set up their own militia, the National Guard, and form their own government, the Paris Commune. Towns all over France followed the example.

Violence also spread into the countryside. Farmers lived in fear of wandering gangs which stole food and damaged property. Angry peasants broke into their lords' homes and burned *records* of their *dues*. A "Great Fear" lay its grip on the country.

First Results

On 4 August the noble deputies in the National Assembly announced that they would give up their privileges. The Assembly took measures against the violence and suggested radical changes to society. But the king resisted them. When it became known in Paris that he was gathering more soldiers in Versailles, crowds of market women armed themselves and marched on Versailles to take the royal family to Paris by force.

to suffer hardship: to have really bad times
to become acquainted with: to get to know
procedure: the way sth. is done
record: written document
dues: charges, money you owe sb.

M 3 **Tennis Court Oath, 1789.** Painting by Jacques-Louis David

M 4 **Storming of the Bastille 14 July.** Contemporary Drawing

M 5 **The Great Fear** Contemporary Drawing

Tasks

1. List the reasons that led to the outbreak of the revolution.
2. Discuss what Louis could have done in 1789 instead of giving in.
3. Show what the arguments of the Third Estate were (M2).
4. Explain how the situation of the king changed in the course of the year 1789.

The Rights of Men and Women

After privileges for the nobles and the clergy were abolished the National Assembly led a debate about civil rights. It had started long before the revolution. During the revolution "liberté, égalité, fraternité" became the *slogan* of the people. Thc National Assembly changed its name to "Constituante" in order to show that its task was to write a constitution.

slogan: a short phrase used by a political party

Liberty

In the second half of the eighteenth century a number of writers set out their ideas to improve society. The philosopher Voltaire wrote that France would not be free as long as the king of France was an absolute monarch. He was impressed by the English example and wrote in 1750 that the English people had a king and a parliament, which guaranteed the people freedom to go where they wanted, to read what they liked, to follow the religion they chose and to be tried properly by law.

Equality

Some writers thought that equality was even more important than freedom. Jean Jacques Rousseau claimed in his book "The Social Contract" that all men are born free, but they are in chains everywhere. In 1760 he wrote in "Kings and Republics" that a republic is always better than a monarchy, because even the best kings do what they like but people in a republic appoint only men of talent and experience to the highest posts. He also said that all men are born equal and should remain equal.

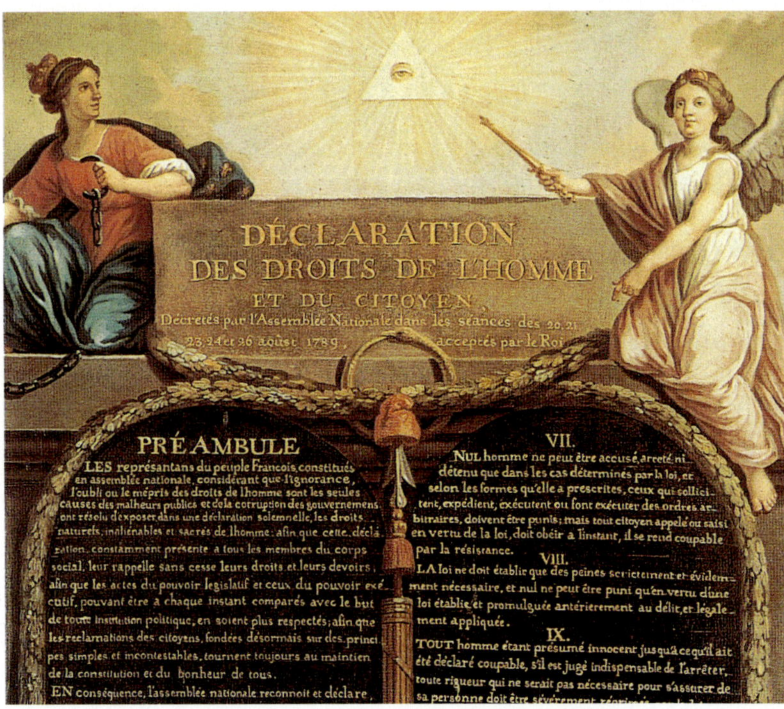

M 1 The Declaration of the Rights of Man and the Citizen
Painting by J. J. LeBarbier, 1790

Fraternity

The ideas and results of the American revolution influenced the development in France. Organizing a state in a peaceful and cooperative way was what the revolutionaries wanted. Everybody was to be everybody else's brother. A wave of patriotism swept over France.

The Rights of Man and the Citizen

The French saw the seventeen articles of the Declaration as the death certificate of absolutism. It became the foundation of the constitution the Assembly created afterwards. The deputies in the National Assembly wanted the document to be valid throughout the entire world. It went even further than the English Bill of Rights of 1689 and marked a new beginning in the relationship between the individual and the state. In effect it turned out to be the very document which recognized rights as high values. Even nowadays people refer to this document in their fight for human rights all over the world.

M 2 Olympe de Gouges (1748–93)

M 3 Extracts from the Declaration of the Rights of Man and the Citizen

The National Assembly began its work to write a constitution by making a "Declaration of the Rights of Man and the Citizen" (August 1789):

"1. Men are born and remain free and equal in rights.
2. The aim of all political association is the preservation of ...liberty, property, security, and resistance to oppression
3. The power to rule comes from the whole nation...
4. Liberty consists in the freedom to do everything which injures no one else...
5. Law can only prohibit such actions as are hurtful to society. Nothing may be prevented which is not forbidden by law.
6. Law is the expression of the general will. It must be the same for all.
9. Every man is innocent until he has been declared guilty."

www.fordham.edu/halsall/mod

M 4 Extracts from the Declaration of the Rights of Woman

Olympe de Gouges, a butcher's daughter and a writer, wrote her "Declaration of the Rights of Woman" in September 1791. Later on she was charged with treason and executed:

"1. Woman is born free and lives equal to man in her rights.
2. The purpose of any political association is the conservation of the natural rights of woman and man; these rights are liberty, property [...]
3. The power to rule comes from the nation which is nothing but the union of woman and man.
4. Liberty and justice consist of restoring all that belongs to others; thus, the only limits on the exercise of the natural rights of woman are perpetual male tyranny; these limits are to be reformed by the laws of nature and reason.
6. All female and male persons must contribute to the formation of the law."

Chris E. Paschold, Albert Gier, Die französische Revolution, Stuttgart 1989, p. 185, translated by RJK.

Tasks

1. Examine the painting and explain what the painter thinks of the Rights of Man (M1).
2. Check in which way the Rights of Man oppose absolutism (M3).
3. Compare the Rights of Man to the Rights of Woman (M3, M4).

to confiscate: to officially take away sb.'s possessions
resistance: opposition
to accept: to agree with sth.
sansculottes: (French) people not wearing fashionable clothing
treason: the crime of trying to destroy one's country or government or helping its enemies
humanity: the quality of being as kind as possible to people
to conduct: to organize a particular activity
in flagrante delicto: while doing sth. bad
to be doomed: to be certain to fail
severity: the state of being extremely serious
yoke: situation that restricts people's freedom

France Becomes a Republic

Changes in the Church

Before the new constitution was finished, a new problem arose. The National Assembly had abolished the clergy and *confiscated* all church land in order to sell it and pay back the state debts. In return the state paid the priests. When the National Assembly demanded that they swear an oath to the constitution, it met *resistance.* Half of the priests and a lot of the farmers rejected the idea. They were supported by the king.

The New Constitution

The reforms seemed to be finished when the new constitution was introduced on 3 September 1791. The electorate was divided into two parts, the "active citizens", four million men over twenty-five who paid high taxes and were allowed to vote, and the "passive citizens", who did not pay enough taxes to vote. Considering those (women, people under age twenty-five, passive citizens) who could not vote, two-thirds of the French population could not participate in politics.

The constitution was founded on Montesquieu's principles of the separation of power into three branches, which even the king had to *accept.* Louis still had considerable influence inside the executive branch. Furthermore, he could delay legislation. He was the official head of state. However, it was clear that Louis rejected the limitations placed on him.

M 1 The King in the Cage of the Constitution
Contemporary caricature

The Flight to Varennes

By 1791 about 40,000 nobles had fled the country, most of them to border towns in Germany. They hoped that they would be able to organize resistance against the new order with the help of German nobles. On 21 June 1791 Louis and his family tried to flee to Germany to join forces with the emigrants. But they were detected in Varennes and escorted back to Paris. By the time of their arrival the *sansculottes,* a large group of Paris radicals, had put up a poster at the city palace: "Flat for rent". The deputies dismissed the king at first, but then changed their minds and made him swear to the constitution instead of making far-reaching changes. Through his attempt to flee the king lost public acceptance and many people said he should be dismissed.

War Breaks Out

The discussion about the king grew heated when the monarchs of Austria and Prussia declared that they would save the French monarchy militarily if they had to. Their declaration caused the French to unite against them and the king. A large majority in the National Assembly declared war. But the enemy proved to be stronger at first. When Austria and Prussia threatened to destroy Paris completely if any harm came to the king, Louis was suspected of being a traitor.

The sansculottes stormed the Tuileries and killed the royal guard. Throughout the month of September they massacred thousands of opponents of the revolution. A new more radical stage was reached. The National Assembly dismissed the king and imprisoned him and his family. Then the Assembly dissolved itself after giving the following National Convention the responsibility to write a new, republican constitution. The new parliament tried the king for *treason*. He was executed in public on 21 January 1793. Soon the military crisis in France worsened and people were called to arms in masses.

M 2 The Execution of Louis XVI

a) In the first of two speeches Saint Just tried to prove to the members of the Convention that they had the political authority to try the king:

"I shall undertake, citizens, to prove that the King can be judged. One day men will be astonished by the fact that *humanity* in the eighteenth century was less advanced than in the time of Caesar. Then a tyrant was slain in the midst of the Senate [...]. And today we respectfully *conduct* a trial for a man who assassinated a people, caught in *flagrante delicto,* his murderous hands soaked with blood!"

b) After the king himself had spoken, Saint Just spoke again, this time urging the deputies to condemn Louis XVI:

"Today will decide the fate of the Republic. It is *doomed* if the tyrant goes unpunished. The enemies of the common good will reappear, meet, and hope. The forces of tyranny will pick up their pieces like a reptile renewing its lost tail. All evil men are for the King. Who here then can join him? False pity is on the lips of some, anger on the lips of others. Everything serves to either corrupt us or frighten us down to our souls. Be steadfast in your *severity* and rest assured of the People's gratitude in the times to come."

http://facstaff.uww.edu/jaffej/great_trials/saintjust.htm

c) As a member of the Convention British-born Thomas Paine, who had written the leaflet 'Common Sense' in the American Revolution and had then become a French citizen, answered Saint Just in the debate over the king's fate:

"My hatred of absolute monarchy is known. Nevertheless I am certain that if Louis Capet had been born in and lived in a respectable neighbourhood, he would not have acted unsocially. We regard him to be worse than his predecessors because our eyes are open now. He cannot be made responsible for the situation if the national assembly that restored him to the throne without the consent of the people is not made responsible as well. The people have beat down royalty, never, never to rise again; they have brought Louis Capet to the bar. There remains only one question to be considered: what is to be done with this man? For myself, I freely confess that apart from all the corruption of his reign there is one circumstance in his life which ought to cover for some of his wrongdoings. Without his support the United States of America would never have been able to shake off the unjust and terrible *yoke*. Let then these United States be the safeguard and asylum to Louis Capet."

www.4literature.net/Thomas_Paine/Paine_Opposes_the_Execution_of LouisXVI, adapted by RJK.

Tasks

1. Explain why Austria and Prussia interfered in the French Revolution.
2. Assess the way Louis XVI was treated by the people and by the politicians (M1).
3. Collect the reasons given for and against the execution of the king (M2).
4. Comment on the arguments for and against his execution (M2).

M 1 **Maximilien Robespierre (1758–1794)**

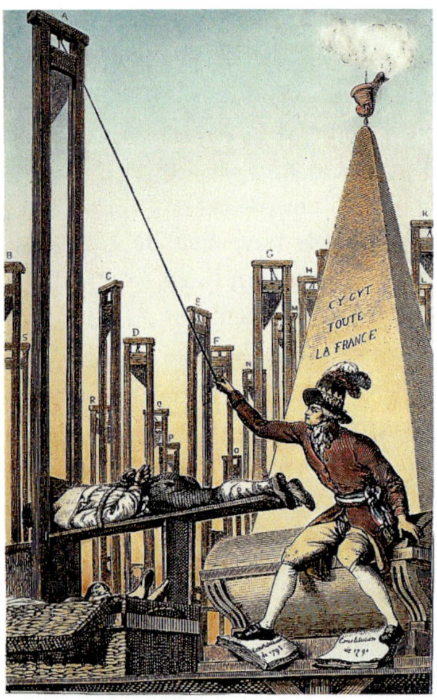

M 2 **"Here Rests all France"**
Satirical leaflet, 1793

The Reign of Terror

Maximilien Robespierre (1758–94) led the French Revolution to its climax and turning point. He rose to power after the fall of the Bastille and became the dominant figure from 1792 until he was guillotined on 28 July 1794.

Politics in Paris

In the fourty-eight sections of Paris "patriotic federations" were formed. One of these groups, the "Club of the Friends of Human Rights" supervised how human rights were dealt with by the authorities. The club was led by Danton and Marat, two men who followed Rousseau's philosophy both using their voices and their *demagogic* abilities to the full. Together with other groups like the Jacobins, the Cordeliers and some men from the Gironde, they formed the Democrats in the first National Assembly.

The Jacobins and the Girondins in the Assembly split over the question of war against the European monarchies. The most *influential* member of the Jacobins was Robespierre, who soon after became their leader. Speaking about *virtue* was something he liked more than political action. Marat once called him "l'incorruptible", pointing out the characteristic which helped him succeed. It was Robespierre's suggestion that no member of the Constituante could be elected to the Legislative Assembly in 1791. Because of this prohibition more radical revolutionaries were elected to the parliament than before. They then voted for war.

Crisis of the State

As a member of the Convention Robespierre voted for the death of the king. Then he increased his attacks on the Girondins and supported the uprising in Paris. After Danton was murdered he led the Convention's Committee of Public Safety, a group of twelve revolutionaries who ruled through emergency measures.

The war, hunger riots and domestic problems brought France to a state of civil war. In addition, some of the people of Paris wanted more radical solutions. In order to defend and save the country Robespierre called all Frenchmen to take up arms ("levée en masse"). On their way to the front the new soldiers sang a song called the "Marseillaise", which is now the French national anthem.

The Reign of Terror

Robespierre introduced terror as a principle of government. He wanted to develop the ideas of 1789 and establish true liberty, equality and fraternity. Opponents to the new system were sentenced to death by revolutionary tribunals and executed immediately. More than 12,000 were officially guillotined, but many more died in other ways. The Convention decreed the destruction of a whole city and set up a memorial to it with the inscription: "Lyons made war on liberty; Lyons no longer exists."

In addition he imposed a new calendar with 1792 being the year one of the revolution. In order to create an entirely new society, he invented

demagogic: using emotion, not reason, to persuade people
influential: having influence and power
virtue: high moral standards
spring: (here) source or origin of sth.
to subdue: to bring sth. under control by force

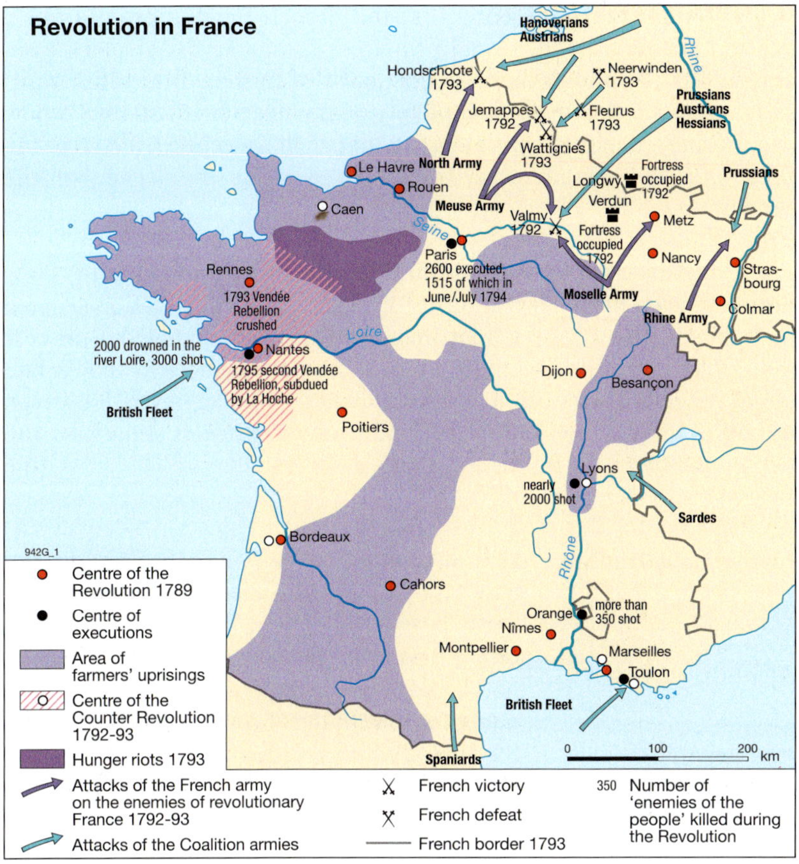

M 3

a new cult replacing religion. In an attempt to cut off all tradition he changed the names of 6,000 towns, of animals and plants.

But he had become too powerful. When the crisis had passed in July 1794 and terror was no longer needed, the deputies of the Convention feared for their lives, voted for Robespierre's arrest and had him guillotined.

M 4 Virtue and Terror

Robespierre explained the nature of his philosophy of terror:

a) "We want a country in which the government looks after the welfare of every individual. One's duty is to punish traitors, to help the needy, respect the weak, defend the oppressed, do good to one's neighbour and behave justly."

Colin Shepherd, Societies in Change. John Murray London 1992, p. 144.

b) "If the *spring* of popular government in time of peace is virtue, the springs of popular government in revolution are at once virtue and terror: virtue, without which terror is fatal; terror, without which virtue is powerless. Terror is nothing other than justice, prompt, severe, inflexible; it is therefore an emanation of virtue; it is not so much a special principle as it is a consequence of the general principle of democracy applied to our country's most urgent needs, [...] Let the despot govern by terror his brutalized subjects; he is right , as a despot. *Subdue* by terror the enemies of liberty, and you will be right, as founders of the Republic. The government of the revolution is liberty's despotism against tyranny."

www.fordham.edu/halsall/mod/robespierre-terror.html

Tasks

1. Collect information on Robespierre's career from this text and the Internet.
2. Explain Robespierre's role in the course of the French Revolution.
3. Describe the leaflet (M2).
4. Analyse the state of France in 1793 (M3).
5. Define the attitude of the radical Jacobins to the people of France.
6. Assess Robespierre's ideas on government (M4).
7. Say why Robespierre was not successful in the end.

M 1 **Thomas Paine (1737–1809)**

The *Legacy* of the Revolution

It became obvious very early that the French Revolution was not a passing incident. Its ideas and principles spread across borders, even before Napoleon took them to most parts of Europe. Many historians say it changed the world completely; some even say it started a new age. Because it marked such a great change, it was controversial at the time and has remained so today. So what is the legacy of the revolution?

The Controversy between Edmund Burke and Thomas Paine

Soon after the three revolutions of 1789 the political situation seemed to stabilize. Not knowing that they were only *witnesses* to a process that would go on for a longer time, some people thought that it had already ended. They started to assess what had been achieved. However, not all of them were of the same opinion. The extracts show how the two *contemporaries* Burke and Paine disagreed.

M 2 Reflections on the Revolution in France

Edmund Burke wrote a letter to a young French aristocrat explaining how he felt about the French Revolution. The letter was published as a book in 1790:

"Abstractedly speaking, government, as well as liberty, is good; yet could I in common sense, ten years ago, have *felicitated* France on her enjoyment of a government [...] without *inquiry* what the nature of that government was, or how it was *administered*? Can I now congratulate the same nation upon its freedom? Is it because liberty in the abstract may be classed amongst the blessings of mankind, that I am seriously to felicitate a madman, who has escaped from the protecting *restraint* and wholesome darkness of his cell, on his restoration to the enjoyment of light and liberty? Am I to congratulate a *highwayman* and murderer who has broke prison upon the recovery of his natural rights?

When I see the spirit of liberty in action, I see a strong principle at work [...]. I must be tolerably sure before I venture publicly to congratulate men upon a blessing that they have really received one [...].

I should, therefore, suspend my congratulations on the new liberty of France until I was informed how it had been combined with government, with public force, with the discipline and *obedience* of the armies, with the collection of an effective and well-distributed *revenue*, with morality and religion, with the solidity of property, with peace and order, with civil and social manners. All these (in their way) are good things, too, and without them liberty is not a benefit whilst it lasts, and is not likely to continue long."

Edmund Burke, Reflections on the Revolution in France, 1790 (from www.knuten.liu.se/~bjoch509/works/burke/reflections.html).

M 4 **Edmund Burke (1729–1797)**

M 3 An Answer to Mr Burke's Attack

Thomas Paine replied to Burke's arguments in a book published in 1791. When it appeared in print in Britain, Paine was tried and convicted of trying to overthrow the government:

"We now come more particularly to the affairs of France. Mr. Burke's book has the appearance of being written as instruction to the French nation; but if I may permit myself the use of an extravagant metaphor [...] it is darkness attempting to illuminate light.

'We have seen,' says Mr. Burke, 'the French rebel against a mild and lawful monarch, with more fury, outrage, and insult, than any people has been known to rise against the most illegal *usurper* [...]'. This is one among a thousand other instances, in which Mr. Burke shows that he is ignorant of the springs and principles of the French Revolution. It was not against Louis XVI. but against the *despotic* principles of the Government, that the nation revolted. These principles had not their origin in him, but in the original establishment, many centuries back: and they were become too deeply rooted to be removed, and the *Augean stables* of parasites and plunderers too *abominably* filthy to be cleansed by anything short of a complete and universal Revolution [...]. In the instance of France we see a Revolution generated in the rational *contemplation* of the Rights of Man, and distinguishing from the beginning between persons and principles.

But Mr. Burke appears to have no idea of principles when he is contemplating Governments. 'Ten years ago,' says he, 'I could have felicitated France on her having a Government, without inquiring what the nature of that Government was, or how it was administered.' Is this the language of a rational man? Is it the language of a heart feeling as it ought to feel for the rights and happiness of the human race? On this ground, Mr. Burke must compliment all the Governments in the world, while the victims who suffer under them, whether sold into slavery, or tortured out of existence, are wholly forgotten. It is power, and not principles, that Mr. Burke *venerates*; and under this abominable *depravity* he is disqualified to judge between them. Thus much for his opinion as to the occasions of the French Revolution."

Thomas Paine, The Rights of Man. Being an Answer to Mr Burke's Attack on the French Revolution, part 2 of 16. Paris 1791-92 (from www.ushistory.org/Paine).

legacy: a situation that exists now because of actions in the past
witness: a person who sees sth. happen
contemporary: a person who lives at the time in question
to felicitate: to congratulate
inquiry: (BE enquiry) official process to find out sth.
to administer: to manage and organize the affairs of a country
restraint: a rule that limits or controls what people can do
highwayman: a robber
obedience: the act of doing what you are told to do
revenue: the money a government receives from taxes
usurper: a person who takes sb.'s position illegally
despotic: using great power, often in a cruel way
Augean stables: in Greek mythology a task assigned to Hercules. King Augeas had the largest herd of cattle in Greece and kept it in stables which had never been cleaned. Hercules had to clean them in one day.
abominable: extremely unpleasant and disgusting
contemplation: the act of thinking deeply about sth.
to venerate: to have or show a lot of respect for sb.
depravity: the state of being morally bad

Analysing Historical Texts:

1. Describing the texts

a. Name the authors and the roles they played when the texts were written.
b. Define the text type (e.g. letter, note, speech, pamphlet, law, etc.)
c. Describe the situation in which the texts were written.
d. Sum up the main points of the texts in your own words.

2. Analysing the texts

a. Analyse the texts in detail and state the authors' intentions.
b. Examine the facts the authors mention and those they do not mention.
c. Point out misconceptions in the texts, if there are any.
d. Look at the content and the language of the texts. Show what both say about the authors.
e. Explain the main points of agreement and disagreement between the authors.

3. Evaluating the texts

a. Assess how much influence the texts had on the situation/the proceedings.
b. Find arguments you approve or disapprove of.
c. Discuss the validity of the arguments.
d. Comment on how much you learn from the texts.

Napoleon

Born in Corsica in 1769, Napoleon started his brilliant military career at the age of nine, when he was sent by his parents to a military academy in France, which he left as a young lieutenant when he was sixteen. In the course of the revolution he had changed sides from time to time in order to pursue his career, which led to his becoming a general at the age of twenty-four.

M 1 **The First Consul, 1799**
Painting by Jean-A.-Dominique Ingres, 1804.

Did at the begining mistakes and his brother saved him. Later he convinced all of his idears.

He crowend himself by taking it away from the pope's hands and put it by himself on his head

decisiveness: ability to decide
coup d'état: a sudden, illegal and often violent change of government
ensuing: happening as the result of another event
undisputed: sth. that cannot be questioned
to sue: to make a legal claim

First Steps to Power

In 1793 Napoleon had suppressed a royalist revolt for the Convention. After Robespierre the wealthy citizens returned to power and gave France a new constitution with a government of five directors. They ordered Napoleon to put down a demonstration of hungry people in 1795. Due to his energy and *decisiveness* he was soon promoted to the rank of major general and given command of the French troops in the war against Austria, to whom he dictated the peace treaty of Campo Formio in 1797.

Trouble at Sea

was sent to Egypt to get rid of him

While he was on his next military campaign to Egypt, the British fleet under the command of Admiral Nelson defeated the French fleet at Aboukir in August 1798. It was not the only time that the French lost a sea battle. In 1805 Napoleon suffered a final and disastrous defeat at Trafalgar which ended all attempts to win against the English at sea. Admiral Nelson lost his life in the battle, but became a national hero.

Gaining Political Power

After Aboukir Napoleon left his soldiers secretly to return to Paris where he organized a *coup d'état*. He overthrew the directors and made himself first consul in November 1799. In power he officially declared the revolution to be over. Four years later he risked a referendum to be elected as lifelong first consul. The risk was not very great because he had had a lot of military and political success before, including the victorious battle of Marengo against the Austrians and the *ensuing* peace treaty of Lunéville. He had also made peace with Britain in 1802 and the Russian tsar withdrew his troops from western Europe. Napoleon had become the *undisputed* leader of his country. The signing of a concordat with the pope brought back the Catholic church to France, however under the control of the state. A second referendum in 1804 made him Emperor of the French. He was then crowned by the pope at Notre Dame in Paris. France was a monarchy again, but the country had changed.

Domestic Policies

Under Napoleon noble emigrants came back to France and the wounds from the revolution slowly healed. He set out to make dramatic reforms. The government was organized under a new centralized prefect system. Prefects ran the 83 regions, making sure that Napoleon's commands were obeyed in each of the departments. The education system was reorganized, giving more boys an opportunity to learn. State schools were set up which were not controlled by the church. A currency reform solved the financial problems. The most important step was the introduction of the "Code Napoleon", a complete change of the legal system. The new laws were simple and ensured many of the rights that citizens had gained during the revolution. But he also introduced censorship of the press again.

M 2 **The General, 1796**
Painting by Antoine-Jean Gros

M 3 **The Imperator, 1805**
Painting by François Gérard, 1810

M 4 A Collection of Laws from the Code Civil

Some laws from the Code Napoleon:

"1. People are equal before the law.
2. Feudal rights and privileges are ended.
3. Religious freedom is guaranteed.
4. A husband owes protection to his wife, a wife must be obedient to her husband.
5. Wives can only own property with their husband's written permission.
6. A wife may only *sue* for divorce if her husband's mistress actually lives in the family's household.
7. Fathers are allowed to imprison their children for up to one month.
8. There is freedom of thought."

Tasks

1. Collect the reasons that enabled Napoleon to take over power.
2. Explain why Napoleon wanted to become emperor.
3. Say what role religion played in Napoleonic France.

principality: a country ruled by a prince
conquest: the act of taking control of a country or a city
to compensate: to provide sth. good in order to balance a loss
to inflict: to cause sth. unpleasant to happen
responsibility: a duty to fulfil of so that you will be blamed if sth. goes wrong
shortcoming: a fault in a plan or system
impetus: a force that encourages a process to move more quickly

The Revolution and Europe

Opposition to the Revolution

Many French nobles who wanted to get away from the threats of the revolution fled to one of the German *principalities* on the right bank of the Rhine. From there they influenced the German princes to start a war against revolutionary France. But after Napoleon had taken over power, the tide quickly turned. He won battles and seemed unbeatable due to his strategic talent. Even the renewed alliance of Russia, Prussia and Britain could not hinder his *conquests* from Spain to the river Elbe. After the final defeat of Prussia in 1806 he began a reorganization of central and eastern Europe, in which his ally, the king of Saxony, ruled the Grand Duchy of Warsaw (formerly Poland) and Prussia was occupied by French troops.

The Principal Decree of the Imperial Deputation

Napoleon wanted to crush Austrian influence in the German principalities to gain hegemony over Europe. The three southern principalities of Baden, Württemberg and Bavaria which had helped him against the Austrians became kingdoms or grand duchies and were given much more land. He "mediatized" forty-five free cities and the lands of 1500 imperial knights into forty medium-sized states, sixteen of which were joined in the Confederation of the Rhine (1806) and made French allies. In order to *compensate* the German princes who had lost land to France on the west bank of the Rhine he "secularized" church lands on the east bank and distributed it among the Protestant princes. All these measures meant the end

M 1

of the Holy Roman Empire. When the Habsburg emperor realized that he had lost his empire, he set aside the crown but retained the title of Emperor of Austria to keep the same rank as Napoleon.

Reorganization of Europe

After his defeat in the sea Battle of Trafalgar Napoleon dropped his plan to attack Britain directly. He turned east, winning the Battle of Jena and Auerstedt, thus *inflicting* a devastating defeat on Prussia, which collapsed. Poland was renamed the Grand Duchy of Warsaw and ruled by the king of Saxony. Napoleon secured his reign in Europe by marrying some of his family members to members of the leading aristocratic families. His brother Jerome was made king of the newly founded Westphalia, formed from Prussian and other territory. He wanted it to be a model state for the results of the French Revolution. So he also introduced the Code Napoleon.

M 2 **Karl Friedrich vom Stein** (1757–1831) started the reforms.

The Prussian Reforms

The defeat against the French showed that Prussia could only survive if reforms were undertaken. Many Prussians, who had been looking forward to French reforms, were soon disappointed because of the negative consequences of the occupation. However, a handful of progressive civil servants started reforms. They wanted to unite the people behind the crown, so that Prussia could regain the power it needed to beat Napoleon. Their main targets of change were society, the economy and the military. They wanted to awaken a sense of *responsibility* in the people. The reforms thoroughly modernized Prussia, because farmers were liberated, towns got the right to govern themselves, people could choose their professions freely and Jews were given equal rights. Everybody had to serve in the army and the system of education was improved. The main aim was to use every citizen.

M 3 **Karl August von Hardenberg** (1750–1822)

M 4 **Reorganization of the Prussian State**

Karl August of Hardenberg (1812):

"Despite its many *shortcomings* the French Revolution has given the French a new *impetus.* All the sleeping power has been awakened, the bad things have been destroyed, alongside with many good things. […] The misunderstanding that the revolution could be held up by strict persecution has promoted it, so that it has spread. The power of the ideas of the revolution is so big and has been accepted so widely that the states which don't accept them will either die or be forced to introduce them.

It is our aim to carry out a revolution led by the wisdom of the government, a revolution that allows people to become better. The pure form of democracy will possibly be invented in the year 2440, but it is our guiding principle to introduce democratic elements in a monarchical society by means of a good revolution."

Walter Demel, Uwe Puschner, Deutsche Geschichte in Quellen und Darstellung, Bd.6, Stuttgart 1995, p. 87 f. transl. by RJK.

Tasks

1. Compare the situation in Germany before and after the changes (M1).
2. Find out who profited from the Confederation of the Rhine and who didn't.
3. Collect information on the Prussian reforms.

recollection: memories
campaign: a series of attacks and battles in a war
corpse: dead body

The Wars of Liberation

The Continental System

Despite his military success on land Napoleon could not prevent his fleet from losing sea battles against the British. Napoleon was so disappointed at having to drop his plans to attack Britain from the sea that he even considered building a tunnel under the Dover Strait.

But he changed his tactics. From 1806 on he tried to weaken England by a trade war. The ports of Europe were closed for English goods. A year later even Russia joined in. However, people needed British goods like cloth, coffee or tea. In order to close the European harbours completely Napoleon attacked Spain and Portugal but he was unable to get them under control. In the north Hamburg became the gateway for British goods, despite the fact that it was under French control. If they got hold of these goods the French publicly burnt them. The

M 1 Continental Blockade
Burning smuggled goods in Frankfurt/Main, 1810

coastline of Europe, however, proved to be too long for Napoleon's strategy.

Opposition

In many parts of Europe people became discontent with Napoleon's reign. When he tried to make his brother Joseph king of Spain in 1808, the Spanish resisted and began to fight for their freedom. They did not do it in the usual way but invented "guerilla" warfare, which meant that there were no open attacks of a Spanish army but partisans attacked anywhere at any time. In a number of areas farmers' uprisings took place like the one in Southern Tyrol led by Andreas Hofer. The French reaction was violent throughout.

The End

Napoleon soon seemed to have gone too far. The turning point came in 1812 when he tried to occupy Russia with an army of 600,000. He lost most of his soldiers there due to the weather and the Russian strategy. They even burnt their capital in order to keep Napoleon from benefiting from its conquest. Only 5,000 soldiers got out of Russia safely at the end of the campaign.

Prussia and Austria now started the Wars of Liberation and were supported by the tsar, who did not stop fighting after he had defeated Napoleon and driven him out of Russia. In the Battle of the Nations at Leipzig the allies beat Napoleon in 1813 and occupied Paris in 1814. He had to vacate his throne. From exile on the island of Elba, he returned for another 100 days as emperor. After losing the Battle of Waterloo he was banned to St. Helena in the South Atlantic where he died in 1821.

The ideas of the revolution, however, had spread all over Europe. The "Code Napoleon" had become the law in many places and many peoples had discovered their wish to form nations of their own.

M 2 Napoleon's Grand Army on its Retreat from Russia, 1812
Contemporary painting

M 3 *Recollections* of Participants of the Russian War

a) Armand de Caulaincourt (1837):

"The emperor was always anxious to obtain everything at the least possible expense and the result was [...] everything had been loaded on wagons in the hope of being able to take possession of horses from the countryside. This had always been done in previous *campaigns* but in Russia there was no means of doing so. Horses, cattle, inhabitants had all fled and we found ourselves in the middle of a desert."

b) Général Comte de Segur (1873):

"I had gone all day with nothing to eat, and I spent that night – the coldest of any – without food, in a hut open to the wind, surrounded by *corpses*. This room was next to a huge barn and during that bitterly cold night between four and five hundred took refuge inside. At least three quarters of them froze to death, even though they had lain one on top of the other around several fires."

Adapted from: Brooman, Revolution in France, p. 76-77.

Tasks

1. Discuss the meaning of the Continental System for Britain and for France (M1).
2. Find reasons why the people of Europe turned against Napoleon.
3. Explain why Napoleon's attack on Russia failed (M2, M3).
4. Discuss in which way fighting against Napoleon changed the people in Europe.

Industrialization

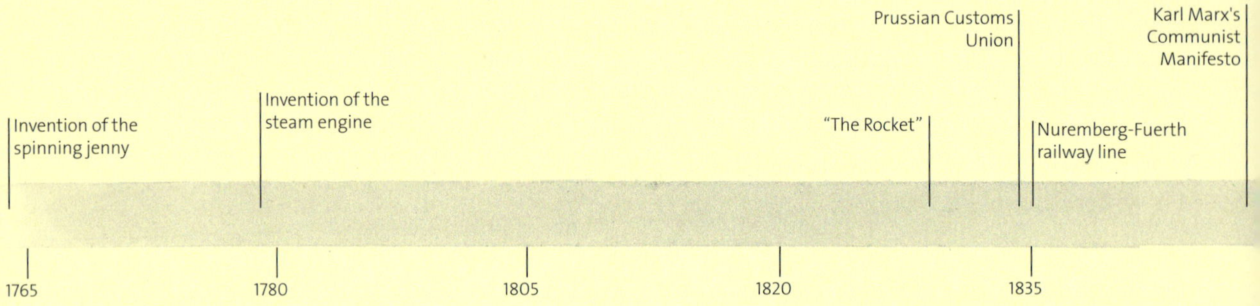

Banner of the German Social-Democratic Party

Model of the Steam Engine by James Watt, 1769

Child Labour: Children Working in a Coal Mine

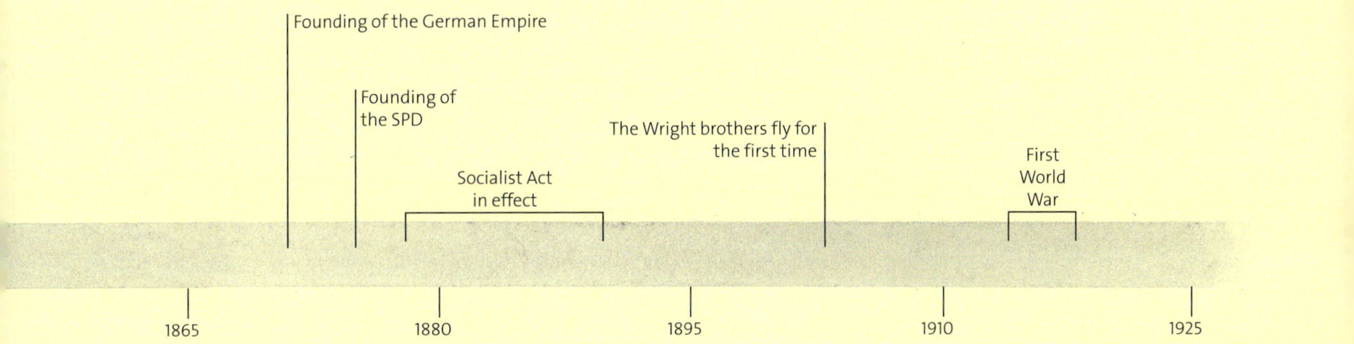

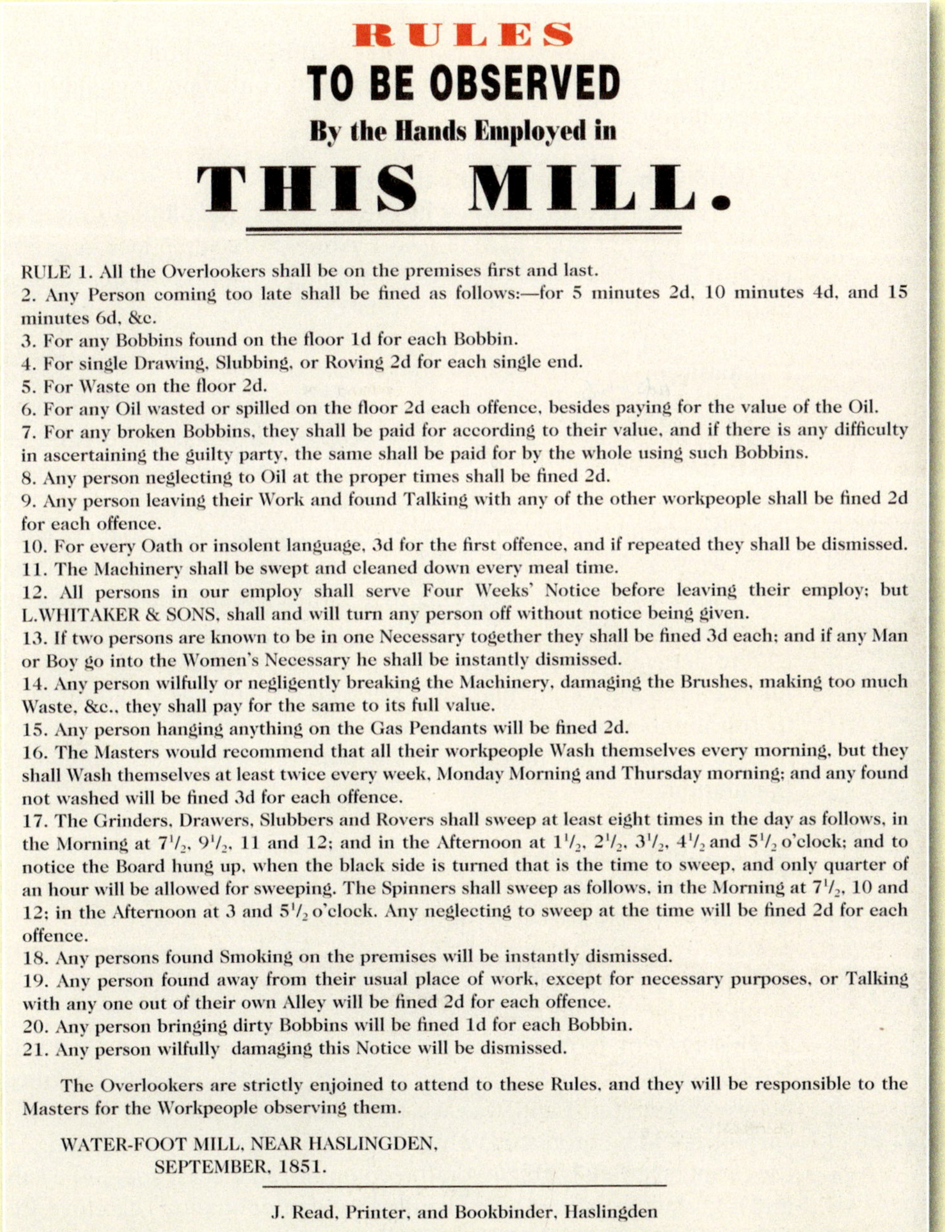

RULES
TO BE OBSERVED
By the Hands Employed in
THIS MILL.

RULE 1. All the Overlookers shall be on the premises first and last.
2. Any Person coming too late shall be fined as follows:—for 5 minutes 2d, 10 minutes 4d, and 15 minutes 6d, &c.
3. For any Bobbins found on the floor 1d for each Bobbin.
4. For single Drawing, Slubbing, or Roving 2d for each single end.
5. For Waste on the floor 2d.
6. For any Oil wasted or spilled on the floor 2d each offence, besides paying for the value of the Oil.
7. For any broken Bobbins, they shall be paid for according to their value, and if there is any difficulty in ascertaining the guilty party, the same shall be paid for by the whole using such Bobbins.
8. Any person neglecting to Oil at the proper times shall be fined 2d.
9. Any person leaving their Work and found Talking with any of the other workpeople shall be fined 2d for each offence.
10. For every Oath or insolent language, 3d for the first offence, and if repeated they shall be dismissed.
11. The Machinery shall be swept and cleaned down every meal time.
12. All persons in our employ shall serve Four Weeks' Notice before leaving their employ; but L.WHITAKER & SONS, shall and will turn any person off without notice being given.
13. If two persons are known to be in one Necessary together they shall be fined 3d each; and if any Man or Boy go into the Women's Necessary he shall be instantly dismissed.
14. Any person wilfully or negligently breaking the Machinery, damaging the Brushes, making too much Waste, &c., they shall pay for the same to its full value.
15. Any person hanging anything on the Gas Pendants will be fined 2d.
16. The Masters would recommend that all their workpeople Wash themselves every morning, but they shall Wash themselves at least twice every week, Monday Morning and Thursday morning; and any found not washed will be fined 3d for each offence.
17. The Grinders, Drawers, Slubbers and Rovers shall sweep at least eight times in the day as follows, in the Morning at $7^{1}/_{2}$, $9^{1}/_{2}$, 11 and 12; and in the Afternoon at $1^{1}/_{2}$, $2^{1}/_{2}$, $3^{1}/_{2}$, $4^{1}/_{2}$ and $5^{1}/_{2}$ o'clock; and to notice the Board hung up, when the black side is turned that is the time to sweep, and only quarter of an hour will be allowed for sweeping. The Spinners shall sweep as follows, in the Morning at $7^{1}/_{2}$, 10 and 12; in the Afternoon at 3 and $5^{1}/_{2}$ o'clock. Any neglecting to sweep at the time will be fined 2d for each offence.
18. Any persons found Smoking on the premises will be instantly dismissed.
19. Any person found away from their usual place of work, except for necessary purposes, or Talking with any one out of their own Alley will be fined 2d for each offence.
20. Any person bringing dirty Bobbins will be fined 1d for each Bobbin.
21. Any person wilfully damaging this Notice will be dismissed.

The Overlookers are strictly enjoined to attend to these Rules, and they will be responsible to the Masters for the Workpeople observing them.

WATER-FOOT MILL, NEAR HASLINGDEN,
SEPTEMBER, 1851.

J. Read, Printer, and Bookbinder, Haslingden

Rules from Water-Foot Mill near Haslingden in Lancashire, 1851

invention: production of sth. new that has not existed before
improvement: something made better
to exeed: to be greater than...
cottage industry: people working at home
vaccination: medicine that is given to immunize a person or animal
famine: little or no food for a long time
supply: an amount of sth. that is provided or available
fertilizer: substance added to soil to make plants grow
fallow: not used for growing crops
to breed (bred, bred): to mate, to couple

M 1

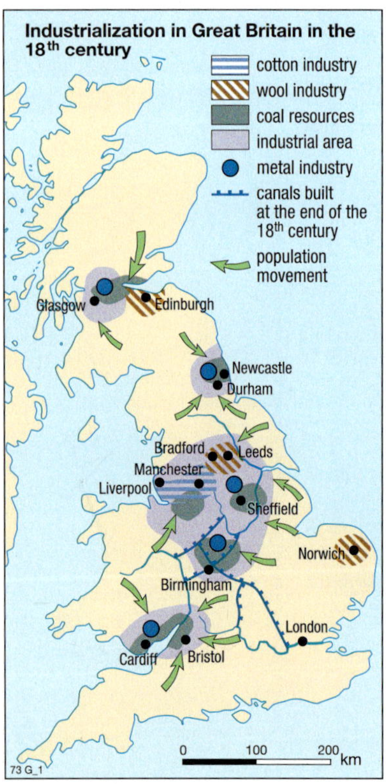

Industrialization in Great Britain in the 18th century

The Industrial Revolution

Drastic Changes

From 1750 to 1850 the population almost doubled. Technical *inventions* like the steam engine or the spinning jenny and later *improvements* of the loom sped up production processes and increased production.

The steam engine, which did not depend on location or climate, brought about the most significant change. Its power *exceeded* human muscle power many times. Therefore, handicraft (*cottage industry* as well as manufactory production) and man's relationship to nature and the environment changed drastically.

A new era dominated by machines had begun – industrialization. The changes were so dramatic and fast that contemporaries spoke of a "revolution".

England – the Cradle of Industrialization

There is no clear explanation why the Industrial Revolution started in England and not anywhere else in Europe. Still, some factors might explain England's lead in industrialization compared to other regions in Europe.

Population

Not only improvements in medical treatment, such as *vaccination* and hygiene, but also the fact that more people married and had children (there had been restrictions on marriage in the Middle Ages and Early Modern Times) led to population growth.

More people moved into towns and cities to find work, so there were more workers for the newly developing industries after 1750. However, this also caused major changes in agriculture, because people living in urban areas could not grow their own food.

The clergyman and mathematician Thomas Malthus wrote in "Essay on The Principle of Population" (1798) that there was a natural limit to the number of people which was enforced by epidemics, war or *famine*. Accordingly, nature kept a balance between food *supply* and population.

Agricultural Changes

Traditionally farmers worked on open fields. They changed the crops they grew yearly to keep the land productive. This was necessary, because they did not have any chemical *fertilizers*. A village usually had three large fields plus a common, where every local farmer could bring a number of animals to graze.

This type of farming was problematic for several reasons: Little fodder for the animals could be produced, so they had to be killed before the winter. Land was wasted when it lay *fallow*. Hardly any surplus could be produced, which could have been sold or traded. All the farmers' animals grazed on the common, so diseases spread easily and high-quality animals *bred* with those of poor quality. Therefore, the richer landowners did much better outside the open fields with their disadvantages. In addition, they could afford to experiment.

The good results did not come overnight, it took more than 200 years to see improvement in agriculture. Farmers learnt by experience how to end the inefficient production of open field farming. Sir Richard Weston discovered that planting turnips and clover helped the soil recover its fertility. So over four years a different crop was planted on each field. This system was known as the Four Year Rotation or Norfolk Rotation. Traditional farmers resisted this new system, so it took quite a while to become widespread.

to broadcast: (here) to throw by hand
to thresh: to separate grain from the rest of the plant
to winnow: to blow air through grain in order to remove its outer covering
to reap: to cut and collect a crop from a field

Inventions and Economical Thinking

Things kept changing: In 1701 John Tull invented a seed drill to sow straight lines of seed in the soil instead of *broadcasting* it on top. *Threshing, winnowing* and *reaping* machines were invented in 1826. In 1856 John Fowler of Leeds invented a steam plough.

Machinery and new methods in growing crops were not the only factors which led to the "agricultural revolution". Animal breeding also improved. One pioneer, Robert Bakewell produced larger sheep on his Leicestershire farm. Earlier, sheep had been bred mainly for wool. Bakewell bred big, fat sheep for food. He was less successful in breeding better cattle. But his ideas influenced others who produced such cattle and later bigger pigs and stronger horses.

M 2

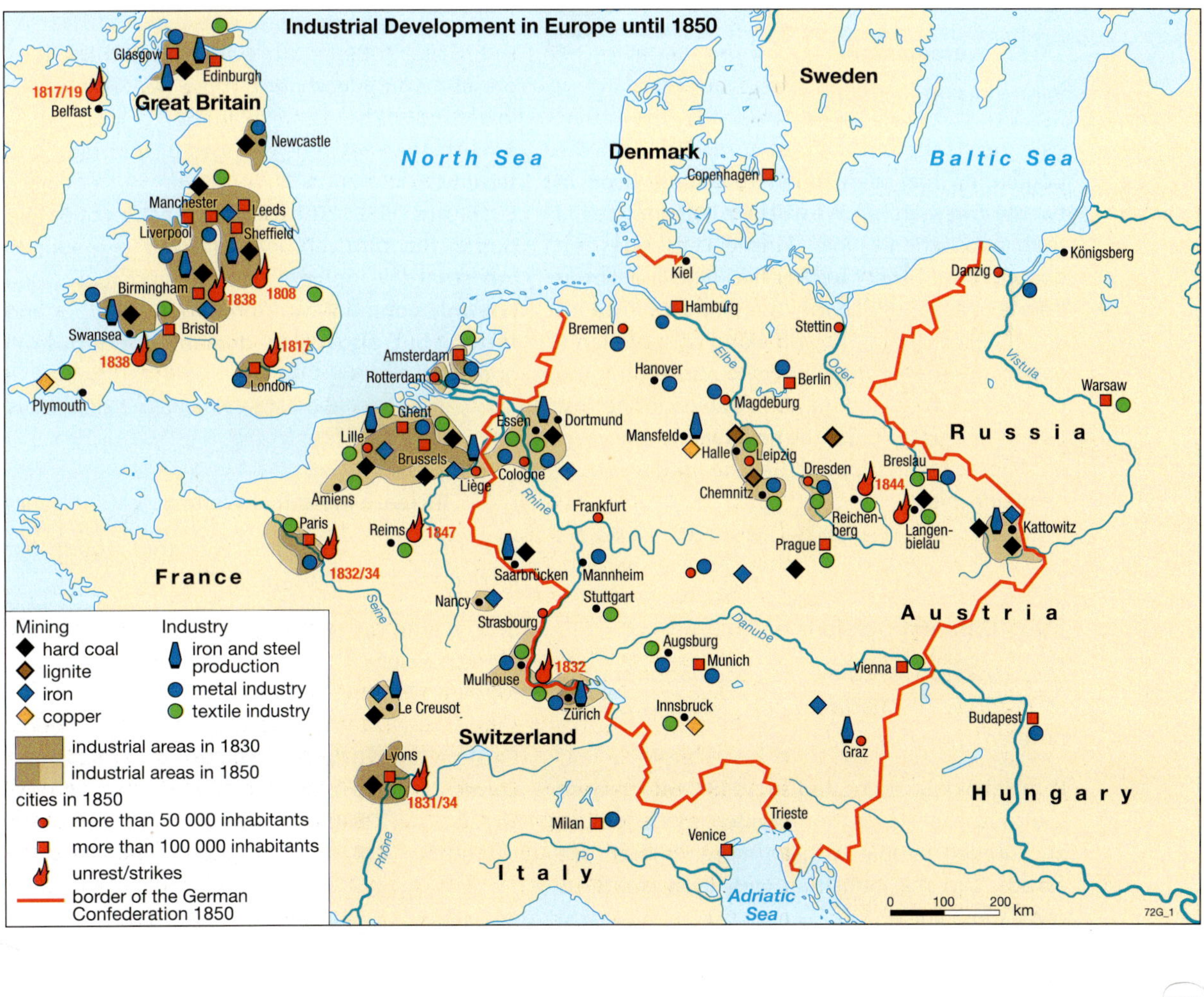

M 3

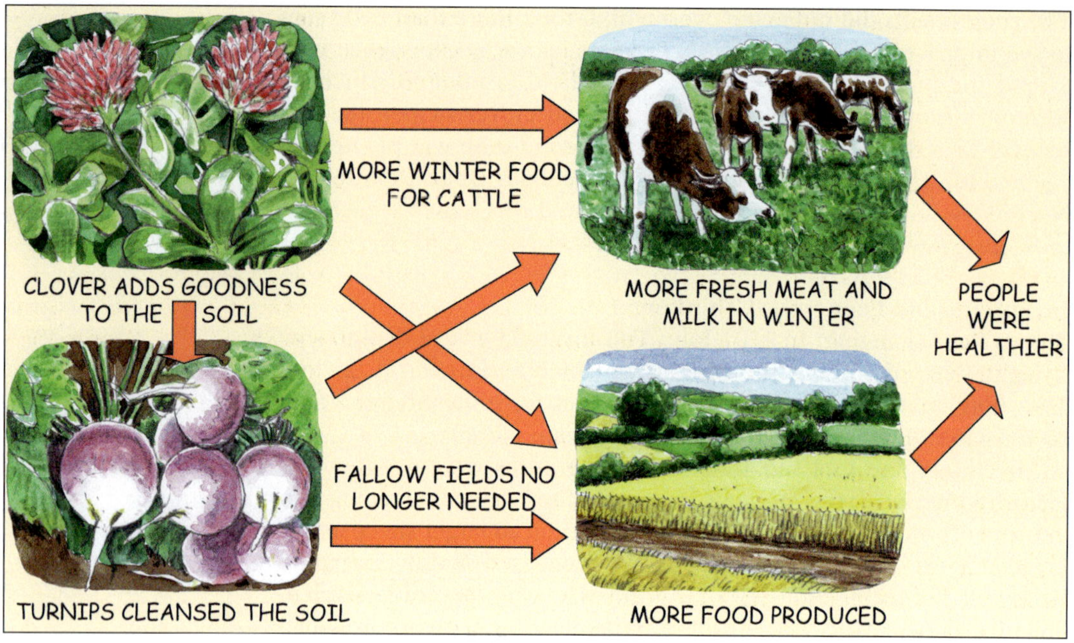

M 4 Overpopulation

Thomas Malthus, 1798:

"In the United States of America [...] the population has been found to double itself in twenty-five years [...]. We will take it as our rule [...] that population, when unchecked, goes on doubling itself every twenty-five years [...]. Let us now take any spot of earth, this island for instance [...]. If I allow that [...] by breaking up more land, and by great *encouragements* to agriculture, the produce of this island may be doubled in the first twenty-five years, [...] in the next twenty-five years it is impossible to suppose that the produce could be *quadrupled.*"

R. J. Cootes / L. E. Snellgrove, Expansion Trade and Industry, Hong Kong 1993, p. 44.

M 5 Different Opinions

Nobody is sure why the British population started to outgrow its "natural limit". Historians have different opinions:

H.J. Habakkuk suggested in 1958 that because the Industrial Revolution created more jobs, it encouraged people to have more children. He asked: "Did the Industrial Revolution create its own labour force?"

D.V. Glass, 1965: "Such evidence as there is at present would lean much more heavily towards lower *mortality* as an explanation of population growth than towards changes in marriage and fertility."

E.J. Ewans, 1983: "The rise in population of Britain during the 18th century [...] acted as a *spur* to industrial development in Britain since it provided not only potential workforce for workshops and factory but also rising demand for industrial goods."

Adapted from H. Macdonald, From Workshop to Empire. Britain 1750–1900, Hong Kong 1995, p. 57.

M 6 Increase in Animal Weight

The House of Commons was told about the increase in animal weight in 1795:

In 1710 the cattle and sheep sold at Smithfield Market weighed, on an average, as follows:
Now (in 1795) they weigh:

	1710	1795
Cattle:	370 lb.	800 lb.
Calves:	50 lb.	143 lb.
Sheep:	28 lb.	80 lb.
Lambs:	18 lb.	50 lb.

IPTS, Materialien zum Bilingualen Unterricht, Geschichte, Bd. 7 (9. Jahrgang Gymnasium), 1998, p. 7.

M 7 Industrial Revolution

The historian Carlo Cipolla writes about the importance of the Industrial Revolution:

"I said before that the only event historically comparable to the Industrial Revolution is the Neolithic Revolution. But apart from every other *consideration,* the Neolithic Revolution developed in the course of thousands of years. It took more than 5,000 years to move from the Middle East to Scandinavia and about 2,500 years to pass through from Mexico to the source of the Ohio river. Man had time to adapt gradually. The Industrial Revolution has invaded the world, turned our very existence upside down and overthrown the structures of all existing human societies in the course of only eight generations. And today it is beginning to press with great *urgency* new problems of such enormity that the human mind can harldy *grasp* them – the uncontrolled increase in population; the hydrogen bomb; the pollution of the atmosphere; the destruction of the natural surroundings by industrial waste; the demand for further mass education; the presence of an ever-increasing number of old people kept alive but rejected by the rest of society; the breaking up of the traditional state; the scientific organisation of uncontrolled centres of power; the unlimited possibilities held out by *geneticists* and biologists of influencing nature and the behaviour of man. Under the weight of these problems the old structures crumble. The conservatives complain that they do not understand what is happening and they *deceive themselves* by trying to keep alive a past which is already dead. Those who understand what is happening do not know of and cannot *conceive* adequate solutions to these pressing and *formidable* problems. The young people protest when they realise the inadequacy of the old institutions and the older generation, but they too have no better diagnoses and no better cures, and they *give vent* to their frustration in surges of violent anarchy and curious hatred against their inheritance, or try to escape reality either by destroying their consciousness or by a desperate search for new religions. Everyone has been taken by surprise. It is the story of the 'Sorcerer's Apprentice' which would be funny if it were not tragic."

Carlo M. Cipolla (ed.), The Fontana Economic History of Europe. Vol.3: The Industrial Revolution, London: Collins; 1973, p. 20f.

encouragement: the act of giving support or hope to sb.
to quadruple: to multiply by four
mortality: the number of deaths in a period of time
spur: (here) motivation
consideration: the act of thinking carefully about sth.
urgency: need to deal with quickly
to grasp: to understand sth. compeletely
geneticist: a scientist who studies in genetics
to deceive oneself: to refuse to admit to yourself that sth. unpleasant is true
to conceive: to form an idea, plan, etc. in your mind; to imagine
formidable: sth. impressive or powerful, because it is very difficult/complicated
to give vent to: to express a feeling, esp. anger, strongly

Tasks

1. List the factors that led to industrialization in England.
2. What does Malthus fear? Explain Malthus's warning in your own words (M4).
3. a) Compare the historians' ideas (M5).
   b) Explain the increase in population yourself.
4. Look at the diagram and explain the advantages of the Four Year Rotation (M3).
5. One problem with the description of the "agricultural revolution" is that it may be wrong. Assess this statement.
6. a) Explain the relationship between natural resources and industrial centres (M2).
   b) Show which factors supported sea trade (M2).
7. Analyse Cipolla's statement about the role of industrialization (M7).
8. Assess the problems caused by industrialization. Take Cipolla's opinion into consideration (M7).
9. Discuss "the new problems" considering the fact that Cipolla wrote this in 1973 (M7).

M 1 **Spinning Wheel**
Thread is made by spinning fibres into yarn.

merchant clothier: a person who sells clothes or cloth
shuttle: a wooden stick that pulls the thread back and forth
pace: the speed at which sb. walks, moves, runs etc.
fine: a sum of money that must be paid as punishment
brisk: busy

M 2 **"Spinning Jenny"**
In 1764 the Briton James Hargreaves invented the first spinning machine, the "spinning jenny".

Driving Force - Textile Industry

Cottage Industry

In 1700 the majority of the population lived in the country as farmers. Not only did they work on the fields and breed animals, they also did other work at home (cottage industry). Very often the entire family was involved. The kind of work varied from place to place but one major field was the weaving of wool. This cottage industry could be found all over Britain.

Usually the families did not own the machines they used. They were provided by a *merchant clothier* who paid the families only for the cloth produced. They were harsh employers, because they had invested their money in the machines and therefore expected as much profit as possible in return.

British wool was of excellent quality and therefore was an important export product. This explains why the textile industry moved first and fastest from the cottage to the factory. Cotton was also an important factor in the growth of the British economy. In the 1600s, cheaply produced cotton was imported from the American colonies. In Lancashire the cotton industry developed more quickly than anywhere else, because the ships from the colonies arrived there.

The production of coke also supported economic development. As there were no customs restrictions within England (unlike in Germany) the great demand for coke and other products within the country could be easily satisfied. Coke powered steam engines, which in turn helped along new inventions and improvements.

Spinning Jenny

The invention of the flying *shuttle* by John Kay in 1733 made weaving twice as fast and productive. As a consequence, four workers using spinning wheels could no longer produce enough thread for a single weaver. In 1761 the Royal Society of Arts set up a contest for a spinning wheel that could produce several threads at once. In 1764 James Hargreaves won with his spinning jenny, a machine that spun sixteen threads at a time. Richard Arkwright invented an even better spinning machine in 1769 and the development in spinning machines continued after that.

In 1785, Edmund Cartwright invented the power loom, powered by a steam engine. Many people laughed at him in the beginning, but after technical improvements the power loom forced many labourers out of work. More than 800,000 weavers in the first half of the 19th century worked in textile production. But between 1820 and 1830 the number of power looms increased from 1400 to 55,000. More and more workers lost their jobs. By 1812 one factory worker operating a machine could produce as much as 200 cottage workers had fifty years earlier.

Working Conditions

Working conditions in most factories were terrible. Factory owners often did not care much about the well-being of their workers, but only about mill profits. The workers – many of them women and children –

had to work at the *pace* set by the machines, not by themselves. A 14-hour working day which included a one-hour break for meals was the average. The room temperature could reach up to 30°C and the wages were low. Even worse for the workers, strict rules were set for the factories. If a worker broke a rule, he was punished according to a list of *fines*. For example, any weaver or spinner who came to work more than five minutes after the last bell was fined 1 shilling, even though the average weekly wage was only 30 shillings.

"Curiosity led me to step into one of the cabins; it was a small one, where nine females were spinning, and one reeling." Dr. Adam Clark.

M 3 **Women Spinning and Their Clothier**

M 4 **Working Conditions**

Samuel Coulson of Leeds: Coulson's children worked in a mill. Here, he answers questions about the work his children did in the "brisk" times:

"At what time in the morning, in the *brisk* time, did these girls go to the mills? – In the brisk time, for about six weeks, they have gone at 3 o'clock in the morning, and ended at 10, or nearly half past, at night.
What breaks were allowed for the rest during those nineteen hours of work? – Breakfast a quarter of an hour, and dinner half an hour, and drinking a quarter of an hour.
What was the length of time they could be in bed during those long hours? – It was near 11 o'clock before we could get them into bed after getting a little food, [then] me or my mistress got up at 2 o'clock to dress them.
Were the children excessively tired by this work? – Many a time; we have cried often when we have given them the little food we had to give them; we had to shake them and they have fallen to sleep with the food in their mouth."

Evidence given to the Commission of Parliament (1831–32), adapted from John D Clare, The Age of Expansion 1750–1914, Nelson, Surrey et al., 1996, p. 56.

Tasks

1. List the most important inventions at the beginning of industrialization.
2. Assess the general effects of the steam engine on population, agriculture and other industries.
3. Describe the development from cottage industry to factory industry in textile production.
4. Compare the spinning wheel (M1) to the spinning jenny (M2).
5. Describe which member of the family does what kind of work (M3).
6. Explain why the working conditions were especially hard for children (M4).

M 1 **Friedrich Harkort (1793–1880)**
The industrialist founded big *plants,* supported social institutions and was a leading politician in the Prussian Parliament. Contemporary Painting.

plant: factory
to trigger sth.: to make sth. happen suddenly
engineering works/factory: a factory that produces machines etc.
to stall: to stop sth. from happening until a later date
hard coal: coal found in the ground
charcoal: coal made from burnt wood
blast furnace: a large structure like an oven in which iron ore is melted in order to take out the metal
to exploit: to use sth. in order to gain as much from it as possible
cart: a vehicle pulled by a horse for carrying loads
stagecoach: a large carriage pulled by horses for carrying people
joint stock company: a company that is owned by all the people who have shares in it
shares: units of equal value sold by a company to raise money
stock exchange: a place where shares in companies are bought and sold
obsolete: no longer used because sth. new has been invented

Industrialization in Germany

Late Start in Germany

Most of the pioneering inventions were made in England. Watt's steam engine, for example, is the invention that *triggered* the industrialization. In 1798, thirty years later, its patent expired. Only then was the first steam engine exported to Germany. It was used in the Ruhr area to mine salt. When this new technology was used to drain water from coal mines, the engine failed. After many efforts Franz Dinnendahl managed to get the engine working. This gave him so much insight into this technology that he founded an *engineering factory* of his own.

It was difficult to start a new business, because guilds still limited the number of businesses. Therefore, many new developments were held back. Often the king or the government of a state would not allow the use of a new invention. These limitations and the protective policies of Great Britain regarding new inventions *stalled* the start of industrialization in Germany.

When *hard coal* replaced *charcoal,* which set much less energy free and had limited availability, it was finally possible to build a *blast furnace* at the Friedrich-Wilhelm-Mill in Mülheim in 1848/49. This was the start of the mass production of raw iron, and led to the importance of the technologically advanced Ruhr area. More improvements in steel production followed. Some were especially successful after the Franco-Prussian war when Germany was able *to exploit* iron ore resources in Lorraine.

Infrastructure in Germany

Almost all of Germany was rural. There were few roads and even fewer paved roads. Most goods were transported by horse *carts* or carried by people on their backs, because roads were either wet and soft in summer, or snowed in and icy in winter.

Additionally, roads and transport connections in Germany suffered from the lack of unity. Road networks were based on each state's individual needs. The connection from one centre of commerce to the next was not necessarily the shortest, often because merchants wanted to avoid customs stations. Before 1834 there were about 1800 customs stations, Prussia alone had 67 on her borders: All hindered the flow of trade and commerce. Even after the introduction of the Customs Union in 1834 there were still 38 customs stations left on the borders.

Railways

Stephenson's invention of "The Rocket" in 1814 started the age of railways in England. In 1830 the first tracks were built south of Essen, but the Prussian king did not permit the use of a locomotive. So the train had to be pulled by horses. Despite opposition the advantages of railways became evident: Goods were transported faster, safer and the arrival of goods became more reliable than by traditional means.

On 7 December 1835, ten years after the first English railway line, the first German railway line was opened between Nuremberg and Fuerth. It was only 6.5 kilometres long. Still, the steam locomotive

M 2 **One of Harkort' s Plants at Wetter Castle, 1834**
Harkort built the first blast furnace: 16 m high, only surrounded by iron bands. Contemporary Painting.

"Adler" was imported from England. Many new lines followed. By the end of the 19th century the distance from Berlin to Hamburg took only five hours by train compared to three days by *stagecoach*.

The Leipzig-Dresden line was a real challenge. There was no company within the Customs Union that could provide the necessary machinery and material. So the business went to Darby & Cort in England. To avoid such a situation in future, investments in the German industry increased. Within only thirteen years, these investments ensured iron of English quality.

The construction of new railway lines required an enormous amount of iron and a larger labour force in many new fields (e.g. stationmasters, people for signal boxes, etc.). Some of these workers came from far away, because there were not enough local workers. The German economy boomed.

The German Boom

It became clear that individuals could not afford to invest the large sums of capital necessary, so the ownership of railway lines had to be taken on by more investors. The solution was found in *joint stock companies*, in which individuals or companies could invest money in return for *shares*. After 1850 the *stock exchange* backed the German coal and steel industry which took the lead over the *obsolete* English plants.

Now the Ruhr area with its vast coal resources became the most important industrial area in Germany. Hamburg and Bremen became Ruhr customers, too, when ships were made from steel rather than wood after 1870.

M 3 **The First German Railway Line** from Nuremberg to Fuerth was opened on 7 December, 1835.

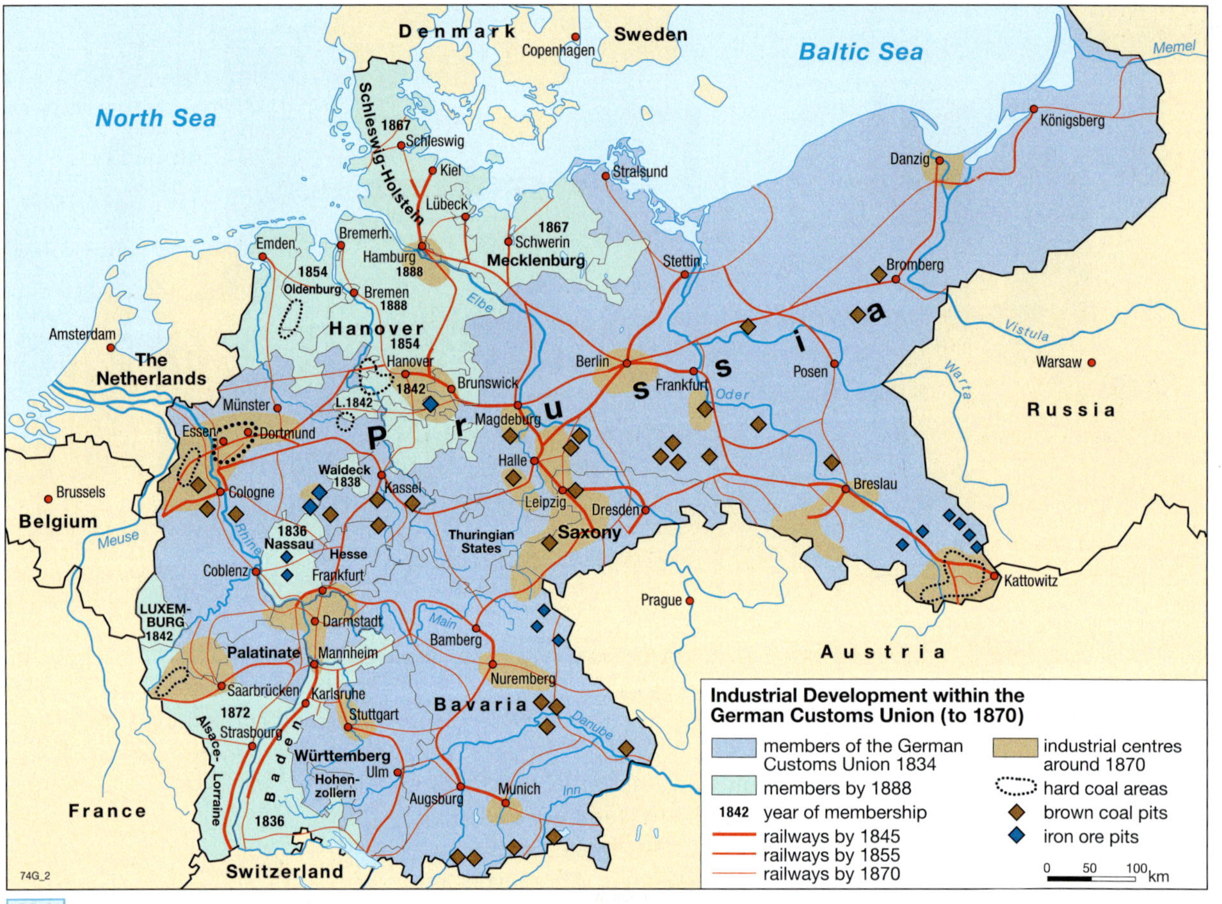

M 4

M 5 Travelling by Train

a) An English statement from 1857:

"It was declared that the railway would prevent cows grazing and hens laying. The poisoned air from the locomotive would kill birds as they flew over them. Houses next to the line would be burnt up from the fire thrown from the engine chimneys. The air would be polluted by clouds of smoke. There would no longer be any use for horses, and there would be no use for oats and hay."

b) A traveller reported in 1830:

"You cannot imagine how strange it seemed to be journeying on without any visible cause of progress other than the magical machine with its flying white breath. The engine was set off at its utmost speed, 35 miles an hour, swifter than a bird flies. The motion is as smooth as possible, too; I could have either read or written. When I closed my eyes the sensation was quite delightful. Yet strange as it was, I had not the slightest sense of fear."

c) A report on a trip on the Liverpool-Manchester Line:

"Today I had the satisfaction, for I can't call it a pleasure, of taking a trip of five miles – and we did it in just a quarter of an hour – that is twenty miles an hour. The quickest motion is to me frightful. It is like flying and it is impossible to get rid of the idea of death if the slightest accident happens. It gave me a bad *headache*. There is not much smoke, but there were *sparks* in the air. One burned Miss De Ross's cheek and another burned a hole in Lady Marian's silk dress. I am glad to have seen this miracle, and to have travelled in it, but this first journey will also be my last."

Adapted from: S. & H. Harrison, The Industrial Age. Questioning History 4. London: MacMillan, 1990, p. 79 and .p. 84.

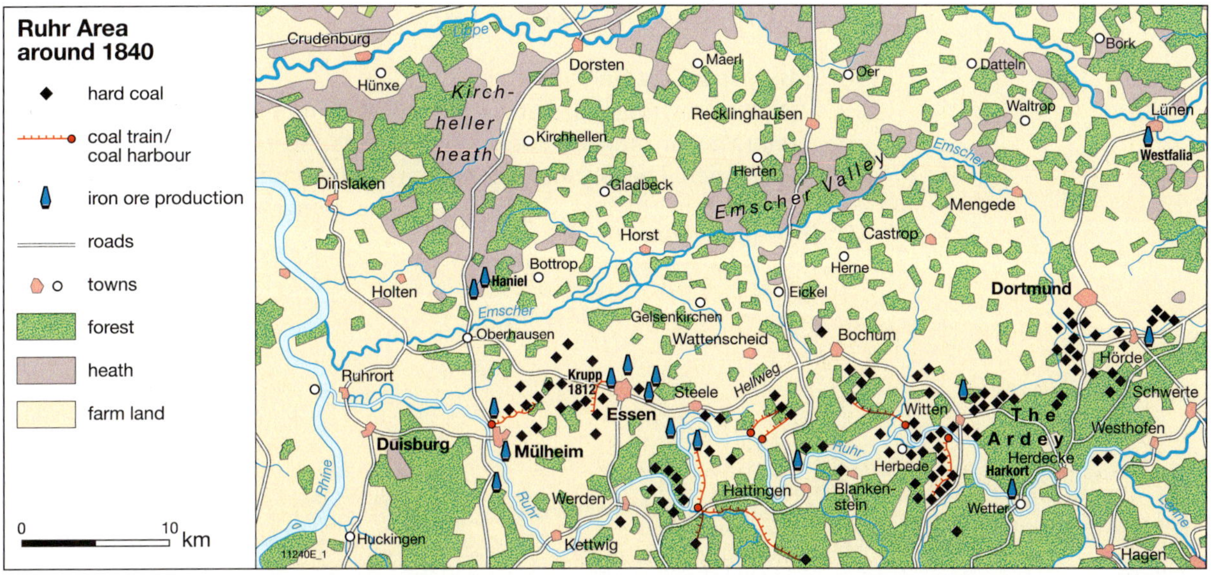

M 6

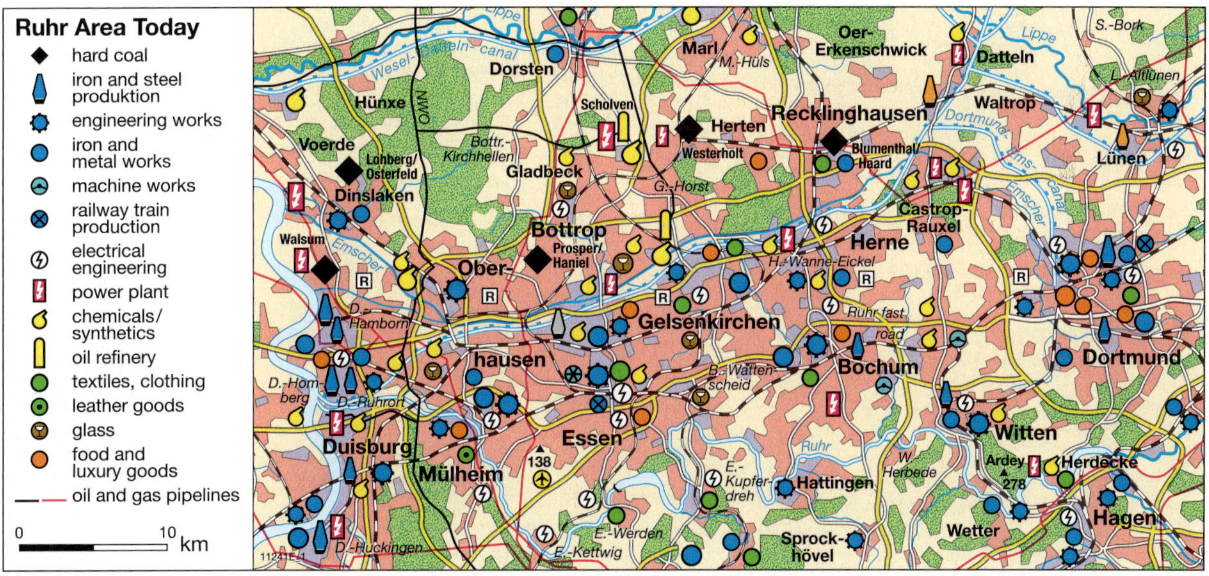

M 7

headache: pain in the head *spark:* a piece flying out of a fire

Tasks

1. Find more information about Friedrich Harkort. Use different sources (Internet, encyclopaedia) (M1).
2. Explain the relationship between industrialization and the development of railways (M4).
3. Assess the importance of railways for industrialization.
4. Explain why joint stock companies became necessary.
5. Compare the different statements (M5).
6. Compare the two maps closely. List the changes (M6, M7).

The Take-off Period

Industrialization Takes Off
Railways were the driving force for economical growth, but new *branches* of industry soon followed: the electrical and the chemical industries. The German economy relied more and more on industrial production, so that Germany stopped being an agricultural country around 1900.

M 1 The Krupp Works, about 1884
The entire plant with its 73 kilometers of railways, living quarters for the workers and their families was bigger than the city of Essen. More than 15,000 people worked in shifts here to make sure the 21 rolling streets, 92 steam hammers and 1195 furnaces, which needed more than 2,500 tons of coal each day, were constantly running and producing.

The invention of the telephone by Alexander Bell and of the electric light bulb by Thomas A. Edison led to the new electrical industry. Werner von Siemens discovered the dynamo-electric principle. This pioneering invention made petroleum, gas lamps, and candles obsolete. Moreover, electrical energy replaced mechanical energy.

Smaller businesses such as engineering works relied on electric power, because steam engines were only profitable for big industrial plants. First, it took several hours for a steam engine to actually produce power and, second, it was only efficient when it was large.

A similar development was also seen in chemistry. Chemists examined the nature of different chemical elements and substances. They produced new substances from oil and tar: paint, gasoline, chemical fertilizer as well as medicine. Theoretical scientists worked hand in hand with practical engineers, a very successful alliance.

Soon Germany was the leading nation in this sector with its inventions and innovations. New industrial plants were built near big rivers, because they could provide cooling water and get rid of waste of all kinds, too.

During this era factories and plants grew to an enormous size. Many became *trusts*, which meant that the combined firms sometimes had more than 10,000 employees. One company could invest in another and vice versa. This process of concentration led to the elimination of competition. So these new trusts dictated prices.

Krupp and Thyssen

Some people became very rich and successful businessmen, for example, Alfred Krupp and August Thyssen.

Friedrich Krupp had founded a cast iron factory, but he never managed to make it a profitable business during his lifetime. His son Alfred Krupp took over the business (it had seven employees at that time) at the age of 14 – he dropped out of school – although his mother owned the business. For several years the business was not very successful. This changed dramatically when around 1830 the development in railways sped up and more cast iron was needed in Germany and in Europe.

In 1852/53 Krupp invented a *seamless* wheel, which became the *core* product of his business, especially because most American railways used these wheels. In addition, Krupp invented and produced different weapons, mostly cannon so the business had about 1000 employees in the 1850s.

August Thyssen was born the third son of a wealthy Catholic family which owned steel mills. In contrast to Alfred Krupp, Thyssen was well educated and trained. In 1883 he bought a neighbouring factory which specialized in machine production. This was the basis for the Machine Factory Thyssen & Co.

In 2000 the companies of Krupp and Thyssen joined together. Today ThyssenKrupp AG is one of the biggest companies in Germany and operates worldwide. It has many different branches, which still include steel production, but it also produces elevators and escalators, automobile parts and high technology products such as monorail trains (Transrapid) and marine vessels.

branch: a special section or department
trust: a group of companies working together to reduce competition, control prices, etc.
seamless: with no spaces between one part and the next
core: most important, central

M 2 Alfred Krupp (1812–1887)
He created a global company, whose social institutions were role models for others.

M 3 August Thyssen (1842–1926)
In 1871 he founded the Thyssen company.

M 4 **„Learning in School"**
Many drawings like these were made for a series of collector's cards in 1899. They show the ideas of the artist for the year 2000.

M 5 **"The Make-Up Machine"**

M 6 **"The Dictation Machine"**

M 7 **The Krupp Works with "not too much smoke".** Photo from 1867

M 8 **Environmental Pollution**

Alfred Krupp wrote in Nice on 12 January 1867:

"For the exhibition in Paris and as presents to high-ranking personalities we need to take new photographs in May when everything is green and there is no wind. You see, in general, I think that small photographs are good enough, still I wish two larger-scale views or even better two views including decoration and life in the squares, yards and railways. I suggest using a Sunday, because there is too much smoke, steam and activities during the week, and the loss of work is also too great.
Whether 500 or 1000 men are necessary, I do not care. It is disadvantageous if too much steam fogs the environment, but it will be beautiful if a little steam comes from as many places as possible. The steam engines and trains are also very impressive just as are the big transport wagons for casting."

Translated and adapted by B. N. from: Historisches Archiv Krupp, Alfred Krupps Briefe und Niederschriften, B. 9, 1866-1879, Bl. 108f.

M 9 **Utopia?**

Alfred Nobel, inventor of dynamite, in a conversation with the pacifist Bertha von Suttner:

"Perhaps my factories will put an end to war even sooner than your Congresses; on the day when two army corps will be able to *annihilate* each other in a second, all civilised nations will *recoil* with horror and *disband* their troops."

http://www.irwinabrams.com/articles/oddcouple.html

to annihilate: to kill sb., esp. an enemy or opponent

to recoil: to pull back from sth.

to disband: (here) to send away

Tasks

1. Describe the picture of the Krupp works in as much detail as possible (M1).
2. a) Show what Krupp's instructions on how to take pictures tell you about environmental pollution in the 19th century. (M8).
   b) Discuss environmental pollution then and today. Are the problems solved?
3. a) Assess Nobel's idea (M9).
   b) Find historical examples which prove or disprove this principle.

a) **Capacity of all Steam Engines**
[in 1000 horsepower (hp)]

	GB	G	F	A	B
1840	620	40	90	20	40
1850	1290	260	270	100	70
1860	2450	850	1120	330	160
1870	4040	2480	1850	800	350
1880	7600	5120	3070	1560	610
1888	9200	6200	4520	2150	810
1896	13700	8080	5920	2520	1180

b) **Capacity of all Steam Engines** (in 1000 hp)

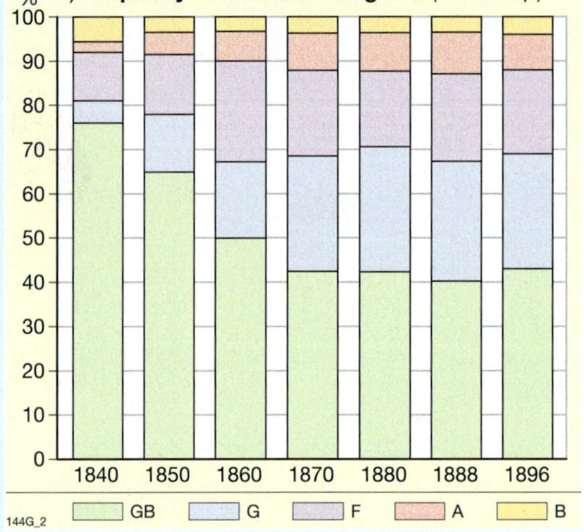

c) **Capacity of all Steam Engines 1840** (in 1000 hp)

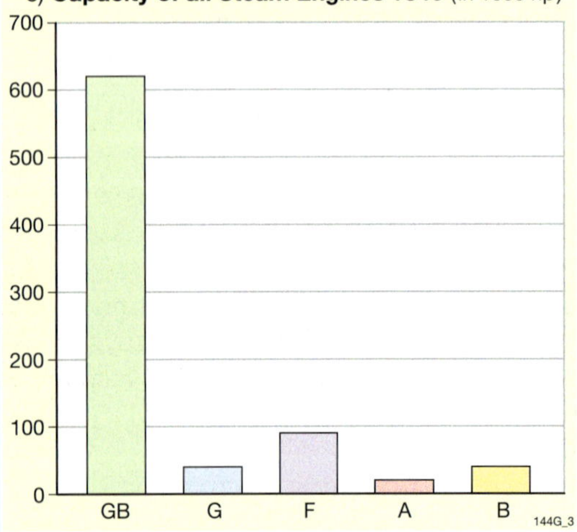

d) **Capacity of all Steam Engines in Germany** (in 1000 hp)

e) **Capacity of all Steam Engines in 1896** (in 1000 hp)

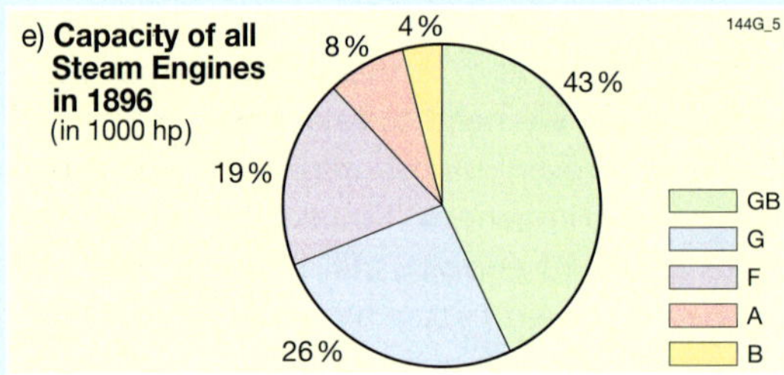

M 1 **Development of Steam Power in Europe 1840 to 1896**

Growth of Efficiency in all Steam Engines

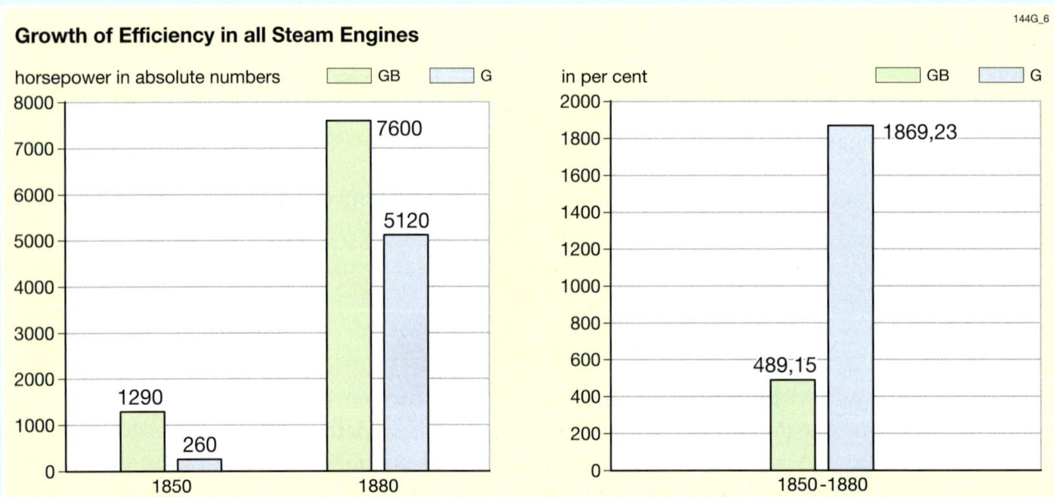

M 2 **Growth of Power of all Steam Engines**

Depicting Statistics

Statistics, whether in form of tables, diagrams or graphs, are part of everyday life. They give very complex information in a very *concise* form, often according to a specific point of view/angle.

Statistics are numbers listed in a particular order. Diagrams and graphs often help to show how these numbers are *interrelated.* A pie chart, for example, shows how big one factor is in comparison to the whole, whereas a bar chart is often used to compare the same thing at different times. In contrast to this, a graph has the advantage of showing a process of development over time.

In former times people did not write everything down. That is why the analysis of statistics is a rather young science. To make statistics about something in earlier centuries historians often have to guess or *laboriously* collect the needed information from many different sources.

concise: clear and short, in a few words
interrelated: closely connected and affecting each other
laborious (adj.): taking a lot of time and effort

There is very little reliable statistical material from the 19th century. Still, statistics are especially helpful to understand the phenomenon of industrialization. Even more helpful are figures that show the differences in development in various European countries. Looking at the data of the power of steam engines, for example, is one way to compare the times when industrialization began and to allow conclusions about where development was faster, earlier, or later.

However useful statistics are, they can also be misleading. A number of famous quotations hint at this fact. Sir Winston Churchill said: "[…] The first lesson that you must learn is, when I call for statistics about the rate of infant mortality, what I want is proof that fewer babies died when I was Prime Minister than when anyone else was Prime Minister. That is a political statistic." Josef Stalin stated at the Potsdam Conference in 1945: "The death of one man is a tragedy. The death of millions is a statistic." Benjamin Disraeli claimed: "There are three kinds of lies: lies, damned lies, and statistics."

Statistics Analysis Worksheet

1. Description

a. Name the topic of the shown statistics.
b. How is the topic presented?
c. Show the differences in the statistics.

2. Interpretation

a. Compare M1 a) and M1 b); in M2 compare absolute numbers and per cent.
b. Explain what additional or more specific information is given in M1 c), d) and e); M2
c. Analyse whether any information is lost.

3. Conclusion

a. Assess the advantages and disadvantages of each form of presentation.
b. Imagine you are the minister of economics in Germany. You have to give a report about the economy in Germany. Argue which of the diagrams you would choose to use.
c. Discuss the statements made by Churchill, Disraeli and Stalin.

Daily Working Hours in Handicraft Workshops and Industrial Factories in the 19th Century

1800-1820: 10-13 hours
1820-1840: 11-15 hours
1840-1860: 12-16 hours
1869-1870: 12-14 hours
1870-1890: 11-13 hours
1890-1910: 10-11 hours
1910-1914: 10 hours

M 1

disability: not being able to use body or mind fully
to contribute: to give sth., esp. money or goods

Living Conditions

Industrial Centres

Many people left the countryside to find work in urban areas. Therefore, many small towns quickly became industrial centres within a few years. New factories were built, new businesses started. Around 1830 there were only two major cities with a population of more than 100,000 inhabitants in Germany (Hamburg and Berlin), by 1850 there were three (plus Munich) and by 1880 there were thirteen. Berlin's population had even increased to more than one million. Neither before nor since has there been a more rapid growth of cities than during industrialization.

Life of the Working Class

Industrialization had negative effects as well. Very few people became rich. The majority remained poor or became even poorer than before. Wages were low and flats were expensive, so many people often shared one room. In addition, working conditions were bad. Big factories could only grow if the production of goods stayed cheap. Therefore, most factory owners did not care about the safety of their workers. Long working hours, dirty work and crowded flats helped diseases to spread.

Things had changed a great deal. Instead of being paid for the piece of work produced, the basis for wages now was time. Therefore, at the beginning of industrialization, people worked at least fourteen hours (sometimes up to seventeen hours) a day. In addition to their working hours, some people had a two-hour walk to the factory (one way).

Wages were low. Alfred Krupp, for example, paid his workers 1.25 marks a day in 1850. In 1873 he paid 3.74 marks. Skilled workers in an industrial factory earned about double what a craftsman earned. Women and children earned least of all and were the cheapest labour available.

Exhaustion was not the only aspect that made work dangerous. Space in the factories was limited and air conditioning was still unknown. Heat, cold, damp, noise and poisonous gases or dust often made the working environment unbearable. Also, workplaces were not primarily designed for people, but for the product being made there. Designing better workplaces would have cost money, which factory owners invested in new machines rather than their workers. These machines had few safety precautions, so there were many serious accidents as well. Poor working conditions caused *disabilities.* Since there was no health care system, a family then had to feed one more person who could not *contribute* to the family income.

M 2 **Child Labour**
A 12-year-old girl in a spinning mill. Photo, 1908.

Child Labour

Children were more of a burden to their families than a blessing. On farms in the countryside, women and children helped in cottage industry. There they played an important role and could work at home. In the industrial centres children meant problems, starting with the mother's pregnancy. Because of the working conditions, about 9% of all children were dead at birth. Those who lived started working at the age of about six years. Because of their small hands they were preferred workers in the textile industry. But the mining industry, too, liked child labourers, because they could crawl or walk through very narrow tunnels. Children had long working hours, very low pay, and many died of exhaustion or in accidents.

M 3 Working Conditions

Conrad Alberti describes the "perfect" worker:

"I want workers who work like machines from dusk till dawn, who do their rather mechanical job in a mechanical way, who eat and sleep as if it was a mechanical process, who drop like dead from their chairs to the straw and who do not get up a minute too early to be on the job at eight sharp. Only this makes a profitable and lasting business. The individual has to become a wheel in the machinery of the business just like a soldier in the army."

Translated and adapted by B. N. from: Conrad Alberti, Maschinen, Leipzig 1895.

M 4 A Child Labourer Reports

Anna Perthen, a worker in the textile industry, tells about her youth around 1880:

"The wages of Father were low, so that Mother always had to go back to work right after having given birth and despite nine children. As the way to the factory was too far for us, we worked at home sewing on buttons. Of the nine brothers and sisters only three survived. Mother's exhaustion and malnutrition might have been the cause of their deaths.

When I was twelve years old, I had to work in the textile factory, where the working hours lasted from 5 a.m. to 7 p.m. in those days. In the afternoons from 4 to 6 we went to the factory school, which took place in an inn next to the factory. Learning was hardly possible, we looked at these two hours more as rest. Work was rather mentally tiring.

When I went home to sleep, I had to get up at 3.30 am, because the way to the factory was very long. At times I lodged with somebody and went home only on Saturdays. In the town where the factory was we slept in an attic, where there were so-called long plank beds and straw mattresses next to each other. We were lucky, because older women, who looked after us, were there, too.

I was glad that I earned money, but often the disappointment was bitter. The wages were low. The two hours of schooling were of course taken off our money. When I had paid for lodging only very little was left, and on Saturdays Father was already waiting to take the rest of my money.

When I was fourteen, I went to a factory together with my parents, but we still had to work at home on Sundays and at night. When a six-week strike began to achieve shorter working hours I was sent to a different factory. Father, who was active in the strike, was fired and did not find any more work anywhere. So Mother and I were left to worry about the other siblings. I stayed in that factory long after I was married; because as was the case for most poor girls, after the wedding more grief and problems started. They did for me, too."

Translated and adapted by B. N. from: Arbeiterinnen kämpfen um ihr Recht, Autobiographische Texte rechtloser und entrechteter "Frauenspersonen" in Deutschland, Österreich und der Schweiz im 19. und 20. Jh, 1975, p. 84f.

Tasks

1. a) Analyse the working hours. What do they tell you about the development during the industrialization (M1)?
   b) Find out whether there were any other factors that might have influenced the number of working hours (M1).
2. a) Explain what Conrad Alberti wants to say (M3).
   b) Discuss his opinion.
   c) What does it tell you about the status of workers?
3. a) Describe the girl's day (M4).
   b) Compare it to your own.
4. a) Describe the picture of the little girl (M2).
   b) Imagine what she is thinking.

Attempts to Solve Social Problems

bourgeois (adj.) / bourgeoisie (n.): middle class
trade union: organization of workers to represent their interests, improve working conditions, etc.

Workers

Karl Marx and Friedrich Engels, who had a middle class background, started a new movement called communism after having seen the suffering of workers in England and Germany. The two men claimed that the only thing workers could sell to earn a living was their working power. They did not have any money or own any productive means (such as machines, raw material or land). Those belonged to the capitalists, who determined wages. In order to earn as much profit as possible they always underpaid their workers, so working power was never valued enough.

Marx's theory states that there is a predetermined order of societies in the history of mankind. First there is a primitive society, then one based on slavery, followed by a feudal system, which in turn is replaced by a capitalistic *bourgeois* society. A revolution to overthrow the capitalistic society by a communist one would lead to a free society without a class system, a ruler, subjects, owners (capitalists) or poor people.

The idea was a revolution of all workers against all capitalists. Many leaders of *trade unions*, socialist groups and parties were influenced by these ideas. In 1847 the Communist League was founded to oppose workers' exploitation. The revolution of 1848 with its goal of more democratic structures supported these new ideas, too. Ferdinand Lasalle founded the General Association of German Workers

M 1 The Strike
The painting was a sensation when presented at the National Academy of Design in New York, because there was a movement to achieve an eight-hour working day in the USA, which was accompanied by many strikes. On 1 May 1886 there was a mass riot of about 350,000 workers in more than 11,000 companies. Painting by Robert Koehler from Hamburg, 1886.

(Allgemeiner Deutscher Arbeiterverein) in 1863. Six years later the Social Democratic Workers' Party (Sozialdemokratische Arbeiterpartei) was founded. These two parties joined in 1875 to become the Social Democratic Party of Germany (SPD).

Factory Owners

After the uprising of the *Silesian* weavers in 1844, factory owners felt an immediate threat and realized that something had to be done. In order to limit the damage, many came up with concepts of their own to deal with workers' problems.

Some turned to paying for health insurance. They started to grant their workers money in case of sickness, some even set up pension systems. Others paid a bonus at the end of the year or for a short holiday.

Alfred Krupp, for example, built houses for his workers and tried to secure a basic school education. But in return he expected his workers to refrain from strikes or other political activities. He, like others, would only grant help to "good" workers.

M 2 **Karl Marx (1818–1883)**

M 3 **Manifesto**

In the Manifesto of the Communist Party (the English version was published in 1888) Karl Marx said:

"A *spectre* is *haunting* Europe – the spectre of Communism. [...]
The immediate aim of the Communists is the same as that of all the other proletarian parties: formation of the proletariat into a class, overthrow of the bourgeois supremacy, conquest of political power by the proletariat. [...]
The working men have no country. We cannot take from them what they have not got. [...]
Nevertheless in the most advanced countries, the following will be pretty generally applicable:
1. *Abolition* of property in land and application of all rents of land to public purposes. [...]
6. Centralization of the means of communication and transport in the hands of the State.
7. Extension of factories and instruments of production owned by the State [...]
10. Free education for all children in public schools. Abolition of children's factory labour in its present form. [...]
Let the ruling classes *tremble* at a Communistic revolution. The proletarians have nothing to lose but their *chains*. They have a world to win.
WORKING MEN OF ALL COUNTRIES, UNITE!"

www.hartford-hwp.com/archives/26/176.html of 1888 translation, published in Karl Marx and Fredrich Engels, Collected Works, New York, International Publishers, 1976, Volume 6, pp. 476–519.

silesia: (German) Schlesien
spectre: ghost
to haunt: if sth. scary keeps coming to your mind
abolition: the ending of a law, system or institution
to tremble: to shake from fear or cold
chain: a series of connected metal rings

Tasks

1. a) List the aims of communism (M3).
   b) Explain why there were arguments over these aims among workers.
   c) Discuss the ideas you find appealing and which you find unacceptable.
2. a) Describe the painting as exactly as possible. Pay special attention to clothes, action, positions, etc. (M1).
   b) Discuss the atmosphere of the picture.
   c) Draw conclusions from certain groups in the picture (i.e. women, children, workers, etc.).
3. a) Find out about Karl Marx's life.
   b) Find out about Friedrich Engel's life.

Church and Government React

M 1 **Johann Hinrich Wichern (1808–1881)**

Church

Traditionally the church took care of the poor, sick, old, widows and orphans. *Donations* were used to give money, food or board to people in need. The help was mainly directed to individual cases; there were hardly any organized projects. In the face of mass poverty in the 19th century a different approach was needed.

The Protestant teacher Johann Hinrich Wichern (1808–1881) wanted to help neglected children in Hamburg. He founded a boarding school (Rauhe Haus) for the children where they were trained for different jobs. It still exists today. In this way, Wichern started a new kind of clerical charity – called the "inner mission".

The Catholic priest Adolph Kolping (1813–1865) was a trained shoemaker. He realized that craftsmen and journeymen on their travels had problems finding board and lodgings as well as work. He founded the "Catholic Journeymen's Club", which provided unmarried men a heated room with newspapers and books. The clubs gave them general as well as specific job information to improve their training. Since this was a church institution, religious questions were important, too. When Kolping died, 60,000 members were organized in 420 clubs. Kolping houses still exist in many cities today.

Besides these individual attempts to solve social problems the Bishop of Mainz, Wilhelm Emmanuel Kettler (1811–1877), wanted the Catholic Church as well as the German people to see how much rich and poor were drifting apart. For him it was more important to close this gap by means of Christian faith than to attack the material problems with money. His approach influenced many Christian workers' associations and helped to form Christian trade unions.

1883 Health Insurance
benefits: free consultation of doctors, medication and treatment in hospital, sick-pay 50% of wages for 26 weeks
premium: 2-3% of wages, 2/3 employee, 1/3 employer

1884 Accident Insurance
benefits: (in case of accident) doctor's treatment and 2/3 of wages as pension, (in case of death) 20% of wages as pension for the widow
premium: 100% employer

1889 Disability and Old Age Insurance
benefits: disability pension in case of inability to work, old age pension after the age of 70
premium: 1-3% of wages, 50% employee, 50% employer

M 2 **Advertisement** of the German government to promote social security

Government

The government tried to attack the problem from two different sides: a Socialist Law and social laws. In order to win back the trust of workers, Bismarck worked to pass some social laws. Among them were a health insurance and a social security system which still exist today. Additionally, he appointed inspectors in factories to ensure minimum safety precautions and to prevent child labour. But Bismarck's hope that workers would leave the different workers' parties was disappointed.

In 1890 the Socialist Law was *abolished* and the SPD became a mass party. By 1914 it had more than one million members. In 1912 34.8% of the parliament (110 representatives) were Social Democrats, the strongest party in the Reichstag.

M 3 Rerum Novarum

Encyclical of Pope Leo XIII on Capital and Labour (1891):

"In any case we clearly see, [...], that some *opportune* remedy must be found quickly for the misery and wretchedness pressing so *unjustly* on the majority of the working class: [...] Public institutions and the laws set aside the ancient religion. *Hence,* by degrees it has come to pass that working men have been *surrendered,* isolated and helpless, to the hardheartedness of employers and the greed of unchecked competition. [...]

[...] Working for gain is creditable, not shameful, to a man, since it enables him to earn an honorable livelihood, but to misuse men as though they were things in the *pursuit* of gain, or to value them solely for their physical powers – this is truly shameful and inhuman. [...] Hence, the employer is bound to see that the worker has time for his religious duties; that he be not exposed to corrupting influences and dangerous *occasions;* and that he be not led away to neglect his home and family, or to *squander* his earnings. Furthermore, the employer must never tax his work people beyond their strength, or employ them in work unsuited to their sex and age. [...]"

www.vatican.va/holy_father/leo_xiii/encyclicals/documents/hf_l-xiii_enc_1505

donation: sth. that is given as a charity
to abolish: to officially end a law
opportune: suitable, at the right time
unjustly: unfairly
hence: for this reason
to be surrendered: (here) to be without any right or hope
pursuit: the act of looking for or trying to find sth.
occasion: a particular time when sth. happens
to squander: not using sth. in a sensible way

Tasks

1. Discuss the role of the church in the attempts to solve social problems.
2. a) Explain Leo XIII's ideas (M3).
   b) Assess whether his aims were achieved.
3. a) Analyse the government's effectiveness in solving social problems.
   b) Assess the 19th century health and social security system and what is missing (M2).
4. Find out as much as possible about Johann Hinrich Wichern (M1).

The Struggle for Unity and Liberty

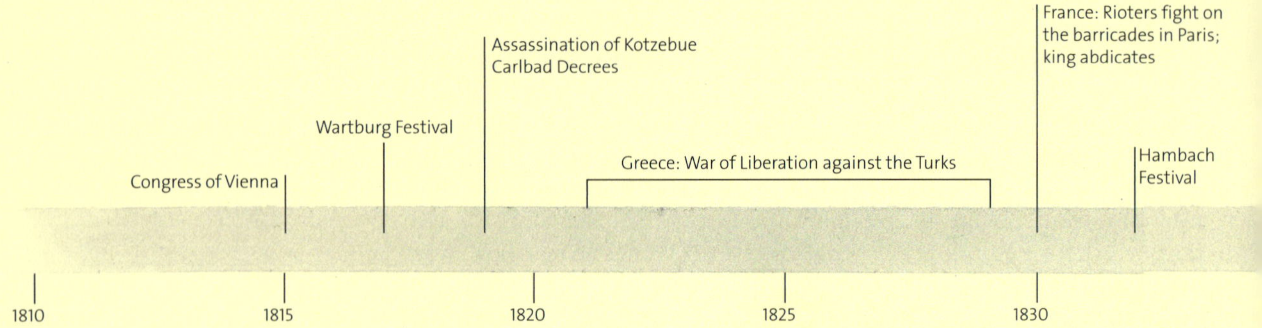

"Liberty Leading the People"
Painting by Eugène Delacroix, 1830

Barricades on the Breite Strasse
Berlin, 1848

Castle in Brunswick Burning, 1830

Göttingen: Protest and dismissal of seven university professors	Silesia: Hunger revolt of the weavers	Revolution

1840 | 1845 | 1850 | 1855 | 1860

The German Confederation

M 1 **Prince Metternich** (1773-1859). Painting

comprehensive: broad, thorough
compensation: payment

M 2 **"Restoring the Old Order"** Caricature, 1819

The Congress of Vienna 1815

Restoring the Old Order

The Congress of Vienna was held by the allies who had defeated Napoleon. Their aim was to calm Europe down after the chaos of the wars with France (1792-1814) and to bring about a lasting peace based on a balance of power among the five major powers in Europe. The leading statesman among the Great Powers was Klemens von Metternich, chancellor of Austria. Convinced that the ideas of the French Revolution were dangerous and destabilizing, he worked for a peace which would keep such ideas under control. The principles of the Congress were:

- restoration: returning to the political situation of 1792
- legitimacy: rightful sovereigns were to receive their thrones again
- compensation: territory taken away was to be restored
- balance of power: the concert of Europe would prevent the hegemony of one power and keep such a power in check
- solidarity: the sovereigns would work together.

The final act of the Congress of Vienna was signed 8 June 1815 by eight powers. It was the most *comprehensive* treaty that Europe had seen. Of course, nationalists, with hopes aroused during the wars of liberation, and supporters of the ideas of the French Revolution were deeply disappointed. In their eyes the Vienna settlement was the product of blind reaction. But the peace organized in Vienna was durable: there was no general European war for 100 years.

The Territorial Reorganization of Europe

All territory was to be restored, and if this was not possible, then *compensation* was to come from territory taken from allies who had stayed loyal to Napoleon. Denmark, for example, lost control over Norway to Sweden. The Austrian Netherlands (Belgium) were given to Holland, which not only compensated Holland, but also created a protective ring of states around France. Austria received compensation for her loss in the Netherlands. Habsburgs also gained control of Parma, Modena, Tuscany. Poland was repartitioned: Russia won the lion's share, while Austria and Prussia divided the leftovers. Great Britain kept Malta in the Mediterranean, took over Tobago and Trinidad in the West Indies and the Dutch Cape Colony in South Africa.

The German Confederation

In Germany, where Napoleon had set up an efficient government in place of the old Holy Roman Empire in 1806, a new confederation of thirty-nine states was organized in a central assembly chaired by Austria in Frankfurt am Main. The individual states remained in control of their own affairs, but Austria assumed a leading role. The confederation did not have an elected parliament, nor were differences among the states in economic systems, finance, taxation, laws, weights and measures resolved. The new confederation ignored popular hopes for a German national state – the interests of the Great Powers were more important.

M 3 **The Congress of Vienna,** Caricature by Josef Zutz, 1815: 1. Emperor Francis I (Austria), 2. Tsar Alexander I (Russia), 3. King Frederick William III (Prussia), 4. Duke of Wellington (Britain), 5. King of Denmark, 6. King of Bavaria, 7. King of Württemberg, 8. Elector of Hesse, 9. Duke of Brunswick, 10. Talleyrand (France), 11. mediatized princes and statesmen.

M 4 **Two Opinions on the Congress**

a) Metternich to an American observer:

"It is true that I do not like democracies. Democracy is in every case a principle of *dissolution,* of *decomposition.* It tends to separate men, it loosens society. I am opposed to this because I am by nature and by habit constructive. That is why monarchy is the only government that suits my way of thinking [...]. Monarchy alone tends to bring men together, to unite them in compact, efficient masses, and to make them capable by their combined efforts of the highest degree of culture and civilization."

b) Speech by Sir James Mackintosh on the Congress of Vienna in the House of Commons, 1815:

"The object of the new system is to crush the weak by the combination of the strong; to *subject* Europe in the first place to an *oligarchy of sovereigns,* and *ultimately* to swallow it up in the *gulp* of universal monarchy; where civilization has always *perished,* with freedom of thought, with controlled power, with national character and spirit, with patriotism and *emulation,* in a word, with all its characteristic *attributes,* and with all its *guardian* principles."

Quoted in: Erich Wilmot, The Great Powers, 1814-1914, Watson-on-Thames 1992, p. 45 and p. 15.

dissolution, decomposition: falling apart, rotting
to subject: to put sth. under the control of sb.
oligarchy of sovereigns: a small group of rulers
ultimately (adv.): finally
to gulp: to swallow sth. all at once
to perish: to die
emulation: competition
attributes: features
guardian: protecting

Tasks

1. Explain the conflict between Metternich's ideas and the principles of the French Revolution ("liberty, equality, fraternity").
2. Name the groups supporting Metternich's ideas and those opposing them. Find support for your arguments in the sources.

M 1 **"The Greek Revolution"**
Painting by Eugéne Delacroix on the Greek uprising, about 1826

to abdicate: to give up the throne
blight: plant fungus
stunning: surprising

European Unrest 1815–1848

The attempt of the Congress of Vienna to keep Europe calm failed, as the signs of unrest all over Europe during this period showed.

Date	Country	Event
1820	Spain	rebellion of the liberals; triggered by part of the army
1820	Italy	the Carbonari revolt against the Austrians (Naples)
1820	Portugal	revolution led by the army
1821	Italy	revolt in Piemont against King Victor Emmanuel
1821-29	Greece	war of liberation against the Turks
1830	France	rioters fight on the barricades in Paris; king *abdicates*
1830	Poland	uprising in Warsaw against Tsar Nicholas I
1845/46	Ireland	great famine; terror wave by the "Young Ireland" group
1847	Italy	uprising in Messina against the Habsburgs

In countries where the authorities were strong, revolutionary uprisings had little chance: In Italy, the Carbonari rebels were put down by the Austrian army, in Poland rebels against the Russian tsar were no match for his troops. But in Greece the Great Powers Russia, France and Great Britain helped the Greeks in their struggle against the Turkish Ottoman Empire, and the revolutionaries were successful.

In France the king tried to restrict voting rights and introduce press censorship in 1830, but was forced to *abdicate* when the majority of French citizens resisted. A "citizen king", Louis Philippe, replaced him.

In Britain voting rights were extended under the Reform Act of 1832. Ireland suffered a devastating famine in 1845 caused by a potato *blight*, a situation made worse by British authorities who refused to take early measures against it. All these signs of political unrest, whether successful or not, were evidence that Metternich's plans to maintain the old order were unlikely to work.

The Customs Union

One of the most important developments during this time was the founding of the "Zollverein", a German customs union. Because the thirty-nine states in the German Confederation were still separate countries, customs duties had to be paid on goods passing from one state to another. Friedrich List, an economist from southern Germany, realized that these customs duties made trade expensive and difficult. He proposed that the states form a customs union within Germany. On 1 January 1834 Prussia founded a larger free trade zone: It included 26 million people, was called the German Customs Union, and was recognized as an important economic and financial structure in the confederation. By 1842 the customs union grew even larger and showed *stunning* success, especially in improving trade relations and railroad building within the free trade area.

Austria had refused to join in the early days of the customs union. Later, Prussia actively prevented Austria from joining, realizing that economic power was an important tool and could be used to challenge Austrian leadership in the confederation.

M 2 "Clearing the Forest"
Caricature from "Fliegende Blätter", 1848

M 3

Tasks

1. Show how the artist supports the Greek revolution in his painting (M1).
2. Make a note of the factors influencing the success or failure of unrest during this time.
3. Assess the role of the German Customs Union (M2, M3).
4. Evaluate the fact that Austria did not join the customs union and show how this affected politics within the German Confederation (M3).

M 1 **"Wartburg Festival"**
Drawing, 1819

Examples of Unrest in Germany 1815-1847

The Establishment of Student Societies

Students were among those who disliked the Metternich System in Germany. Many had taken part in the Wars of Liberation against Napoleon. Starting in 1815 they formed patriotic groups known as "Burschenschaften". They organized secret meetings to discuss making Germany a united and democratic country. The two ideas of unity and liberty seemed to go together. Representatives of fourteen German universities met in Jena on 18 October 1818 and founded the "Allgemeine Deutsche Burschenschaft", a federation of all German students. On their clothing they wore "German colours", the same colours a heroic regiment had worn in the 1813 Battle of Leipzig: black, red and gold. Metternich regarded the student organizations as dangerous and looked for a way to forbid them.

From the Wartburg Festival 1817 to the Carlsbad Decrees 1819

On 18 October 1817 about 500 students from Jena attended a festival at Wartburg Castle near Eisenach to celebrate the Battle of Leipzig (October 1813) and the start of the Reformation (October 1517). During the meeting speakers criticized the old system and burned symbols of repression and censorship, like a policeman's *pigtail* and a copy of the German Act of Confederation. The students' demonstration seemed quite harmless, but German rulers became nervous and Metternich was alarmed.

On 23 March 1819 Carl Ludwig Sand, a theology student at Jena University, killed the journalist and playwright August von Kotzebue at his home in Mannheim. Kotzebue had made fun of the students' liberal and patriotic ideals in his magazine "Literary Weekly". Sand was executed on 20 May 1820. His deed was controversial: some called him a fanatic, others thought of him as a martyr to German freedom. Using the assassination as an excuse, Metternich moved to silence the liberal and national movement in Germany.

M 2 **"The Thinkers' Club"**
Caricature, about 1820

The Carlsbad Decrees were adopted on 20 September 1819 by the frightened rulers of the Confederation. The Decrees put censorship on all printed matter of fewer than 320 pages, placed the universities under strict supervision and set up a commission at Mainz to investigate "revolutionary plots and demagogic connections". A "*demagogue* hunt" followed as the police spied on liberal students and professors. The liberal movement was unable to express its demands in public and lost support.

pigtail: hair braided together, symbolizing authority
demagogue: a leader who misleads the common people
Palatinate: German "Pfalz"

The Hambach Festival 1832

On 27 May 1832 30,000 southern liberals and radicals met at Hambach Castle in the *Palatinate* to demand national unification and a republican government in Germany. Hundreds of flags with the German colours were shown, in addition to national flags of other countries, including France and Poland.

The Göttingen Seven 1837

Great Britain and Hanover had been ruled in personal union since 1714. This ended in 1837 when Queen Victoria ascended the British throne. Ernst August II became King of Hanover, broke with the constitution and restored absolute monarchy. Seven university professors in Göttingen protested the king's coup d'état in an open letter. The king dismissed the men from their university positions – a move which made the scandal worse.

M 3 "The Hambach Festival" on 27 May 1832. Drawing

M 4 At the Hambach Festival

Speech (excerpt) by lawyer Johann Georg August Wirth at the Hambach Festival:

"The country that speaks our language, the country where our hope resides, where our love delights, where our joys thrive, where the secret of all our sympathies and all our longing rests, this beautiful land is being ravaged and plundered, torn and enervated, gagged and disgraced. Rich in all the resources of nature, it should be the home of joy and contentment for all its children; yet, its blood sucked by 34 kings, it is the domicile of hunger, misery, and poverty for the majority of its residents."

Adapted from: German Historical Institute, From Vormärz to Prussian Dominance, 1815-1866, Washington D.C. 2006, translated by Jeremiah Riemer.

Tasks

1. Explain the connection between the Wars of Liberation and the students' ideas.
2. Discuss how realistic Metternich's fear of the student societies was.
3. Describe the effect of the Carlsbad Decrees on political life in the German Confederation.
4. Explain the criticism of the Metternich System which the caricature (The Thinkers' Club) makes fun of (M2).
5. Compare and contrast the various examples of political unrest during the period 1815-1847, stating reasons for the success or failure of these efforts.
6. Name two factors Wirth uses to define Germany.

M 1 **"Paris 1848"**
Storming the Seat of Government in Paris, February 1819

The Revolution of 1848

Revolutionary activities began in Italy in January, but it was the Paris uprising in February 1848 which set off revolutionary ideas in Europe. French citizens resented the king's use of press censorship and the army to stay in charge. Because suffrage was limited to only 250,000 citizens, liberals had no seats in parliament and could not express their complaints. So reformers held political *banquets* to discuss changes instead. When a banquet set for 22 February 1848 was forbidden, the public protested. Troops shot at the demonstrators, Paris rose in revolt, and Louis Philippe was forced to abdicate.

Vienna 1848

News of the events in Paris spread – by March petitions in Vienna demanded freedom of the press, civil rights and a *constitution*. A crowd assembled on 13 March 1848 and called for Metternich's dismissal. Troops were sent to break up the demonstration. Students, members of the city *militia* and some workers set up barricades. Metternich fled to safety in England. The Austrian government responded to the revolution and published a new constitution quickly, but unrest continued.

Berlin 1848

In 1815 a constitution was promised for Prussia, but none was written. At his *coronation* in 1840, Frederick William IV insisted that no written document could come between God, the king and the people of Prussia. Nevertheless, the promised constitution was not forgotten.

When news of the events in Vienna reached Berlin, Frederick William IV relaxed press censorship and promised a new constitution. A crowd gathered on 18 March to thank the king for his last-minute changes. Suddenly, the palace guard fired shots. The crowd quickly set up barricades. Troops then killed more than 230 rioters.

Frederick William, upset and shocked by the tragic events, ordered his troops to return to their barracks. Under public pressure he seemed to give in to the revolution: He rode through Berlin under the black-red-gold flag, the symbol of united Germany. On 22 March the king promised to ask a Prussian national assembly to write a constitution. A week later he appointed two liberals – Ludolf Camphausen and David Hansemann – to his "March Cabinet".

banquet: large, formal dinner
constitution: a written set of laws governing the country
militia: citizen's army
coronation: ceremony in which a king or queen is crowned

The Constitution "from above"

The national assembly began writing a constitution for Prussia, but the assembly, the king's liberal cabinet and a group of conservative landowners soon disagreed. When a revolt in Vienna was put down in October 1848, Frederick William IV called his troops back to Berlin. The Prussian national assembly moved to Brandenburg, where the king's soldiers dissolved it in December. The king rejected the assembly's constitution and imposed one written by his advisors on 5 December 1848. It included a list of civil rights, but the king kept an absolute veto. From 1850 to 1918 elections were held according to a notoriously unfair three-class voting system.

M 2 **"To My *Beloved* Berliners"**

Message of Frederick William IV, on19 March 1848:

"The shout of joy which greeted me from *innumerable faithful* hearts still resounded in my ears when a crowd of peace-breakers mixed with the loyal *throng.* As the courtyard was cleared by the cavalry, two guns went off by themselves, without, thank God, causing any injury. A band of *wicked* men, mainly foreigners, have succeeded in filling the excited minds of my faithful and beloved Berliners with thoughts of revenge for *supposed bloodshed.* My troops, your brothers and fellow countrymen, did not make use of their weapons till forced to do so by several shots fired at them.

It is now up to you, *inhabitants* of my beloved native city, to *avert* a fearful evil. Remove the barricades which are still standing. All the streets and squares shall immediately be cleared of troops. Forget the past, as I shall forget it, for the sake of the great future which is dawning upon Prussia and through Prussia upon all of Germany."

Adapted from: "Der Vorkampf deutscher Einheit", edited by Tim Klein, Ebenhausen 1927, pp. 178-179, translated by Gernot Schikowski.

M 3 **"Barricades in Berlin"**
The "Königsstraße" on the night of 18 to 19 March 1848

M 4 **"The King Gives In"**
Frederick William IV rides through Berlin on 21 March

M 5 **"From Above"**
The Prussian people receive the constitution "from above", 1849

beloved: dear
innumerable: uncountable
faithful: loyal
throng: crowd
wicked: evil, bad
to suppose: to imagine
bloodshed: people losing blood
inhabitants: people living in a place
to avert: to prevent

Tasks

1. Explain the sudden fashion for revolution in western Europe in 1848.
2. Compare the political goals of the revolutionaries in Paris, Vienna and Berlin.
3. Analyse Frederick William IV's explanation for the revolutionary uprising in Berlin (M2).
4. Define the role the king saw for Prussia in the unification of Germany (M2).
5. Look at the pictures in M3-M5 and describe the course of the revolution in Prussia.

M 1 **The Preliminary Parliament**
574 members gather at St. Paul's Church in Frankfurt on 30 March 1848

Problems of the National Assembly

While national assemblies started writing constitutions for the separate German states, many demanded that a German national parliament meet. A *preliminary* parliament met in Frankfurt to prepare the elections to a *constituent assembly.*

The representatives were elected according to universal and *equal* male suffrage. For nearly two-thirds of the German states this was the first such election ever held. However, the election was indirect. Voters chose "electors" who then elected the representatives to the Frankfurt Parliament – a method to keep the election results moderate. On 18 May 1848 over 500 representatives met in St. Paul's Church in Frankfurt. Their task was diverse:

Problems of the National Assembly

Sovereignty: The Frankfurt Parliament elected Heinrich von Gagern its president on 19 May 1848. But the governments of the separate states were still in power. The Parliament had to decide whether it was a *sovereign* assembly or whether the German states had to agree with its decisions. As a compromise the Parliament elected Archduke Johann of Austria its "imperial administrator", a preliminary constitutional monarch. Although the separate states accepted this change, the executive had no real power. It depended on the good will of the rulers of the states. Their good will disappeared as the revolution faded.
Constitution: There was no agreement on a constitution in May 1848. From the beginning, it was uncertain whether a new emperor should be head of state, whether he should have an elected or *inherited* office, what role parliament should play, or how elections should be organized. Working out the final *draft* of the constitution by April 1849 was a solid achievement.
German borders: It was unclear which territory made up the new German national state – whether Austria, or only part of Austria, should be included in the new Germany. Questions of territorial borders were *postponed* until late October.
Human rights: The national assembly began discussing human rights because these had been raised by the revolution in the first place. Also, it was easier to agree on human rights than on other issues. But by spending time on such questions at first, the assembly missed its historical chance. By the time agreement on the constitution and territorial arrangements was reached, the monarchs were back in charge of their separate states again.

Crown Offered to the Prussian King

On 28 March 1849 the Parliament voted to offer the German crown to Frederick William IV. A delegation traveled to Berlin to present their crown to him. The king refused to "pick up a crown from the *gutter*" – harsh terms for a crown offered by the elected representatives of the German people.

When both Prussia and Austria rejected the *proposed* constitution, it was clear that the Parliament could not *survive.* Most of the state governments ordered their representatives to return home.

preliminary: coming before
constituent assembly: group which writes a constitution
equal: each vote counts the same
sovereign: having independent power
inherited: passed from parent to child
draft: plan, version
to postpone: to put off
gutter: edge of street carrying water and waste
to propose: to suggest
to survive: to live on

M 2 **"Refusal"**

The President of the Frankfurt Parliament von Gagern with Borussia. She asks, "Why are you crying, little boy?" He replies, "I've carved a crown for your little 'un, but 'e doesn't want it!"
Caricature, 1849

M 3 **Frederick William and the Revolution**

a) Fredrick William IV wrote about his fear of world revolution to Queen Victoria:

"The consequences [of the revolution in France] are clear and certain. If the revolutionary party pushes through its programme – 'the sovereignty of the people' – my relatively small crown will be destroyed, but also the much more powerful crown of your majesty, and a fearful burden will be laid upon the people, a century of unrest, lawlessness and godlessness will follow."

http://www.st-andrews.ac.uk/jfec/cal/1848/documents/world-rea.htm (April 2006)

b) Frederick William IV refuses the crown of Germany on 15 May 1849 :

"I was not able to *submit* a favourable *reply* to the offer of a crown by the German National Assembly because that *body* does not have the right, without the *consent* of the German governments, to *bestow* the crown they offered me, and because, in addition they *tendered* the crown under the condition that I would accept a constitution which could not be *reconciled* with the rights and safety of the German states."

Quoted in: L.L. Snyder, Documents of German History, 1958.

to submit: to give
reply: answer
body: assembly, group
consent: agreement
to bestow: to give
to tender: to offer
to reconcile: to bring agreement

Tasks

1. Choose the problem the Frankfurt Parliament had to deal with which you consider the most difficult to solve and explain your reasoning.
2. The Frankfurt Parliament is criticized for its long debates which seldom seemed to reach conclusions. Agree or disagree with this criticism, explaining your thinking.
3. Analyse the caricature of von Gagern with Borussia (M2).
4. Assess Frederick William IV's fear at the outbreak of the revolution in 1848 (M3a).
5. Analyse Frederick William's refusal to accept the German crown. Compare and contrast with his fears (M3).
6. Evaluate the effect of the 1849 constitution which was never actually put into practice.

M 1 **"The times are changing, and with them, customs."**

22 March 1848: "Hat off!"

22 February 1849: "Hats off!"

Analysing Cartoons

Mainly Visual Sources

Caricatures and historical cartoons offer lots of information at one glance. Caricature comes from the Italian word "caricare", meaning to *exaggerate.* These pictures make fun of people and things by exaggerating their features and weaknesses. The artists often take a stand, either for or against their subjects.

Because caricatures are visual, rather than *merely* textual, they became a popular way of informing people who could not read about political events. Cartoons are a good source for finding out how people who lived at the time of historical events felt about these events and political figures. But, like all types of sources, we have to learn how to interpret them.

to exaggerate: to overstate, overemphasize
merely: only, just

Commenting on Historical Events

The main figures, events, successes and failures of the Revolution of 1848 were popular topics for caricatures at the time. The two cartoons on the opposite page deal with Frederick William IV's reactions to revolutionary events. To analyse them you need to know that the king removed his helmet and bowed his head to the coffins of those who died in the March 1848 uprising in Berlin. In February 1849, when representatives of the German National Assembly asked him to become the new German emperor, he refused.

Cartoon Analysis Worksheet

1. Describing the cartoon

a. List the objects or people you see in the cartoon.
b. Identify the cartoon caption and/or title.
c. Find the main words or phrases used by the cartoonist (Note: Here no other words appear besides the titles.)
d. Record any important dates or numbers that appear in the cartoon. Don't forget the date of the cartoon.

2. Assessing the information

a. Name the objects on your list which are symbols.
b. Explain what each symbol means.
c. Explain why the words used in the cartoon are significant.
d. List adjectives that describe the emotions portrayed in the cartoon.

3. Interpreting the cartoon

a. Describe the action taking place in the cartoon.
b. Explain how the words in the cartoon clarify the symbols.
c. Explain the message of the cartoon.
d. Name special interest groups which would agree or disagree with the cartoon's message. Explain why.

The End of the 1848 Revolution

M 1 The Execution of Robert Blum. Engraving, 1849

The Reaction in Austria and Prussia

By the summer of 1848, pressure on the Austrian government came from many sides. National groups wanted to determine themselves and demanded independence from Austria. German revolutionaries in Austria expected to take part in politics in future.

The emperor took control again with his army. In June 1848 Austrian troops put down a Czech revolt in Prague, and in July in Italy. The imperial army marched back into Vienna in October 1848, driving out the city government of democratic and socialist workers, artisans and students within five days. General Windischgrätz, who commanded the troops, showed no mercy. Robert Blum, a member of the Frankfurt Parliament from Saxony who had helped fight on the barricades in Vienna, was shot by a firing squad. Austrian and Russian troops put down the movement for independence in Hungary in June 1849.

In Prussia, too, conservatives got back the upper hand. The king ordered his troops to return to Berlin in September 1848 and appointed a conservative minister-president. In November the king dissolved the Prussian national assembly and ended all hopes for a democratic constitution. Instead he presented his own constitution "from above" – the constitution was written without consulting any representatives of the people. Frederick William IV now directly opposed the revolution. When members of the Frankfurt Parliament travelled to Berlin to offer him their crown on 3 April 1849, he refused.

The Legacy of the Revolution

Austrian members left the Frankfurt Parliament when it decided to offer the crown to the Prussian king. When he refused, the remaining members realized that they could no longer reach an agreement with the German rulers about the people taking part in politics and national unity. So most of the Parliament's members gave up and returned home. Only about 100 men in the democratic and republican groups met again in Stuttgart as a "rump parliament", but the Württemberg military put an end to that as well. In Baden a group of dissidents held out longer than in other places because first, the troops there took sides with the rebels and second, the fortress in Rastatt was easy to defend. When the fortress finally fell, fifty-one leaders of the rebellion were executed, 845 revolutionaries were put in jail. Many fled or emigrated to the United States. Others committed suicide – for example, Bassermann in Baden.

The hopes of liberal citizens from March 1848 were completely disappointed in 1849. For years, political opposition in Germany came to a halt. However, although the revolutionaries of 1848 failed to achieve their goals, the revolution did have long-term effects. Feudal rights were abolished, the liberation of the peasants could not be turned back. The Frankfurt Parliament's constitution had been written down. Even though the German monarchs refused to accept its ideas at the time, the document became a model for the constitution of the first German republic in 1919. Also, national unity remained a topic of public debate after 1849 and could not be ignored.

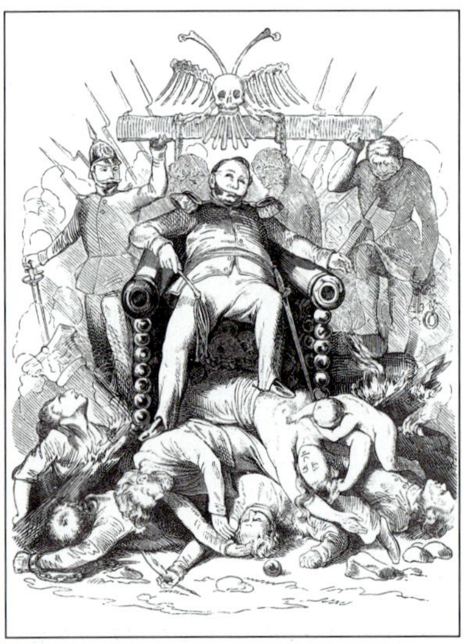

M 2 "After the Prussian Army Put Down the Revolt in Baden: The Red Monarchy"
Frederick William IV sits on a newly designed throne. Caricature, 1849

M 3 **"Another Dance of Death".** Woodcut by Alfred Rethel, 1849

M 4 "Solution of All the Political Problems"

Carl Schurz (1829–1906), a 48er who emigrated to the United States and became a political leader there, explained why he became more radical during the Revolution of 1848:

"Our democratic club was *composed* in almost equal parts of students and citizens, among whom there were many of excellent character, of some *fortune* and good standing, and of moderate views, while a few others had worked themselves into a state of mind *resembling* that of the terrorists in the French Revolution. Kinkel [a professor of law in Bonn] was the recognized leader of the club, and I soon became a member of the *executive* committee. At first the establishment of a constitutional monarchy with universal suffrage and *well-secured* civil rights would have been quite satisfactory to us.
But the reaction, the *threatened* rise of which we were observing, gradually made many of us believe that there was no safety for popular liberty except in a republic. From this belief there was only one step to the further *conclusion* that in a republic, and only in a republic, all evils of the social body could be cured and the solution of all the political problems be possible."

Carl Schurz, The Reminiscences of Carl Schurz, New York 1913, Vol.1, pp. 133–137.

M 5 Positive Effects of the Failed Revolution

The historian William Carr wrote in 1991:

"Before 1848 only a small section of the German middle class was politically and nationally conscious [...].
Without the ground swell of public opinion favourable to unification which the Revolution had created, the achievements of Bismarck in the 1860s would hardly have been possible."

W. Carr, A History of Germany, 1815–1990, London 1991, p. 57.

to compose: to make up
fortune: success
resembling: similar to
executive: leading
well-secured: guaranteed
threatened: dangerous
conclusion: decision

Tasks

1. Give reasons for the failure of the Revolution of 1848 in Germany.
2. Explain how the monarchs regained control over their countries in 1848.
3. Discuss the caricature's subtitle "The Red Monarchy" (M2).
4. a) Analyse Rethel's "Another Dance of Death" (M3).
   b) Agree or disagree with Rethel's point of view and explain your reasons.
5. Assess Carl Schurz's reasoning for becoming a republican (M4).
6. Evaluate the long-term results of the Revolution of 1848 in Germany (M5, text).

Imperial Germany

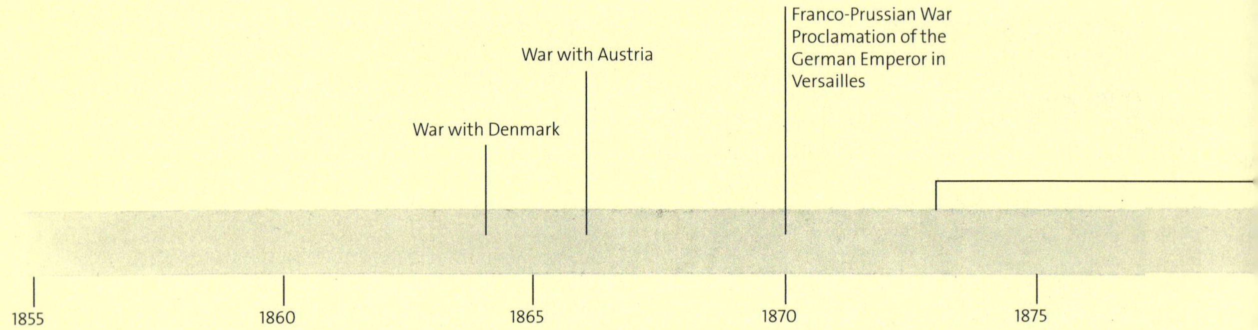

"Blacksmith Bismarck Forges German Unity". Woodcut, about 1895

A working-class family in its living room-kitchen-bedroom, Photograph, 1907

Painting of the Opening of the Reichstag and Coronation of William II, 1888

Year of Three Emperors:
William I
Frederick I
William II

Bismarck leaves office

Alliance System

1885 1890 1895 1900 1905

M 1 **William I (1861–1888)**
Photograph

insane: mentally ill
conscripts: men required to do military service, draftees
standing army: army on permanent duty
in spite of: without considering
envoy: diplomat who represents his country, (here) at the Confederation in Frankfurt

M 2 **Bismarck (1815–1898)**
Photograph, 1862

Prussia – Leading Power in Germany

Status of the German Confederation

After the failure of the Revolution of 1848, the question of how to organize Germany once again was raised. The German Confederation was re-established, but it was clear that the confederation would have to be reformed. Two major powers competed for hegemony in the confederation: Prussia and Austria. Which would triumph in the new situation?

Prussia: From Military Reform to Constitutional Crisis

In 1858 King Frederick William IV of Prussia was declared legally *insane.* His brother became regent and then in 1861 King William I. At first, many hoped that William would be more flexible than his brother – this period is called the "New Era" because of these hopes. William swore his loyalty to the constitution (although Frederick William had warned him against this) and even appointed several liberal ministers to his cabinet. But William had been trained from his youth as a military officer – his role in the Berlin uprising in 1848 had been unpopular (he was called the "machine gun prince" because of his willingness to shoot at demonstrators). As one of his first orders of business, he decided to reform the army.

There were several good reasons for reform: the Prussian army had a smaller number of troops than the French, Austrian or Russian army; also, troop numbers had remained the same since 1814, so that more than two-thirds of the *conscripts* in Prussia did not have to serve. This made military service harsh for the smaller number of men who did have to serve.

Prussian Minister of War Albrecht von Roon presented a plan in 1860 which increased the size of the *standing army* during peacetime, lengthened conscription from two to three years, and weakened the status of the militia (Landwehr). The liberal majority in the Prussian parliament did not approve of William's plans. When he tried to put them into effect *in spite of* parliamentary opposition, the parliament refused to approve the budget. The king was at a loss and even considered abdicating. At this point Minister of War Albrecht von Roon suggested Otto von Bismarck as the person who could help in the crisis.

Otto von Bismarck

As the son of a landowning aristocrat, a Junker, Bismarck's conservative thinking was well known. He had served as Prussian *envoy* to the Frankfurt Parliament, as Prussian ambassador in St. Petersburg and in Paris. When he assured the king in 1862 that he would support the military reform in spite of parliament's opposition, the king appointed him Prussian Minister-President. Bismarck announced that the Prussian constitution had a "gap" – the constitution did not foresee a conflict between the king and the parliament. In such a situation, according to Bismarck, the power to govern rested with the king, because he could exercise it. Using this excuse, Bismarck led Prussia without parliamentary approval for the following several years.

M 3 Bismarck's Promise to the King

a) Bismarck discusses his appointment as Prussian Minister-President with King William I on 22 September 1862:

"[The king said:] 'I do not want to govern if I cannot do so in a way in which I am responsible to God, to my conscience and to my subjects. I cannot if I have to govern according to the will of the present majority in the parliament, and I can no longer find any ministers who are willing to lead my government without submitting themselves and me to the parliamentary majority. I have therefore decided to abdicate.' [...] The king asked [...] whether I would be willing to support the military reform as minister [...] even in opposition to the parliamentary majority and its resolutions. Upon my agreement he finally declared: 'Then it is my duty to try to continue the fight with you.' I could *persuade* him that the problem was not about conservative or liberal [politics] [...] but about monarchical or parliamentary rule and that the *latter* had to be prevented even if a period of dictatorship was necessary. I said: 'In this situation even if I disagree with what your majesty orders me to do, I will tell you my opinion openly, but if you insist on your opinion, then I will rather go down with the king than *abandon* your majesty in the fight against parliamentary government.'"

Bismarck, "Die gesammelten Werke", ed. by Hermann von Petersdorff, Berlin 1924–1935, Vol. 15, p. 178, translated by D.N.

b) Bismarck to the budget commission of the Prussian Parliament, 29 September 1862:

"We [Prussians] are too hot-blooded, we *have a preference* for putting on *armor* that is too big for our small body; and now we're actually supposed to *utilize* it. Germany is not looking to Prussia's liberalism, but to its power; Bavaria, Württemberg, Baden may *indulge* liberalism, and for that reason no one will assign them Prussia's role; Prussia has to *coalesce* and concentrate its power for the opportune moment, which has already been missed several times; Prussia's borders according to the Vienna Treaties [of 1815] are not favorable for a healthy, *vital* state; it is not by speeches and majority *resolutions* that the great questions of the time are decided – that was the big mistake of 1848 and 1849 – but by iron and blood."

Bismarck, "Die gesammelten Werke", ed. by Hermann von Petersdorff, Berlin 1924–1935, Vol. 10, p. 139–140, translated by Jeremiah Riemer.

M 4 Bismarck in the Parliament of the North German Confederation. Caricature, Vienna, 1870

to persuade: to convince
the latter: the last named, (here) parliamentary rule
to abandon: to desert, to leave alone
to have a preference: to like sth.
armour: covering (usually metal) to protect the body from weapons
to utilize: to use
to indulge: to enjoy, to give in to
to coalesce: to unite
vital: living
resolutions: parliamentary decisions

Tasks

1. Explain the Prussian constitutional crisis in 1862.
2. Interpret William I's unwillingness to govern together with a parliamentary majority.
3. Assess Bismarck's willingness to assist in the situation.
4. Summarize and clarify Bismarck's influence on William I in the conversation (M3a).
5. Analyse Bismarck's view of the role of Prussia and the failure of the Revolution of 1848 (M3b).
6. Assess the Viennese opinion of Bismarck (M4).

M 1 **"Battle of Düppel"**
Painting, 1864

successor: person who follows another in an office
to amend: to change
ethnic: having a common cultural background (customs, language, history, etc.)
to be humiliated: losing pride, seeming foolish
reparations: payment for wartime expenses or losses (paid by the loser to the winner)
to annex: to add a territory to another state

M 2 **"William I in the Battle of Königgrätz" 1866**
Detail from the painting by Christian Sell, 1866

The Road to German Unity

Germany was finally unified in three wars: the German-Danish War 1864, the Austro-Prussian War 1866, the Franco-Prussian War 1870–71. It is to Bismarck's credit that none of the wars involved a conflict with more than one great power at a time.

The War with Denmark 1864
When the Danish king died in 1863, his *successor* and the Danish parliament *amended* the constitution to include the duchy of Schleswig, which had a majority of *ethnic* Danes. This action violated the London Protocol of 1852 which guaranteed that the duchies of Schleswig and Holstein (which had a majority of ethnic Germans) would stay together.

Other European powers were unable to engage in the conflict: Russia was occupied with the Polish uprising of 1863, Britain stuck by her guarantees of the London Protocol. Bismarck convinced Austria to support Prussia in the German Confederation. Austrian and Prussian troops defeated Denmark and forced her to give up the duchies. In the peace treaty of Gastein (1865), both allies agreed to administer the duchies cooperatively: Austria was to administer Holstein, Prussia Schleswig.

The War with Austria 1866
Prussia and Austria soon disagreed over the administration of the duchies. Austria raised the question in the German Confederation, which Prussia saw as a violation of the Treaty of Gastein. In turn, Prussia invaded Holstein (15 June 1866) and demanded that Austria leave the German Confederation. An alliance among Austria, Hanover, Electoral Hesse and the southern German states declared war on Prussia. Prussia won the decisive battle against Austria and her allies at Königgrätz, or Sadova, on 3 July 1866; on 23 August the war ended with the Treaty of Prague. The victory demonstrated Prussian military superiority in two areas: the use of railways and more efficient rifles. Moltke and Roon's modern military overwhelmed the traditional Austrian army.

Bismarck's pre-war diplomacy had secured French neutrality (Napoleon III received an unclear promise of payment) and Italian support (in April 1866 Italy agreed to attack Austria if war with Prussia began within three months – Italy's reward was to be Venetia).

When Prussian victory was clear, William I wanted a victory parade through Vienna, but Bismarck insisted that Austria should not *be humiliated.* Also, Prussia demanded no *reparations.* Austria lost little territory, but Venetia returned to Italy as promised. France was not paid for her neutrality: Bismarck refused to honour his unclear pre-war promise and the short war ended before Napoleon III could take part in it. Bismarck's policies were called "Realpolitik" – political decisions based only on harsh realities.

Following the Treaty of Prague (1866) Schleswig and Holstein were *annexed* by Prussia, as were Hanover and Electoral Hesse, which had sided with Austria. Led by Prussia, a North German Confederation of twenty-two German states north of the Main did away with the old confederation. The German states south of the Main signed a secret defensive alliance with Prussia in case of attack. Essentially, Germany was divided into three parts: Prussia with the North German Confederation, the southern German states, and Austria. With no role in Germany any longer, Austria turned to *consolidating* the new Austro-Hungarian Empire and her diplomatic interests in the Balkans and southeast Europe.

Public opinion in Prussia was reversed: now nationalists *enthusiastically* supported the military budget. The Prussian parliament even approved Bismarck's actions during the constitutional crisis after the fact.

M 3 A Change in Opinion about Bismarck

a) Rudolph von Ihering, a liberal and professor of law, on the war with Austria (1 May 1866):

"A war has probably never been started with such shamelessness, with such *cruel* ease as the war Bismarck is trying to start with Austria. Such an outrage against all the principles of law and morality is deeply shocking. [...] What will we have to go through, what horrible future awaits us [...] German armed against German, a civil war, a *conspiracy* [...] without any appearance of legality, without any participation by the people, just brought about by some diplomats!"

b) Rudolph von Ihering (19 August 1866):

"I bow down before the genius of a Bismarck [...] What we unknowingly regarded as outrageous *presumption* is now revealed as an *indispensable* means to an end [...] I would give one hundred men of liberal opinions and powerless honesty for one such man of action."

H. Michaelis, Königgrätz. Ein geschichtlicher Wandel, 1952, p. 177, translated by D. N.

M 4 Bismarck's Political Principles

Bismarck in a private letter, 11 May 1857:

"If I were convinced that it is in the well-considered interest of Prussian policy to do so, I would be equally content to see our troops fire their weapons on the French, the Russians, the English or the Austrians. In times of peace I consider it *reckless* to *sap one's strength* by causing annoyance to others without combining it with a practical political purpose."

Bismarck, Die Gesammelten Werke. Bd. 14. p. 464 ff., translated by D. N.

to consolidate: to make sth. strong
enthusiastically: (adv.) with spirit, excited by
cruel: causing suffering
conspiracy: a group planning and acting in secret
presumption: overstepping proper behaviour
indispensable: absolutely necessary
reckless: irresponsible, careless
to sap one's strength: to weaken oneself

Tasks

1. Explain why Denmark tried to annex Schleswig in 1863.
2. Analyse Bismarck's diplomatic tactics before the war with Austria (1866).
3. Interpret Bismarck's refusal to impose severe treaty conditions on Austria.
4. Look at M1 and M2. Explain why paintings of battles were popular at this time.
5. Interpret Ihering's change of opinion in his diary entries from 1866 (M3 a and b).
6. Discuss the advantages and disadvantages of Bismarck's political realism (M4).

M 1 **"Germany's Future"**
„Will Germany fit under one hat? I think it's going to fit under a spiked helmet." Caricature, Vienna, 1870

M 2 **"Prussia chains Alsace to Himself"**
French caricature by Cham, 1871

The Franco-Prussian War 1870–1871

The Hohenzollern Candidacy

The Spanish throne fell vacant in 1868 and a Catholic member of the Hohenzollern family, Leopold of Hohenzollern-Sigmaringen, was suggested as a candidate for the crown.

Napoleon III feared France would be surrounded by a Hohenzollern Prussia and Spain. (In the 16th century Habsburg rule in Spain and Austria had endangered France.) Faced with strong French opposition, Leopold withdrew his candidacy, and Prussian King William I, head of the Hohenzollern family, agreed. That could have ended the affair, but Napoleon wanted a diplomatic victory. He ordered his ambassador to Prussia, Count Benedetti, to ask William to promise that no Hohenzollern would ever ascend the Spanish throne. Benedetti approached the king on the promenade at Bad Ems, where William was on a spa. William refused the request in written form and informed Bismarck in Berlin that he could publish "all or part of" his reply in the press. Bismarck shortened the telegram so that the king seemed to insult the French ambassador (as well as the French emperor). Bismarck's timing was important, as publication of the dispatch fell on 14 July – the French national holiday. Napoleon's attempted diplomatic triumph turned into a disaster. On 19 July 1870 France declared war on Prussia.

War and Peace

The southern German states went to war along with Prussia. Napoleon had hoped that they would remain neutral, but he was unaware of their secret defensive alliance with Prussia from 1867. A wave of nationalism swept up the northern and southern German states. The Prussian army and its allies *mobilized* faster than the French forces. The decisive battle was won by the German forces on 2 September 1870 at Sedan, where Napoleon himself and 100,000 French soldiers were taken prisoner. But Napoleon's capture led to revolution in Paris – an unforeseen development.

Moderate French republicans proclaimed the Third Republic (4 September 1870) and organized resistance to the Germans. Suddenly, the war became a national struggle, creating enormous difficulties for the German troops now facing guerrillas. Not until 21 February 1871 did the French National Assembly in Bordeaux accept defeat in a preliminary peace treaty in Versailles. The bitterness and frustration caused by the unexpectedly long conflict continued in the Treaty of Frankfurt: France had to let Germany annex the provinces of Alsace and Lorraine, to pay reparations of 5 billion francs, and to accept German occupation of eastern France until the sum was finally paid.

The German Empire

Before the war was over, the new German Empire was proclaimed in the Hall of Mirrors at Versailles on 18 January 1871 – a further humiliation for the French government and people. For Germany a new era, called the "Gründerzeit", began with the founding of the empire.

M 3 Proclamation of German Empire in Versailles, 18 January 1871. Portrait by Anton von Werner, 1885

M 4 Opinions about the New Germany

a) Comment of The Times on the new German Empire, 20 January 1871:

"Within living memory German nationality was *utterly* dead, and up to 1866 the country was linked with foreign and hostile communities. In 1871 Germany starts independent, *ardently* patriotic, almost purely national. She is about to have the most powerful instrument of unity, a great popular Assembly, an institution which seems in these days to have a more strongly centralizing influence than any despot can command."

Michael Gorman, The Unification of Germany, Cambridge: Cambridge University Press, 1989, p. 98.

b) Benjamin Disraeli (British opposition leader) in the House of Commons, 9 February 1871:

"This [Franco-Prussian] war represents the German Revolution, a greater political event than the French Revolution of the last century [...]. Not a single principle in the management of our foreign affairs [...] any longer exists. There is not a diplomatic tradition which has not been swept away [...]. The balance of power has been entirely destroyed, and the country which suffers most, and feels the effects of this great change most, is England."

Hansard, Parliamentary Debates, Series 3, Vol. 204, London 1871, Col. 81–82.

to mobilize: to assemble troops at the start of a military action
utterly: (adv). completely
ardently: (adv). intensely

Tasks

1. Debate whether Napoleon III's demands in the Hohenzollern candidacy were reasonable.
2. Interpret the cartoons M1 and M2.
3. Describe the picture of the proclamation of the German Empire (M3).
4. Consider the effect of the wars of unification on the political climate in the new German Empire.
5. Compare and contrast the opinions about Germany (M4).

M 1 The new German Flag, with the colours of Prussia (white and black) and the former Imperial cities (red), and **the Imperial War Flag.** The Imperial eagle with Prussian shield and crown of the Holy Roman Empire was the official symbol of the German Empire.

M 2 The Victory Column erected in Berlin on 2 September 1873 to commemorate the wars of 1864, 1866 and 1870–71.

to initiate: to begin the process of passing laws

Politics in the New Germany

Germany after 1871: Authoritarian or Democratic State?
The new German constitution was based on the Constitution of the North German Confederation of 1867. It included a mixture of authoritarian and parliamentary features.

The German Empire unified twenty-five separate countries. Their rights and privileges were guaranteed by the Federal Council, the assembly of the individual states. Without the council's approval, no law could be passed.

Prussia, with two-thirds of the population and territory of the new Germany, played a hegemonial role. But Prussia had only seventeen out of fifty-eight seats – not a majority – in the Federal Council. However, one-fourth of the seats in the council (fourteen votes) were enough to stop a law from passing. Prussia's special role was clear in other ways: the Prussian King was automatically German Emperor, the Prussian Minister-President was automatically Chancellor.

Problems with the Parliaments
The Reichstag was the popular assembly. Its members were elected by equal, direct, and secret ballot. All men over the age of twenty-five could vote (universal suffrage). The candidate who received a majority of votes in his district was elected. Members of the Reichstag received no payment for their parliamentary duties, so they had to earn an income by other means. The Reichstag had no influence on the government, as the chancellor was appointed by the emperor and was only responsible to him. The chancellor appointed the state secretaries, the officials who were in charge of the administration. The emperor could dissolve the Reichstag and call for new elections. However, the Reichstag had the right to *initiate* new laws, to ask questions and demand answers from the government. Reichstag approval was necessary to pass any law, including the budget. The chancellor had to find a majority in each newly elected Reichstag so that laws could be passed.

In Prussia (as in many of the separate states) the three-class electoral system for the Prussian Chamber of Deputies was indirect, unequal, and oral. Not surprisingly, this system led to more conservative results than the electoral system for the Reichstag. With time this structural problem – the differences in parliamentary majorities in the Reichstag and the Prussian Chamber of Deputies – made finding coalitions in both parliaments a problem. As long as Bismarck stayed in office he tried to manipulate the assemblies according to his needs. But over the years it became more difficult.

In 1871 it was unclear which of the constitutional organs would be most powerful – the emperor and his government, the Federal Council, or the Reichstag. The constitution seemed to favour the Federal Council and through it the rulers of the twenty-five separate states. In later years the role of the Reichstag increased as the press reported and discussed its debates. Public opinion could even put pressure on the emperor – a fact which William II discovered rather late.

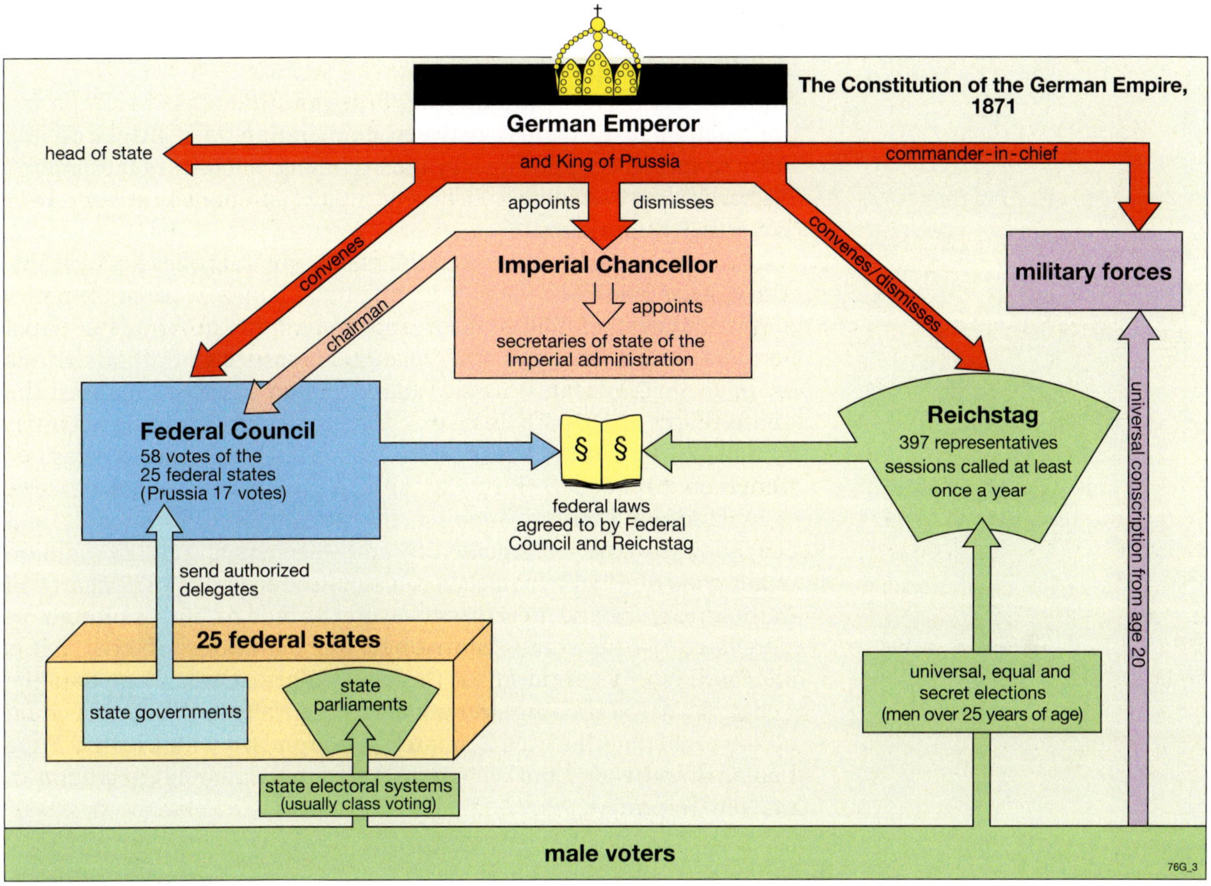

M 3

M 4 **"So-called Freedom"**

Jacob Burckhardt, Swiss historian, in a letter to a friend, on the lack of real freedom in Germany, 1872:

"Our Berlin *masters* are, I believe, full of anxiety, not *on account of* foreign countries but on account of their basically false position *in face of* the nation. The *external apparatus* of so-called freedom has been allowed to come into existence, but they are secretly *resolved* to act for all time according to their own will."

Helmut Böhme, The Foundation of the German Empire, Oxford, 1971, pp. 35–39.

masters: leaders (ironical)
on account of: because of
in face of: regarding
external apparatus: outside machinery
resolved: determined, firmly decided

Tasks

1. Look at the flags and symbol of the new Germany and interpret them (M1).
2. Explain which features of the German Constitution of 1871 were authoritarian and which were democratic (M3, text).
3. Analyse which of the constitutional organs seems most powerful. Explain your reasoning.
4. Assess Burckhardt's opinion about the new constitition (M4).
5. Critics of the 1871 Constitution have called it "only a constitution in form, not in substance." Agree or disagree with this argument.

M 1 **At the Helm of the Ship of State.** Caricature, 1879

Domestic Problems in the New Germany

The "Kulturkampf"

In both the Reichstag and the Prussian Chamber of Deputies, politicians had to choose between cooperating with Bismarck and being rewarded or opposing him and becoming "enemies of the empire." Bismarck's first attempt to deal with domestic opposition after 1871 led to the "Kulturkampf".

The defeat of Austria reduced the number of Catholics in Germany. At the same time Pope Pius IX, fearing Italian unity, warned Catholics of the dangers of nationalism and stated the doctrine of papal *infallibility*. Bismarck and other Protestants suspected Catholic priests of supporting Poles in Prussia. When German Catholics founded the Centre Party in 1870-71, Bismarck tried to restrict Catholic activities by passing laws in the Prussian parliament. Some of these measures were then extended to Germany through the Reichstag.

In German "culture" implies the arts as well as schools and education, so laws were passed to keep teachers and public opinion under control. Civil marriage was also introduced. By 1875 nearly all Catholic orders and newspapers were forbidden and hundreds of clergymen arrested and imprisoned. As *violations* of civil rights increased, so did criticism of the laws. When it was clear that the Centre Party was gaining strength and that loyalty to the church could not be broken in this way, Bismarck compromised with the new Pope Leo XIII and ended the dispute in 1878. But Catholic integration in the new empire was slowed.

M 2 **Between Berlin and Rome.** Caricature from "Kladderadatsch", 1875.
"The last move was unpleasant for me, but the match is still not lost. I have another good move in reserve."
"That will be your last, and you will soon be checkmated – at least in Germany."

The Socialist Law

Bismarck used two assassination attempts on William I in 1878 as an excuse to fight another "enemy of the empire" – the Social Democrats. The Reichstag was disbanded, new elections were held and a law forbidding the Social Democratic Party organization, treasury, meetings and publishing house was passed. However, candidates could still stand for election.

These measures against the party were as ineffective as those against Catholics during the Kulturkampf. By 1890 the party won three times more votes than in 1878. Disagreement with the new emperor William II about renewing the law led to Bismarck's dismissal in 1890.

M 3 Socialist Law

Social-Democrat August Bebel on the effects of the Socialist Law:

"The police continued to expel Socialists [from their home districts] and pick on them, but the success of these measures was not what our saviours of the state expected. Extremely bitter, those persecuted moved from city to city seeking out party members who took them in with open arms. They passed their anger and bitterness on to their hosts and encouraged them to unity and action. Many secret local contacts would not have been made without the agitation of the expelled. It seemed like the persecution of the Christians in the first centuries after the birth of Christ."

Aus den Erinnerungen August Bebels, in: Geschichte in Quellen, Das bürgerliche Zeitalter, 1815–1914, München 1980, S. 434, translated by D. N.

M 4 The Socialist Jack-in-the-box

Caricature from "Punch", 28 September 1878

infallibility: not being able to make a mistake

violations: not respecting sth.

Tasks

1. Analyse Bismarck's opposition to groups he characterized as "enemies of the empire". Suggest alternatives to Bismarck's domestic policies.
2. Explain the view of Bismarck's political methods shown in cartoon M1.
3. Look at the cartoons in M2 and M4. Explain which caricature is more optimistic about Bismarck's ability to keep his political opponents under control.
4. Analyse Bebel's opinion about the unexpected effects of the Socialist Law (M3).

M 1 **"Our Flag Nevertheless"** Lithografie, 1871. It was forbidden to wear or show the French colours in Alsace-Lorraine. These three women have found a way to protest the restriction.

Social Structure in the New Germany

Ethnic Minorities

Two and one-half million Poles made up the largest ethnic minority in the new empire. From 1871 on Poles were to be *"Germanized"* to keep them from leaving Germany or founding a separate Polish state. Various laws were passed to make certain that German was the only language used in schools and in public places. The measures *backfired*, strengthening Polish nationalism rather than weakening it.

The Danish population of North Schleswig faced similar treatment. However, opponents of "Germanization", including young men who wanted to avoid Prussian military service, simply emigrated to nearby Denmark.

In Alsace-Lorraine the integration of the French also caused problems. German officials in the annexed territory distrusted the local people. Thus, many members of ethnic minorities felt like only second-class citizens in Germany.

Social Differences in the New Germany

Although the German Industrial Revolution made the aristocracy with its large farms outdated, this group nevertheless played a prominent role in society, mainly through its contacts to Imperial court circles. But it was the middle class which formed the economic backbone of German society.

The middle class was made up of different groups. Most prominent were wealthy businessmen, bankers and industrialists – the upper middle class. Few of the very wealthy accepted noble titles – most were confident enough of their own achievements. Well-educated professionals, such as doctors, lawyers, upper secondary teachers and professors had to pay for expensive homes, clothing, and children's educations to stay prominent. These families might also marry their children into aristocratic families. Their sons often became reserve officers, positions open only to aristocrats before the 19th century, by volunteering for one year and passing the examinations. A reserve

M 2 **Strousberg, a Railway "robber baron" and his Family.** Painting, about 1910

M 3 **A working-class family in its living room-kitchen-bedroom.** Photograph, about 1907

officer could wear an officer's uniform in public, serve in military campaigns, and had to follow a military code of behaviour. "The officers are the highest social class," reported a Norwegian observer in 1907. Men in uniform were often seen in the streets, medals were desirable decorations, and the military was admired in all of Germany. Military discipline was a model for civilian life.

The largest group within the middle class – artisans, shop owners, small businessmen, lower civil servants, employees in business, in trade and industry – was the lower middle class. This group showed pride in a legendary work ethic of *meticulousness, punctuality,* loyalty, incorruptibility and *diligence.*

The lower class was made up of unskilled workers who had left farming jobs to find work in industry. The hard work *took its toll* – by the age of fifty, workers faced unemployment, poverty and social decline. With daily lives characterized as *monotonous,* hopeless and empty, this group felt like third-class citizens in Germany.

M 4 ***"Preoccupation*** **... with the Idea of War":**

The German historian Prof. J. A. Cramb in a lecture in London in 1913:

"There is, for example, the annual appearance in Germany of very nearly seven hundred books dealing with war as a science. This points, at once, to an extreme *preoccupation* in that nation with the idea of war. I doubt whether twenty books a year on the art of war appear in this country, and whether their circulation, when they do appear, is much more than twenty!"

Eric Wilmot, The Great Powers 1814–1914, Walton-on-Thames 1992, p. 295. Prof. J. A. Cramb in a lecture in London in 1913, quoted by J.C.G. Röhl, From Bismarck to Hitler, 1970.

M 5 **Military Influence.** Postcard, about 1910

"Germanize": to make someone more German
to backfire: to have the opposite effect
meticulousness: paying attention to details
punctuality: always being on time
diligence: working hard
to take a toll: to pay a high price
monotonous: one-sided, boring
preoccupation: thinking about sth. for a long time

Tasks

1. Refer to M1 to show the effect of Germany restrictions on French people in Alsace-Lorraine after 1871.
2. Discuss why members of ethnic minorities felt like only second-class citizens after 1871.
3. Assess the differences in social classes in Germany after 1871 (M2, M3, text).
4. Analyse Professor Cramb's concern with German books on the art of war (M4).
5. Discuss whether the postcard in M5 was meant to be taken seriously or not.

M 1 Louise Otto (1819–1895)
When Louise Otto started a newspaper, an 1850 law made it illegal for women to publish newspapers ("Lex Otto").

M 2 Helene Lange (1848–1930)
Photograph

Liberty – for Women, Too?

Women fought on the barricades and died during street battles in 1848, they participated in the meetings which demanded reforms from German rulers. But when the German National Assembly was elected, no woman could vote or stand for election. Most people could not imagine German women participating in political affairs – they were limited to family life. Nevertheless, some women insisted on their right to be included in political life.

Class Differences among Women

German women had no political rights in the 19th century. They could not even belong to political clubs or organizations legally until 1908. Working-class women had to earn money because working men's wages did not support a family. They worked as servants, nursemaids, cleaning women, laundresses, factory workers, and in cottage industry.

It was socially unacceptable for middle-class women to earn money. They depended on their families to survive. Most moved from their fathers' authority to their husbands' when they married. *"Old maids"* or widows could not support themselves because they lacked proper training. Women's education was poor: girls attended schools with lower standards than boys' schools, they could not get proper school-leaving certificates or study at a university. The only acceptable work for an unmarried middle-class woman was as a *governess, social companion,* or teacher.

These class differences led women to seek their rights differently. Middle-class women tried to improve their situation through education and better job opportunities. Louise Otto, for example, helped found the General German Women's Organization in 1865 to further such goals. Helene Lange (1848–1930) demanded suitable schools for women and, in 1905, "equal pay for equal work". The writer Hedwig Dohm (1831–1919) insisted on the right to vote, claiming in 1876, "Classes which do not have voting rights are in the power of those which do." Her arguments went too far for most men and women. Some felt that the time had not yet come for women to vote, others thought that women's rights were of minor importance in the new Germany.

Some but not all Social Democrats agreed that women should be able to vote, although not all were convinced. Clara Zetkin (1857–1933), publisher of the magazine "Equality", considered women's suffrage necessary to free the entire working class. August Bebel and Wilhelm Liebknecht supported this goal as early as 1875, claiming, "A party which writes equality on its banner insults itself by refusing political rights to half of humanity." Still, the SPD did not include women's suffrage in its party platform until 1891.

Slow Progress for Women's Rights

Many in the 19th century believed that the right to vote should only be given to citizens who had proved (by the property they owned or the taxes they paid) that they had earned it. When voting rights were extended to men who did not own property or pay taxes in the 1871 constitution, those men who felt they had earned their right to vote even tried to abolish universal male suffrage. When some men could deny other men the right to vote, it was *ridiculous* to consider it for women. The importance of the military in German life also worked against women's suffrage. All men had to serve in the German military, women did not. The argument that military service and suffrage were connected was repeated throughout the 19th century. Politics was for men alone.

Women's rights made only slow progress. In 1892 girls were allowed to finish upper-level school examinations (at boys' schools) in Prussia. By 1900 women were allowed to *audit* lectures in Prussian universities, if university trustees and professors agreed. Women were not permitted to take state examinations. In 1908 they could *join* political clubs and organizations, but were not allowed to vote or stand for election. Women's suffrage was granted in 1918 after the fall of Wilhelmine Germany only because the party platform of the SPD, then the largest political party in the Reichstag, had supported it.

M 3 Clara Zetkin (1857–1933)
Photograph

old maids: women who did not marry
governess: woman employed in a private home to train and teach children
social companion: person employed to live or travel with another
ridiculous: laughable, silly
to audit: to listen to
to join: to unite
midst: middle
upheavals: uprisings
share: part
to invoke: to call on, to refer to

M 4 "I am not a ... liberated woman"

Louise Otto explained her principles in the first edition of her newspaper (1849):

"In the *midst* of the great *upheavals* in which we all find ourselves, women will be forgotten if they forget to think of themselves!
Join with me, my sisters, so that we are not left behind, as everything around us is moving forward. We want to demand and earn our *share* in saving the world that will at long last come to all of humanity, of which we are one half. [...]
I *invoke* my life, my work as a writer since 1843 – anyone who is familiar with it knows that I am not a so-called 'liberated' woman, someone who has discredited the words 'women's liberation' by making woman into a caricature of man."

Margrit Twellmann, Die Deutsche Frauenbewegung im Spiegel repräsentativer Frauenzeitschriften. Meisenheim am Glan 1972, pp. 34-35. Translation: Thomas Dunlap.

M 5 Women's Rights

Hedwig Dohm (1876):

"Because women bear children they should have no civil rights. I say because men bear no children they should have no civil rights. I think each of these sayings is as meaningful as the other."

Hedwig Dohm, Das Stimmrecht der Frauen, 1876, p. 124, translated by D. N.

Tasks

1. Summarize briefly women's difficulties in getting political rights in the 19th century.
2. Find out more about Louise Otto, Hedwig Dohm, Helene Lange, or Clara Zetkin and report to the class.
3. Identify Louise Otto's goals for women in 1849 (M4).
4. Interpret Hedwig Dohm's argument (M5). Explain why Dohm was considered radical in her time.

M 1 **"Au Revoir"**
Caricature from "Punch", 27 September 1873

Principles of Bismarck's Alliance System

The unification of Germany at first destabilized Europe. France had been humiliated by defeat, high reparations and the loss of Alsace-Lorraine. A war of revenge seemed to be the next logical step for France. British diplomacy aimed to maintain stability on the continent so that Britain could pursue colonial affairs without worrying about European wars. Russia seemed neutral and almost friendly towards Germany, while Austria, no longer interested in German affairs, was likely to seek an understanding. According to Bismarck, who was German Chancellor and Foreign Secretary, German foreign policy had three principles:

- The German Empire was *"saturated"*: Germany after 1871 claimed no territory in Europe or in colonies abroad.
- The German Empire had to keep neighbouring powers from forming alliances against her. Bismarck called such a situation his *nightmare*. France had to be isolated.
- The German Empire had to keep the powers in the centre of Europe calm by *directing* tensions to the outer edges – the periphery – or to the colonies.

The Alliances (1873–1890)

In the 1873 Three Emperors' League, Germany, Austria-Hungary, and Russia agreed that republicanism and socialism were common enemies and promised to cooperate in future.

In 1877–78 a war between Russia and the Ottoman Empire nearly *escalated* into a conflict with Britain and Austria-Hungary. Bismarck *mediated* the dispute as an "honest broker" at the Congress of Berlin in 1878. Although a peaceful Balkan solution was found, the Russians were disappointed by Bismarck's lack of support for their goals. Slav nationalists also criticized Bismarck's role.

In 1879 the Dual Alliance, a defensive alliance between Germany and Austria, was signed for five years (it eventually lasted until 1918). It stated that if Russia attacked either Austria or Germany, the remaining partner would provide military assistance; if France attacked Germany, Austria would remain neutral.

In 1881 Russia returned to an alliance with Germany and Austria (whom she had abandoned after 1878) in the Three Emperors' Alliance, which stated that if Germany, Russia, or Austria were at war with another power, the partners would remain neutral. In addition, the powers agreed to

- keep the Black Sea closed to foreign warships,
- only permit territorial changes in the Balkans if the partners agreed beforehand,
- divide the Balkans into spheres of influence (with Russia in the east, Austria in the west),
- let Russia enlarge Bulgaria and Austria annex Bosnia-Herzegovina.

The alliance was renewed after three years in 1884, but a new dispute over Bulgaria made it obsolete by 1885.

In the 1882 Triple Alliance, Germany, Austria, and Italy agreed that if a partner were attacked by two or more powers, the other partners

M 2 **"Bismarck's Balancing Act"**
Caricature, 1888

would provide assistance. In a war between Austria and Russia, Italy would remain neutral. If France attacked Germany, Italy would provide assistance. If Italy were attacked by France, Austria and Germany would assist her.

In the 1887 secret *Reinsurance* Treaty, Germany and Russia agreed to remain neutral if either were at war with a third power. Neutrality did not apply if Germany attacked France or Russia attacked Austria. The treaty also recognized Russian interests in Bulgaria. The agreement was made for three years, but was not renewed in 1890.

Bismarck also encouraged the Second Mediterranean Agreement in 1887 (Germany did not participate) in which Britain, Austria, and Italy guaranteed the *status quo* in the Mediterranean and Near East. This treaty was really directed against Russia, which might try to create a crisis in Bulgaria or the rest of the Balkans.

Evaluation of the Alliance System

By a series of complex treaties and diplomatic agreements, Bismarck was able to consolidate the position of the German Empire in Europe without war for twenty years. However, the alliances sometimes seemed confusing and contradictory. After he left office in 1890 future chancellors did not manage German foreign policy as persuasively as Bismarck had. His successors' lack of *foresight* meant that the alliances could work against Germany by forcing her to keep her promises instead of acting on her own interests.

to saturate: to fill to the maximum capacity
nightmare: bad dream
directing: pointing, leading
to escalate: to grow larger and more dangerous
to mediate: to help others solve a problem
reinsurance: buying insurance for an already made insurance policy
status quo: things as they are at the moment
foresight: ability to see sth. clearly before it happens
to stunt: to keep sth. from growing
striking: clear
to put store upon: to value sth. highly
intelligible: clear to understand
to denounce: to criticize

M 3 Assessments of Bismarck's Foreign Policy

a) Historian Gordon A. Craig (1978):

"Bismarck chose his aides with care and with an eye to their intelligence, their technical skills, and their judgement; he protected their rights against attacks from outsiders. [...] But it was always his policy, and they were always only instruments; and he placed so much emphasis on this that, in the long run, he *stunted* initiative and judgement in his Foreign Service. [...] There is no more *striking* proof of [this...] than the result of the debate over the renewal of the Reinsurance Treaty in 1890, after his fall from office. One might have supposed that [the men of...] his diplomatic corps would have tried to defend the tie with Russia, *upon* which he had always *put* such *store.* They neither did so nor seemed even to appreciate what was at stake. Familiar only with the problems of their own posts, they were incompetent to make judgements about greater issues of policy."

Gordon A. Craig, Germany 1866–1945, Oxford 1978, pp. 137ff.

b) Historian Koppel Pinson (1966):

"Bismarck's [foreign] policy was limited [...] and *intelligible,* and therefore essentially peaceful in character. After the victory of 1870 Bismarck realized that the new German Reich needed a long era of peace. He therefore was satisfied to contain German energy within the European continent. Even the Balkans were not considered by him to be a direct field of German interest. [...] Bismarck had concrete and tangible 'interests'. A policy based only on 'prestige' or 'power' was *denounced* by him in a speech in the Reichstag of February 6, 1888, as completely unrealistic."

Koppel Pinson, Modern Germany, New York 1966, p. 295.

Tasks

1. Explain Bismarck's "nightmare" of coalitions.
2. Consider the situation of France (M1) and outline a French strategy against the isolation brought on by Bismarck's foreign policy.
3. Analyse the strengths and weaknesses of Bismarck's alliance system (M2, text).
4. Compare and contrast Pinson's and Craig's views on Bismarck's achievements in foreign policy (M3).

Bismarck Monuments

Monuments are historical evidence we can see every day, but we need to place them into a larger context. Each monument has its own history and shows how people felt about historical events at the time the monument was erected. Perhaps more importantly for us, the way a monument is respected and cared for shows how people feel about these events today.

Try analysing a monument on a field day excursion.

Bismarck monument in Hamburg

The world's largest Bismarck monument, designed by sculptor Hugo Lederer, stands 34 meters high in Hamburg St. Pauli. It is on a base built by architect Emil Schaudt. The 625-ton granite colossus shows Bismarck as a Roland figure leaning on a sword and looking westward toward the mouth of the Elbe and England, rather than eastward toward Berlin. Hamburg's city fathers wanted a large monument to impress William II. But the emperor disliked Bismarck and Hamburg (Bismarck criticized him after 1890 from nearby Friedrichsruh); also, he disapproved of Social Democratic successes in Hamburg elections.

But William's favourite seaport, Bremen, had erected a monument to his unloved father, Frederick I. Hamburg businessmen hoped that their monument to Bismarck would increase the money from the German Empire spent to improve the seaport and harbour facilities in their city. Private citizens raised 500,000 German marks to pay for the monument. When the dedication ceremony was held in 1906, the emperor did not attend. The cost of repairing the monument in 2007 is estimated to be about two million euros, which makes the city of Hamburg ask whether the monument is worth it. As one reporter wrote, "Hardly a postcard shows it, no city brochures praise it – it stands there, dirty, in a blind corner … like something set aside."

M 1 Roland statue

From a modern dictionary:

"Roland statue: larger-than-life statue of a bare-headed knight with a drawn sword placed on or near a market place or main square in the 13th to 18th centuries.
The meaning and origin of the name has been lost. Roland statues referred to legal matters, to courts which heard legal cases, or to city rights and freedoms."

Adapted by D.N. from: Meyers Neues Lexikon, Mannheim 1993, vol. 8, p. 234.

M 2 Bismarck monument in Hamburg St. Pauli

Bismarck monument near Ascheffel
The Aschberg statue near Ascheffel, Schleswig-Holstein, differs from the Hamburg monument. It was built in 1900 by Adolf Brütt and was meant to stand guard at the foot of a 45-meter tower near Apenrade (Denmark today). It is made of hammered sheet-copper and stands seven meters high. Bismarck wears a 19th century cavalry uniform. His right hand holds a sword and the left rests on the Imperial German crown. The statue was moved out of Denmark in 1919, because German nationalists feared that it would be melted down if left on Danish soil. It took until 1930 to remove it from storage and put it up on the 98-meter-high Aschberg. Today, Bismarck faces north towards Denmark, although he originally faced south towards Germany.

M 3 **Bismarck monument near Ascheffel**

Monument Analysis Worksheet

1. Describing the monument

a. Assess the importance of the monument's location.
b. Find out what material it is made of and what it represents.
c. Name the figures or objects which are used on the monument and what they symbolize.
d. Note how the figures or objects are portrayed, their size, where they are placed in the monument, their body language, their clothing, objects placed near them, etc.
e. Write down any inscriptions you find on the monument – texts, quotations, names, etc.
f. Describe the impression the monument makes on you.

2. Finding information

a. Find out as much about the building of the monument as you can: sculptor, architect, date built, sponsors, reasons for building it, name or title of the monument, its artistic style.
b. Find out who supported building the monument and who paid for it.
c. Look for evidence on how people felt about the monument at the time it was built: Find documents dealing with its dedication, its history, public debates about it.
d. Note whether the monument is used in ceremonies or formal occasions, who maintains it, and any nicknames it has.
e. Assess the importance of the location today.
f. Examine why people visit the monument today – ask visitors why they have come and how they feel about the monument.

3. Interpreting the monument

a. Analyse the impression the monument makes on a visitor today.
b. Assess the importance of the monument's symbols to visitors today.
c. Estimate which people will be enthusiastic about the monument today and which groups will not.
d. Formulate what the monument stands for and your response to it in your own words.

New Imperialism and the Scramble for Africa

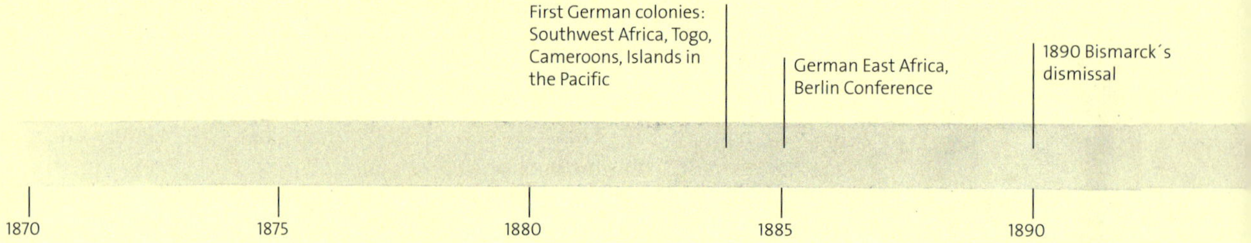

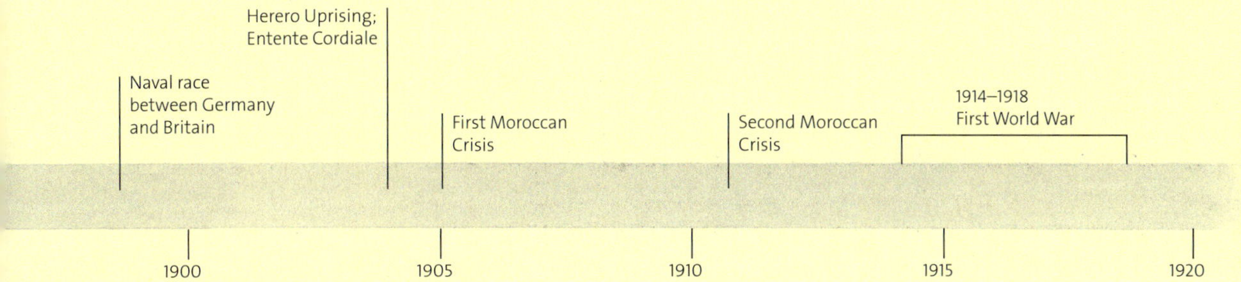

„France will bring culture, prosperity and peace."
Front page of the French paper „Le Petit Journal", 1911

Advertising Sign of the Company Bergmann & Co
around 1899

German Colonial Rule in German Southwest Africa
1904

The "New Imperialism"

The "new imperialism" was characterized by a hectic competition among European nations, Japan and the USA for territorial gains in Africa and Asia. This led these nations into conflicts with native peoples and with each other.

The "Scramble for Africa" changed the map of the continent profoundly. Before 1880 only 10 per cent of Africa was controlled by European powers. Colonies spread along the coast of West Africa from the former slave trade, settlements in southern Africa of the Dutch, English and Portuguese, and Algeria in the north, conquered by the French. By 1900 only Abyssinia and Liberia remained free of European control leaving 90 per cent of all African territory under European rule.

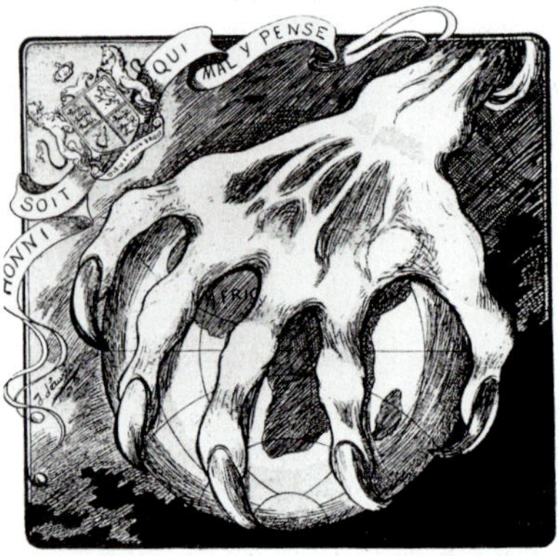

M 1 "The English paw is grabbing the world"
"Honi soit qui mal y pense" ("Shame on him who thinks ill of it"), the motto of the most noble Order of the Garter.
French cartoon, 1899.

Reasons for Expansion

The causes of the new imperialism are still hotly debated and extremely complex. Most European powers saw this expansion as a battle for wealth, power and survival. Although some Europeans bitterly criticised imperialism as a betrayal of Western ideals of freedom and equality, most people and politicians believed that to remain or become a great power seemed to require the possession of an empire.

Businessmen, bankers and investors encouraged imperial expansion and expected their governments to support their interests and activities; Cecil Rhodes and George Goldie asked the British government for help and Carl Peters, a German explorer and merchant, called on Bismarck to protect the gains of his German East Africa company. Their aim was to exploit the continent's natural resources and profit economically from the colonies.

Explorers and missionaries were also interested in visiting some lands. In the 19th century Africa was a mysterious place – "the Dark Continent". Because of diseases and the difficulties of crossing deserts and jungles, Europeans knew little about the interior. Missionaries followed the explorers in order to convert the African people to Christianity. They believed that the natives were *"heathen"* and had to be saved. The civilization of "backward" peoples was also justified with the idea that the white race was *superior*.

M 2 "The White Man´s Burden"

Rudyard Kipling (1865–1936), British author and poet, born in India and best known for the "Jungle Book", awarded the Nobel Prize for Literature in 1907 (1899):

"Take up the White Man's *burden* –
Send forth the best *ye breed* – […]
To wait, in *heavy harness,*
On *fluttered* folk and wild –
Your new-caught *sullen* peoples,
Half devil and half child. […]
Take up the White Man's burden –
[…]
Fill full the mouth of Famine,
And *bid* the sickness *cease;*
And when your goal is nearest
(The end for others sought)
Watch *sloth* and *heathen folly*
Bring all your hope to *nought.*"

Abridged by T.S. from Mc Clune's Magazine, 12 Febr. 1899, New York.

M 3 "The White (?) Man's Burden." Cartoon by William Walker, 1899

M 4 **"Finest Race"**

Cecil Rhodes (1853–1902), British businessman and the colonizer of the state of Rhodesia, today's Zambia and Zimbabwe (1877):

"I say that we are the finest race in the world and that the more of the world we inhabit the better it is for the human race. Just imagine what change there would be if those parts that are at present inhabited by the most *inferior* human beings were brought under Anglo-Saxon influence. Think of the extra employment a new country added to our dominions would give [...].
The *acquisition* of the greater part of the world under our rule would simply mean an end to all wars. [...] Africa is lying ready for us, it is our duty to take it."

Adapted by T.S. from: The last Will and Testament of C. J. Rhodes, London, 1902, p. 58.

M 5 **"Hammer or Anvil?"**

Prince Bernhard von Bülow (1849–1905), German Chancellor 1900, speech before the Reichstag on 11 December 1899:

"In our nineteenth century, England has increased its colonial empire – the largest the world has seen since the days of the Romans – further and further; the French have put down roots in North Africa and East Africa and created for themselves a new empire in the Far East; Russia has begun its mighty course of victory in Asia [...].
The English prime minister said a long time ago that the strong states were getting stronger and stronger and the weak ones weaker and weaker. [...] We don't want to step on the toes of any foreign power, but at the same time we don't want our own feet tramped on by any foreign power (Bravo!) and we don't intend to be shoved aside by any foreign power, neither in political nor in economic terms. (Lively applause.) [...] The *means,* gentlemen, for a people of almost 60 million – *dwelling* in the middle of Europe and, at the same time, stretching its economic antennae out to all sides – to battle its way through the struggle for existence without strong *armaments* on land and at sea, have not yet been found. (Very true! from the right.) In the coming century the German people will be a hammer or an *anvil.*"

Adapted from: Michael Behnen, Quellen zur deutschen Außenpolitik im Zeitalter des Imperialismus 1890–1911, Darmstadt 1977, p. 231 ff., translated by T.S.

heathen: not a Christian
superior: better, more powerful
burden: heavy task and responsibility
ye breed: (that) you can produce
heavy harness: horses have harnesses to pull a heavy load
fluttered: nervous and confused
sullen: dark and unpleasant
to bid sth. cease: to ask sth. to stop
sloth: laziness
heathen folly: the fact of doing sth. stupid because of not being a Christian
nought: nothing
inferior: lower in rank, opp.: superior
acquisition: here: the act of getting land and power
means: method
dwelling: living
armaments: weapons and military equipment
anvil: heavy iron block on which metal is hammered into certain shapes

Tasks

1. Work in groups and develop a diagram that shows the different motives to take part in this scramble for territorrial gains. Be prepared to introduce the different sources and to explain your diagram.
2. Prepare a short presentation on Cecil Rhodes or Rudyard Kipling.
3. According to Kipling, and in your own words, what was the "White Man's Burden" (M2)?
4. What reward did Kipling suggest the "White Man" gets for carrying his "burden" (M2)?
5. How does the cartoon respond to Kipling´s poem (M3)?
6. Discuss in class the reasons why the Europeans wanted to take over Africa (M4, M5).

Acquisition of Colonial Territory in Africa			
	Great Britain	Germany	France
1881	670,953		320,972
1895	5,965,519	2,385,100	2,381,476
1912	6,209,602	2,657,300	6,480,200

Wolfgang J. Mommsen, Imperialismus, Hamburg 1977, p. 37. 147G

M 1

Europeans in Africa

Annexation of Territory and Exploitation in Africa

In 1885 the Berlin Conference agreed upon Africa's division among the European powers. White people came to rule millions of black people and the tempo of expansion was enormous. By purchase and war the colonial powers turned all of Africa into *dependencies* and began to exploit the land and its people. The *annexation* of African territories meant the establishment of new states, and colonial rule was executed by policemen and soldiers, administrators, tax collectors, traders and labour recruiters. Railroads connected the coast with the interior and opened up new markets. New borders were drawn that lasted beyond the colonial period.

The economic exploitation of Africa mainly took place in mines, where the colonists searched for gold, diamonds or copper, and on plantations, which produced coffee, cocoa beans or rubber. The hard work was done by Africans, who were forced to labour and paid poorly. The punishment for disobedience was *harsh* and many Africans were killed or driven off their land. In some places, however, attempts to subdue the native population were not successful and led to long and bloody wars. The overwhelming majority of African leaders strongly opposed this change and decided to fight for their sovereignity and independence. One tragic example was the rebellion of the Herero and Nama in German Southwest Africa.

dependency: area or country controlled by another
annexation: to take control, occupy
harsh: cruel and severe

So kolonisiert der Deutsche,

So kolonisiert der Engländer,

M 2 **Cartoon by Thomas Theodor Heine in the German Journal "Simplizissimus",** 1905.

M 3 Statements from African Chiefs

a) In the face of the French invasion of his territory in 1883 and the demand for permission to build a railway across his territory Lat Dior, the Damel of Cayor in modern Senegal, wrote to the French Government:

"As long as I live, be well assured, I shall oppose with all my might the construction of this railway [...]. That is why, every time I receive a letter from you concerning the railway, I will always answer no, no, and I will never make you any other reply. Even when I go to my rest, my horse Malaw would give you the same answer."

b) In 1890, King Machemba of the Yao in Tanganyika (United Republic of Tanzania) told the German commander Hermann von Wissman:

"I have listened to your words but can find no reason why I should obey you – I would rather die first [...]. If it should be friendship that you desire, then I am ready for it, today and always; but to be your subject, that I cannot be [...].
If it should be war you desire, then I am ready, but never to be your subject [...]. I do not fall at your feet, for you are God's creature just as I am. I am Sultan here in my land. You are Sultan there in yours. Yet, listen, I do not say to you that you should obey me, for I know that you are a free man. [...] As for me, I will not come to you and, if you are strong enough, then come and fetch me."

c) Hendrik Wittbooi, a king in Southwest Africa, told the Germans in 1894:

"The Lord has established various kingdoms in the world, therefore I know and believe that it is no sin or crime that I should wish to remain the independent chief of my land and people."

M 4 Fight between the Herero and German troops 1904

d) In 1895, Wobogo, the king of the Mossi, told the French Captain Destenave:

"I know the whites wish to kill me in order to take my country, and yet you claim they will help me organize my country. But I find my country good just as it is. I have no need of them. I know what is necessary for me and what I want. I have my own merchants. Consider yourself fortunate that I do not order your head to be cut off. Go away now and, above all, never come back."

UNESCO Courier 5/1984 p. 33 ff.

Tasks

1. Try to show the development of the acquisition of colonial territory in Africa in a diagram (M1).
2. Describe the two cartoons and compare their messages. Who is criticized and what for (M2)?
3. Name the arguments the African chiefs present against their suppression by the Europeans (M3).
4. Which picture of the African chiefs do you get from reading these statements (M3)?
5. Explain the picture (M4) and discuss the statement the Africans were helpless in the face of the colonial threat.

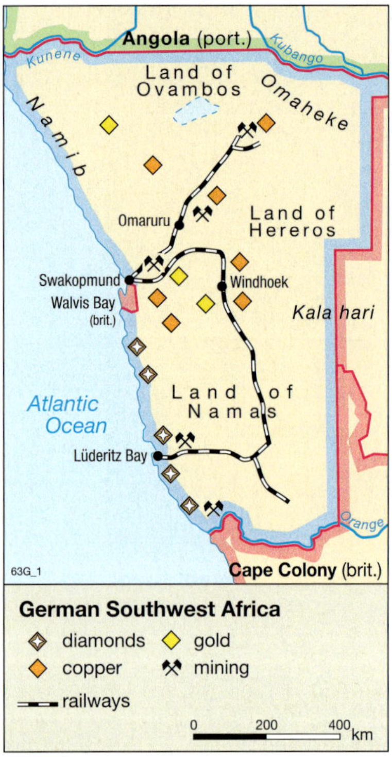

M 1

malnutrition: poor condition of health caused by lack of food
genocide: the murder of a whole race or people

M 2 German soldiers in Southwest Africa, 1904

German Rule in Southwest Africa

A German Colony

In 1884 Southwest Africa became a German colony. During the First World War it was administered by South Africa and in 1990 it became the independent state of Namibia. In 1883 the German merchant Adolf Lüderitz bought land from a native chief and asked the German government to protect his interests in Africa. Although the German Chancellor Bismarck was very sceptical about colonies he agreed. German Southwest Africa was larger than the German Empire of that time and became the only German colony where Germans settled in great numbers. They hoped for a better life and jobs in the mining (diamonds and copper) and the farming business. By 1902 about 2,600 of the 200,000 inhabitants were Germans and in 1914 their number had increased to 12,000. The native Africans living in the colony were the Herero, the Ovambo and the Nama, also called Hottentots.

Herero Uprising

On 11 January 1904, Herero tribal leader Samuel Maharero called for his people to rise up and fight against their German colonial rulers. Angered by the growing number of German settlers, the dividing of their land by new railroads and the killing of their herds of cattle, the Herero killed 100 German civilians and 13 soldiers in just a few days.

Completely unprepared for the unrest, Governor General Theodor Leutwein was unable to keep the uprising from spreading quickly all over the colony. After an unsuccessful six-month bush war the government in Berlin ordered 14,000 German soldiers, equipped with modern weapons like the breech-loading rifle, to the region to put down the rebellion. Heading the force was the hard-line Lieutenant General Lothar von Trotha. After a decisive battle for the Germans on 12 August 1904 near the Waterberg, the surviving Herero fled into the dry Omaheke desert.

Confronted with the very real possibility of dying in the desert, many Herero hoped to surrender to the Germans and headed back to their lands. But on 2 October von Trotha ordered all Herero, armed or unarmed and including women and children, to be shot if they attempted to return. Although the German Emperor William II and Chancellor von Bülow supposedly disagreed with this decision, they apparently did little to stop von Trotha, who was now willing to exterminate the Herero. The Africans who survived were put in chains and taken to camps where they suffered from forced labour, disease and *malnutrition.* Over all 75 to 80 per cent of the Herero population died and this tragic event was to become the first *genocide* of the 20th century.

The Herero in Namibia Today

The Herero never completely recovered from the conflict. Of the nearly 100,000 in Namibia today, many live in poverty or work on the farms of white landowners. In 2001 tribal leaders tried to sue Germany for compensation in U.S. courts, but the claim for $4 billion (3.12 billion euros) didn't go far.

M 3 **Herero Uprising**

a) General von Trotha in an appeal to the Hereros, 1904:

"I, the great general of the German soldiers, send this letter to the Herero people. The Herero are no longer German subjects. They have murdered and stolen, have cut off the ears and noses and other parts of injured German soldiers and now they refuse to fight out of *cowardice* [...].
The Herero nation must [...] leave the country. If they do not leave, I will force them out with cannons. Every Herero, armed or unarmed [...] will be shot dead within the German borders. I will no longer accept women and children, but will force them back to their people or shoot them."

Rust, C., Krieg und Frieden im Hererolande, Leipzig 1904, p. 25, transl. by T. S.

M 4 **Samuel Maharero,**
Chief of the Herero

M 5 **General von Trotha,**
Chief of the German troops

b) Statement of Hendrik Witbooi (Nama chief) on the German administration:

"The German himself [...] makes no requests according to truth and justice and asks no permission of a chief. He introduces laws into the land [... which] are entirely impossible, [...] unbelievable, *unbearable, unmerciful* and unfeeling [...]. He personally punishes our people at Windhoek and has already beaten people to death for *debt* [...] it is not just and right to beat people to death for that. [...] He *flogs* people in a shameful and cruel manner. We stupid and unintelligent people, for so he thinks us to be, we have never yet punished a human being in such a cruel and improper way for he stretches people on their backs and flogs them on the stomach and even between the legs, be they male or female, so Your Honour can understand that no one can survive such a punishment."

c) The following letter was written by Samuel Maharero on 6 March 1904 in reply to a letter of the German Governor Leutwein asking him why he had started the war:

"The beginning of the war is not just in this year begun by me, but by the whites, for you know how many Herero have been killed by white people, especially [by] traders with rifles and [by guards] in prison. And always when I brought the matter to Windhoek, the blood of my people was always valued at no more than a few head of [cattle] [...]. The traders increased the trouble in the way that they [...]gave my people *credit.* After they had done this they robbed them, going so far as to take away by force, to repay themselves, two or three head of cattle for a debt of one pound sterling. These are the things which have caused the war in this land."

b) and c) www.historyteacher.net

cowardice: lack of courage
unbearable: not acceptable
unmerciful: not willing to forgive
debt: sum of money that sb. owes
to flog: to punish sb. by hitting him with a whip or stick
credit: borrowed money

Tasks

1. List the reasons the German general and the African chiefs offer for the outbreak of the war (M3).
2. Work in groups and discuss the role the Germans played in Southwest Africa.

International Tensions

M 1 **"How are we going to shake hands?",** German cartoon from "Simplizissimus", 1912

to heighten: to increase
glorification: extreme praise
spheres of interest: area a power declares interest in

M 2 **"Dropping the Pilot"** English caricature, 1890

Rivalry among the European Powers

The scramble for colonies in Africa or Asia intensified the rivalry among the European powers. The dispute between France and Great Britain over the Sudan almost led to war at Fashoda in 1898 and Anglo-Russian relations often reached the point of war over disagreements in Asia. Russia and Japan actually engaged in a war in 1904/05. All the imperial powers became obsessed with gaining further territory and showing no sign of weakness. An atmosphere of *heightened* patriotism and *glorification* of armed force spread and undermined any forms of criticism and rational thought.

"New Course" in Germany

This was most noticeable in Germany. Chancellor Bismarck, who had subordinated colonial policy to the goal of stability in Europe, was dismissed in 1890. The Reinsurance Treaty with Russia was not renewed and Emperor William II chartered a "new course" announcing that Germany would adopt a "world policy". Attempting to find "a place in the sun" William's policy aimed at building a strong German navy and making Germany a major imperial power by expanding overseas. The new policy, however, showed little success. The only colonies added between 1897 and 1899 were some islands in the Pacific. But at the same time Germany's "world policy" created a great deal of tension and damaged Germany's standing in the world.

The French and Russian governments concluded the Franco-Russian Alliance in 1894. The British engaged in a naval race against Imperial Germany and in 1904 finally settled their differences with France over colonial policy in an agreement called the "Entente Cordiale".

Anglo-French cooperation in the Moroccan Crises (1905–1911) ruined Germany's attempt to gain greater influence in North Africa and when Russia and England finally concluded an agreement on their *spheres of interest* in Asia, the German government felt "encircled". The balance of power in Europe had turned against Germany, which had only one firm ally: Austria-Hungary.

M 3 **Painting of William II** "The Emperor during a Naval Manoeuvre", by Willy Stöwer, 1912

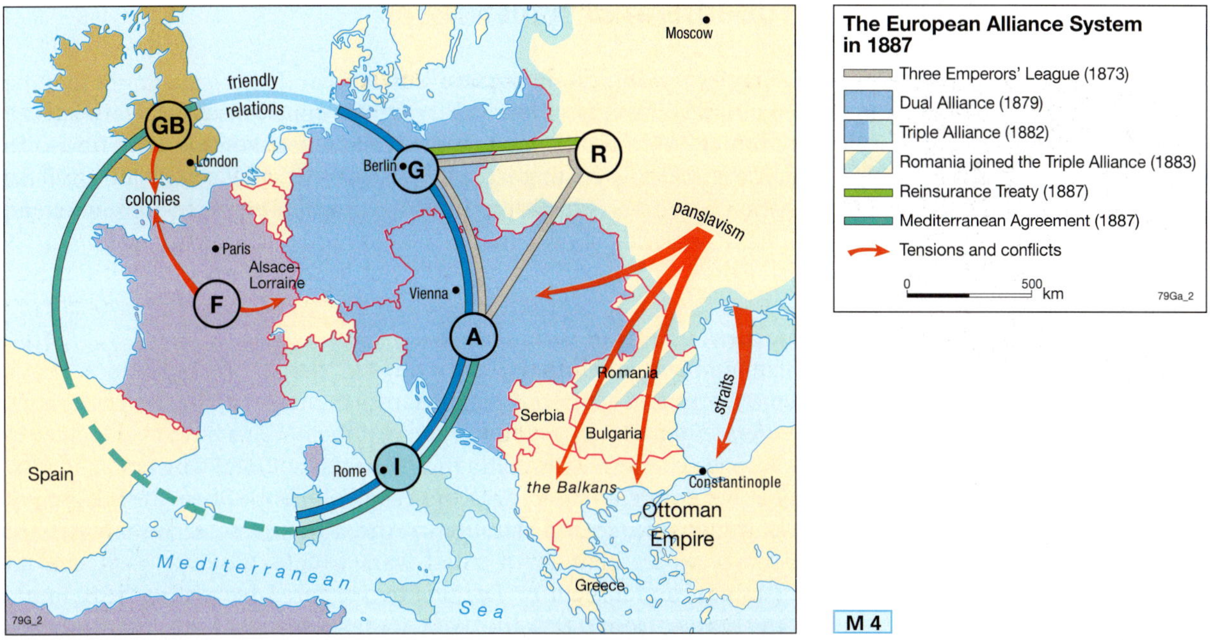

M 4

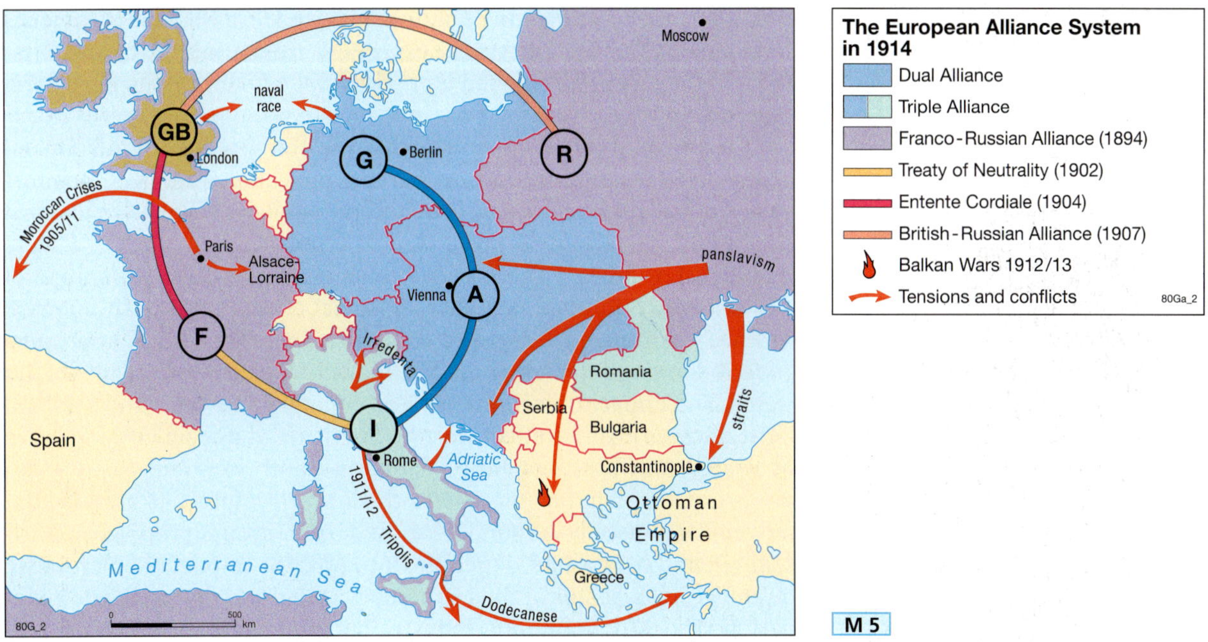

M 5

Tasks

1. Prepare a short report on the Fashoda Crisis and its background.
2. Describe the cartoon "How are we going to shake hands?" and work out its message (M1). Relate it to events mentioned in the text.
3. Show how the artist portrays William II (M3).
4. Compare the two maps and write a short text about the changes in international relations in Europe between 1887 and 1914 (M4, M5).

M 1 **"Light of Civilization"**
Schoolboys at the German School in Togo, about 1900

legacy: sth. from the past that affects life today
impact: powerful effect
harmful: causing damage or injury to sb./sth.
assessment: an opinion or judgement about sb./sth.
decade: period of ten years
groundnuts: peanuts
arbitrary: not based on reason, system or plan and sometimes seeming unfair

The Effects of Imperialism

What *legacy* did colonialism leave to Africa? There is no doubt that the economic, social and political *impact* of imperialism was very strong, although there is still some controversy over the different effects. To some historians its impact was positive or at least not *harmful* for Africa. To others colonialism in Africa only had negative consequences. Latest research shows that a much more balanced *assessment* is necessary.

Positive Effects of Colonialism

The impact of imperialism varied: Some poor nations have enjoyed greater economic benefits from contact with the rich than have others. India, Brazil, and other developing nations have even begun to compete economically with their former colonial powers. The first positive political impact was the establishment of a greater degree of continuous peace and stability in Africa than before. The nineteenth century was a century of tribal wars which caused a great deal of instability and insecurity. The first two or three *decades* of the colonial era, that is from 1880 to 1910, intensified this state of instability, violence and disorder and caused destruction and loss of population. But after the colonial occupation and the establishment of civil services, most parts of Africa, especially from the end of the First World War onwards, enjoyed a great degree of continuous peace and security.

The second positive effect was that the colonial system introduced a new judicial system and a new bureaucracy or civil service into most parts of Africa. The spread of Christianity was closely linked to western education. Certainly, by the end of the colonial regime, there were relatively few areas without at least elementary schools. The spread of western education had far-reaching social effects such as an increase in the westernized educated African elite. This elite now runs governments and makes up the backbone of the civil service in African states. The impact on economics was equally important. The first and most obvious positive effect was the provision of a basic infrastructure of roads, railways, telegraph, telephone and, in some cases, even airports. Completed by the 1930s, this infrastructure was used for the movement not only of goods, the new cash crops (crops grown for selling), and troops, but of people, too. Also the impact of colonialism on the primary sector of the economy was realized during the colonial period. The African mining industry boomed while the cultivation of cash crops such as cocoa, coffee, tobacco, *groundnuts,* sisal and rubber spread.

Negative Effects

But if there were positive effects, the negative effects were even greater. The economic exploitation of Africa's natural resources was and is still quite often controlled by western companies. Often the borders of the African states that emerged were *arbitrary* and many of the states were artificial creations made up of various peoples with different cultures, traditions, origins and languages. The negative consequences can still be seen today. Civil wars within and among African states have become part of daily life. Worse still was the impact of colonialism in the cultural field. Throughout the colonial period, African art, music, dancing and even history were not only ignored but actively discouraged or rejected. Imperialism has destroyed traditions and ways of thinking and has replaced them with the habits and mentality of the western world. As one speaker declared at the Second Congress of Negro Writers and Artists in Rome, in 1959: "Among the sins of colonialism, one of the most *pernicious*, because it was for a long time accepted by the West, was the concept of people without culture."

Disaster or Benefit?

Thus, it is an exaggeration to consider colonialism a disaster for Africa that caused only underdevelopment and backwardness. On the other hand, colonial *apologists* overstate the facts when they see colonialism as an unqualified *blessing* for Africa. The question of whether a colony benefited from colonialism or not has to be examined on a case-by-case basis. Colonial rulers did not see the development of Africans as a priority. The impact of colonialism was positive as well as negative. However, most of the positive effects were accidental by-products of activities or measures *intended to promote* the interests of the colonizers.

The Economic Importance of the German Colonies	
Raw materials imported from the colonies as a proportion of total raw materials imported	**1.6%**
Colonies' share of German Empire's exports	**0.5%**
Colonies' share of German Empire's capital exported	**2.0%**
German settlers in the African colonies until 1913 as a proportion of all the emigrants from the German Reich 1871-1914	**0.03%**

R. v. Albertini, Europäische Kolonialherrschaft 1880-1940, Zürich 1976 141G

M 2

M 3 Two Different Views

a) The English historian P.C. Lloyd:

"It is easy to *cavil* today at the slow rate of economic development during the half-century of colonial rule [...]. Nevertheless, the difference between the condition of African society at the end of the nineteenth century and at the end of the Second World War is *staggering*. The colonial powers provided the infrastructure on which progress in the 'independence' period has depended: a fairly efficient administrative machine, reaching down to villages in the most remote areas, a network of roads and railways, and basic services in health and education."

b) The black Guyanese historian Walter Rodney:

"The argument suggests that, on the one hand, there was exploitation and oppression, but, on the other hand, that colonial governments did much for the benefit of Africans and that they developed Africa. It is our *contention* that this is completely false. Colonialism had only one hand, it was a one-armed bandit."

UNESCO Courier 5/1984, p. 33 ff.

pernicious: harmful
apologist: a person who tries to explain and defend sth.
blessing: sth. that is good or helpful
intended: planned
to promote: to help sth. to grow
to cavil: to complain about
staggering: hard to believe
contention: belief

Tasks

1. Working in pairs, transform the data into text and evaluate the economic importance of the colonies for the German economy (M2).
2. List the textbook's arguments and those of the two historians. Add further aspects that should be considered (M3).
3. Discuss the effects of imperialism and the lessons that should be learned for today's world.

M 1 **"The name is full of bloody history"** Headline "Kieler Nachrichten", 27 July 2006

M 2 **"Dr. Carl Peters – Gedenkt unserer Kolonien"**
Emergency currency, 1921

The Renaming of Streets

The era of imperialism is over and Germany no longer has any colonies. But there are still signs and *reminders* of colonial times. There are monuments or streets named after German colonists in many cities; and they led and still lead to controversial discussions. In Schleswig-Holstein's capital Kiel, such a controversy over the "Carl-Peters-Straße" arose in the summer of 2006. "The name is full of bloody history" was the headline of an article in the local paper and different political groups wanted to rename the street. With the help of the Internet we can inform ourselves about Carl Peters.

The World Wide Web

The World Wide Web offers users access not only to information from universities, libraries, government and the press but also to information from firms or private persons wishing to share their ideas and views. Keep in mind:

- Anyone can put something on the Internet – an unintelligent person or an expert.
- He can say anything he likes – be it true or false.
- He can leave it there as long as he likes – even if it is out of date.

Therefore, it is necessary to check how credible a source is. It is important not to trust everything you read on the Internet. Be careful about which information you use.

Trust

So how do you decide whom or what to trust? Ask yourself the "three Ws": who, where, when? Who has written the information (author's name, organisation, About Us section, URL)? Where is the information coming from? When was the information produced? Has it been updated?

Develop a Search Strategy

1. What exactly is the topic you're searching for? Example: Carl Peters and his actions in Africa.
2. What are the three or four keywords for your topic? Example: German colonist, imperialism in Africa, 19th century, Carl-Peters-Straße in Kiel
3. How can you combine these keywords to start a search? Despite differences among search engines, most of them have tools in common.

(A) Putting a phrase in QUOTATION MARKS tells the search engine to list only sites that contain those words in that exact order.
(B) Using "operators" like AND or OR: For example: "Carl Peters" AND "German colonialism in Africa" returns web pages containing both words.
(C) Using the operator OR returns pages containing only one key term. For example: "Carl Peters" OR "German colonism".
Start your search with a search engine like Google or Yahoo!

Minding the "Netiquette"

- Whenever you download information or texts, graphics, etc. you should be fair to those who created them.
- Do not simply copy and present information without *citing:* You have to document where the material comes from. Not doing so is an academic offence called plagiarism.

How to Cite Correctly

Web pages are cited in the following way: Author's last name, author's first name, title or site of page, name of institution or organization, date of visit to site, URL of page. Example: Boddy-Evans, Alistair, Biography: Carl Peters, About.Com, New York Times Company, 2 March 2007, http://africanhistory.about.com/cs/biography/p/bio_peters. htm?terms=carl+peters

Results

a. Explain the background of the controversy in Kiel.
b. Give an account of Carl Peters's biography.
c. State your opinion and decide whether the street in Kiel should be renamed.

M 3 Carl Peters (1856–1918)
Photograph, about 1900

reminder: sth. that makes you remember
to cite: to quote
to maintain: to keep sth. in a good condition by checking and repairing it regularly
range: limits
to evaluate: to judge how good, useful, or successful sth. is
appropriate: correct or suitable for a particular time, situation, or purpose

Internet Analysis Worksheet

1. Describing the pages	a. Who is responsible for the site? (Look up the author in Google.) b. Who is the site's audience? c. Where and when was it written and *maintained?*
2. Working with the site: Checking the depth and *range* of information	a. Is there evidence of research such as references to other sources? b. Does the author consider opposing points of view? c. Does the site comment on the topic or suggest a specific point of view? d. What do you learn about your topic from the site?
3. *Evaluating* the site	a. Is the site informative? b. Does the site deal with the material in an *appropriate* way? c. What is the site's purpose?

The First World War

28 June Assassination of Archduke Franz Ferdinand in Sarajevo
July Crisis and declarations of war

Sinking of the "Lusitani
by German submari

1910 | 1911 | 1912 | 1913 | 1914

"The governments of Europe stumbled and staggered into war".

Quotation from Lloyd George, English Prime Minister 1916

"Destroy this Mad Brute"
US poster, 1917

"News of a Soldier's Death"
Drawing by Käthe Kollwitz

"Dogfight over France"
Watercolour, 1917

German Propaganda Postcard,
1914

War Cemetry in Douaumont near Verdun
In the building the remains of 100,000 unknown soldiers are stored

1916
Battles of Verdun and the Somme;
war of attrition

1917
Unrestricted submarine warfare,
US enters the war,
Russian Revolution

1918
German spring offensive failed
Sailor's mutiny in Kiel
Proclamation of a republic in Berlin
Emperor William II abdicated
Armistice signed, end of war

1919

1920

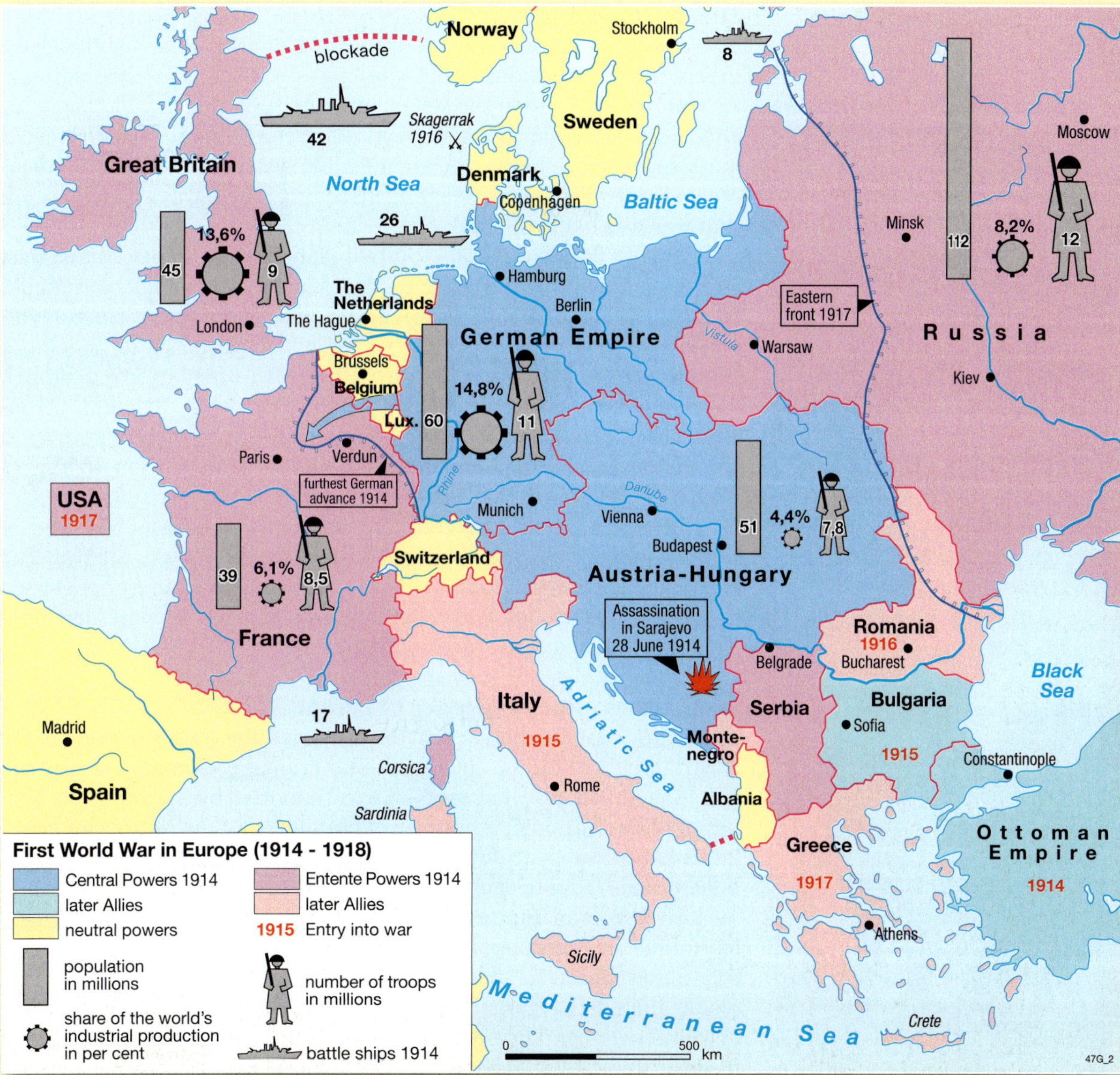

The Road to War

fortress: building or place made stronger and protected against attack
powder keg: small barrel of gunpowder
to ignite: to start to burn
carte blanche: complete freedom to act as one thinks best
to reject: unwilling to accept sth.
to affirm: to state publicly, that sth. is true
to impose upon: to force sth. on someone

The First World War – "Hell's Last Horror"

In August 1914, when war broke out in Europe, the British Foreign Minister Sir Edward Grey said: "The lamps are going out all over Europe; we shall not see them lit again in our lifetime." He was one of the few who realized that this war would be totally different from former ones and would turn out to be, in the words of the British poet, Siegfried Sassoon, "Hell's Last Horror". The Great War or World War I became a global military conflict which left millions dead and shaped the modern world. But who was to blame?

The Origins of the War

The causes of the war were complicated and historians still suggest different interpretations about who was responsible for its outbreak. As you have learned in the last chapter, imperialism also had negative effects on the relationships between European nations. Tensions rose, a massive arms race began and an inflexible system of opposing alliances created an atmosphere of fear and insecurity. There was a general sense that war was likely to break out.

Germany feared an attack on two fronts: from France in the west and from Russia in the east. To win such a war would be difficult, because it meant splitting forces in two. Therefore General von Schlieffen drew up a war plan in 1905 which proposed to knock out France first and then turn against Russia. In order to avoid French *fortresses,* German troops had to invade France via Belgium, whose neutrality was guaranteed by Britain. The Schlieffen Plan was a calculated gamble and included risks. The general thought that it would take Russia at least six weeks to mobilize its forces and prepare for war which would give Germany enough time to beat the French. The second risk was the hope that Britain would not join the war. The acceptance of the plan meant that as soon as the Russian troops started to mobilize, Germany had to attack France. This dilemma left little room for diplomacy to solve conflicts.

M 1 "The Boiling Cauldron"
English Cartoon, published in "Punch", 1908

The Balkans – the *Powder Keg* of Europe

The spark that finally *ignited* the war was the assassination of the Austrian heir to the throne, Archduke Franz Ferdinand, and his wife in Sarajevo. The Bosnian assassin was supported by a group of Serbian nationalists. Although a number of conflicts like the Moroccan crises had been solved peacefully, the Balkans in southeastern Europe were a dangerous trouble spot. The states had been part of the crumbling Turkish Ottoman Empire and powers like Austria and Russia tried to expand into the area. Russia encouraged a movement to form a Pan-Slavic union of all Slavs under the protection of Russia. This would include Bulgarians, Serbs and the majority of the population in Montenegro and Bosnia. Since many Slavs lived in Austria-Hungary its government saw Slav nationalism as a serious threat to the empire and a potential cause of war. The assassination of the Austrian Archduke set into motion a series of fast-moving events – the July Crisis – which eventually led to war.

M 2 "The arrest of the assassin"
Photograph, 1914

1914	Juni 28	Archduke Franz Ferdinand of Austria is assassinated in Sarajevo.
	July 6	Germany gives Austria *'carte blanche'*.
	July 20–23	French President Poincaré visits St. Petersburg and declares that France will be on Russia's side whatever happens.
	July 23	Austria sends an ultimatum to Belgrade (Serbia): (1) … that Serbia was to ban all societies organizing anti-Austrian propaganda (2) that Serbia was to dismiss all officials to whom Austria objected (3) that Austrian police and officials were to enter Serbia to make sure that these two demands were carried out.
	July 25	Russia promises to help Serbia. Serbia accepts (1) and (2) of the Austrian ultimatum, but refuses to accept (3) for reasons of her sovereignty. Austria mobilizes part of her troops.
	July 28	Austria declares war on Serbia.
	July 29	Russia mobilizes part of her troops (against Austria-Hungary). In an ultimatum to Belgium, Germany demands the right for her troops to march through Belgian territory in case of war against France.
	July 30	Russia mobilizes all her forces (directly against Germany).
	July 31	In two ultimata Germany demands that a) Russia demobilize and b) France declare her neutrality in case of war between Germany and Russia.
	August 1	a) Russia does not answer the German ultimatum and b) France mobilizes her forces and *rejects* the ultimatum. Germany mobilizes her forces. Germany declares war on Russia.
	August 2	Great Britain mobilizes her fleet.
	August 3	Germany declares war on France and invades Belgium.
	August 4	Great Britain declares war on Germany because she has violated Belgian neutrality.

M 3 **Chronology of Events during the July Crisis 1914**

M 4 **Article 231**

The Peace Treaty of Versailles (1919) contained a "war guilt clause":

"The Allied and Associated Governments *affirm* and Germany accepts the responsibility of Germany and her allies for causing all the loss and damage to which the Allied and Associated Governments and their nationals have been subjected as a consequence of the war *imposed upon* them by the aggression of Germany and her allies."

Adapted from: Geschichte in Quellen, 1914–1945, S. 134, translated by T.S.

Tasks

1. Try to identify which nation the figures on the cauldron represent. Describe the situation in the cartoon and express its message (M1).
2. Write down the dates of measures which encouraged war and those which were intended to prevent war (M3).
3. As you have seen, different factors helped to cause the war. Historians talk about long-term causes, which build up over a long period of time and make war a possibility, and short-term causes, triggers that actually start a conflict. Try to work out the long-term and short-term causes of the First World War. Be prepared to explain your choice.
4. Discuss this assessment and the question who was to blame for the outbreak of the war (M4).

M 1 **"Soldier's Farewell"**
Photo, 1914

M 2 **"On the Way to the Front"**
Photo, 1914

The Modern War Begins

"The Spirit of 1914"

The war had long been expected and when it finally came patriotic enthusiasm took hold and created the "Spirit of 1914". Most people in Europe seemed to be delighted at the prospect of war. Especially in major cities a general rejoicing became visible. Demonstrations in support of the war took place in the streets and, driven by the propaganda of the time and a sense of patriotism, honour and duty, millions of young men volunteered for military service and marched off to the front singing patriotic songs. The glamour of the uniform, the chance for adventure and the idea that the war would be over by Christmas of 1914 also attracted many men. Others, usually workers, were more critical, but their protests and marches against the war only had a limited effect.

The War in the West

The war began on 3 August 1914, when German troops invaded Belgium. On the one side were the Central Powers: Germany and Austria, later joined by Turkey and Bulgaria. On the other were the Allies or Entente Powers: France, Russia and Britain, later joined by Japan, Italy, China and the United States (1917).

At first it looked as though the Schlieffen Plan would work. The German armies swept into Belgium but their progress was slower than expected. They met strong Belgian resistance at Liège and then the British Expeditionary Force held them up at Mons. Even worse, the Russians mobilized more quickly than expected and on 19 August the Russian army attacked. The Germans had to send two divisions to try to stop them on the eastern front. Despite all this, by 4 September German troops had almost reached Paris. When they were just sixty kilometres from the French capital, the French and British counter-attacked along the River Marne. The Battle of the Marne was the most important battle of the war. It lasted a week and involved two million men. Finally, the Germans were forced back to the River Aisne, where they dug *trenches* and built defences. When the Allies found they could not advance any further, they also dug themselves in facing the German positions. By the end of 1914 these trenches stretched from Belgium to Switzerland. There was little change in these positions until 1918. Both sides were locked in a *stalemate*. The German defeat at the River Marne wrecked the Schlieffen Plan and General von Moltke, the German Chief of Staff, told the Kaiser "Germany has lost the war". William II did not take the consequences and von Moltke resigned.

M 3 **"German Soldier"**
Photo, 1918

Trench Warfare

The war became a static *war of attrition*. Each side tried to break through, to gain land and advantage. In 1915 and 1916 the major battles took place at Ypres, Verdun and at the River Somme. There was no breakthrough in the lines but the fighting cost the lives of millions of soldiers. Life in the trenches was hard. Soldiers had to cope with the extremes of the weather. Heavy rain could leave the trenches knee deep in water and in the hot summer there was no chance for refreshment. Soldiers ate basic food, stood guard and slept in mud. Hunger, rats, lice and the penetrating smell of corpses characterized daily life. Again and again exhausted soldiers were sent "over the top". This meant climbing out of the trenches, crossing the stretch between the lines, the so-called No Man's Land, and attacking the enemy lines. The defenders protected themselves with barbed wire and machine guns. Heavy artillery fire, gas or aeroplane attacks proved to be traumatic and horrifying. Modern warfare was much different from former wars and much more murderous. There was no decisive battle and no quick end to the fighting. Instead, there were unlimited *casualties* and endless killing of millions of soldiers.

The invention of the tank eventually gave protection for the attacking troops and offered a chance to break the standstill. But it took another two years, when finally Allied tanks broke through the defences at Amiens on 8 August 1918. The German army suffered its "black day" and was forced to retreat to the defensive positions along the "Siegfried Line".

The War in the East

In the east, the German army was initially on the defensive, but after the successful battles of Tannenberg and the Masurian Lakes, General von Hindenburg could stop the Russian advance. In 1915, German and Austrian troops moved into Russia and brought the Russian Empire to the brink of collapse. Although its soldiers fought bravely, the huge Russian army could not stop the invaders. Badly equipped and led by incompetent generals, the Russians suffered enormous losses and the fighting spirit was low. Mutinies in the army and riots and strikes at home prepared the ground for the Communist Revolution in October 1917. The new government, headed by Vladimir Lenin, made peace with Germany and had to accept the harsh terms of the Treaty of Brest-Litovsk in March 1918. Russia agreed to pay reparations for war damage, lost its western provinces and accepted an independent Ukraine. Germany could now transfer armies to the western front where they were *urgently* needed. But it was too late to change the course of events.

trenches: a long, deep hole dug in the ground
stalemate: situation in which neither side can win or make any progress
war of attrition: wearing the other side down by killing so many men that they could not be replaced
casualties: killed, wounded or missing soldiers
urgently (adv.): needs to be dealt with or happen immediately

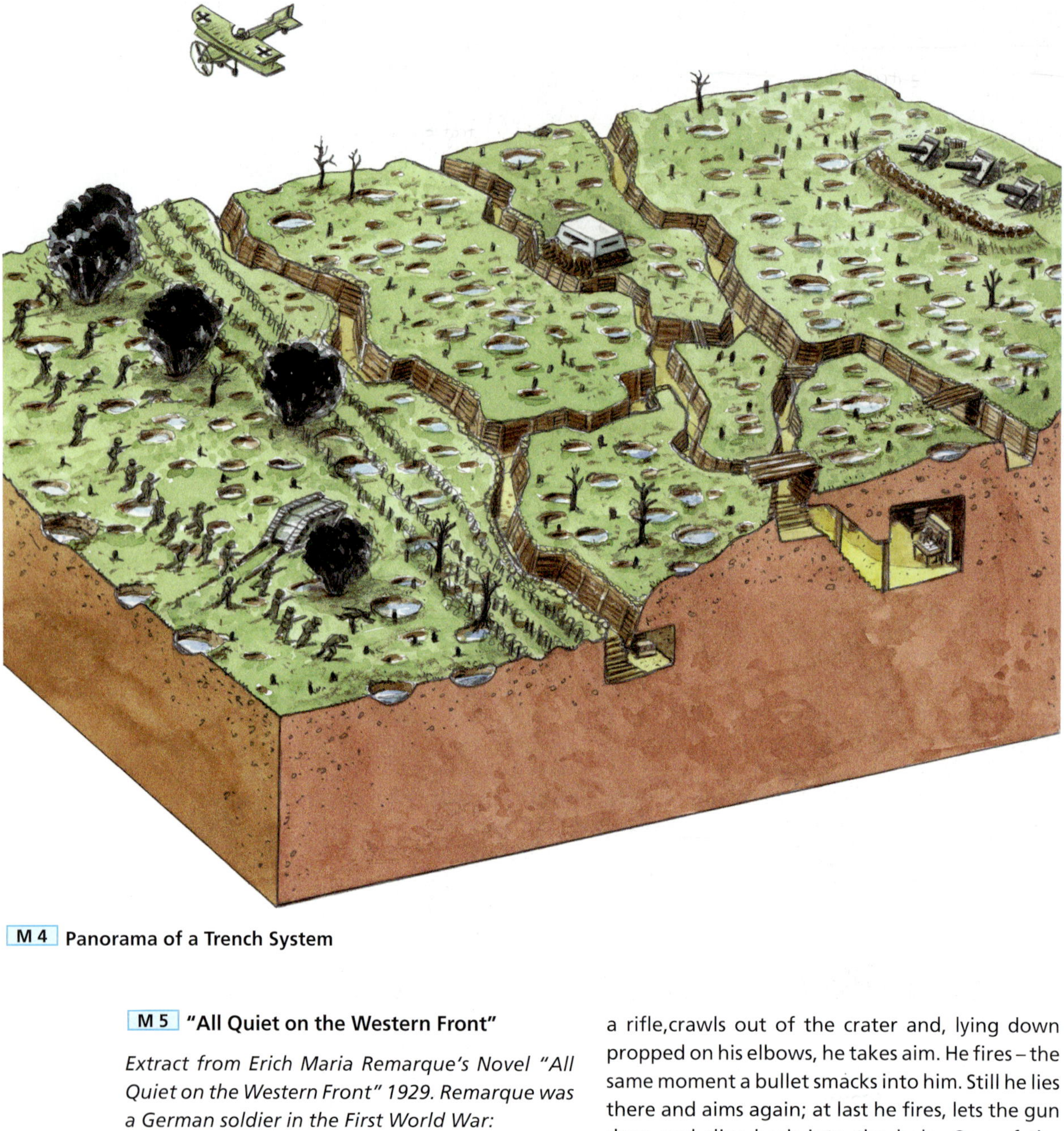

M 4 **Panorama of a Trench System**

M 5 "All Quiet on the Western Front"

Extract from Erich Maria Remarque's Novel "All Quiet on the Western Front" 1929. Remarque was a German soldier in the First World War:

"We occupy a crater and get surrounded. Two fellows with a flame-thrower move towards us. One carries the tin of petrol on his back, the other has a hose from which the fire *spouts.* If they get near enough to use it, we are done for, since we cannot retreat across the open ground.
We open fire on them, but they work nearer; things look bad. Bentinck is lying in the hole with us. When he sees that we cannot escape, he takes a rifle,crawls out of the crater and, lying down propped on his elbows, he takes aim. He fires – the same moment a bullet smacks into him. Still he lies there and aims again; at last he fires, lets the gun drop and slips back into the hole. One of the flamethrowers is hit, he falls, the hose slips, squirting fire on all sides and he burns.
Bentinck has a chest wound. After a while a *shell fragment* hits him and smashes away his chin. The same fragment carries on to tear open Leer's hip. He bleeds quickly, like an empty tube; after a couple of minutes he collapses."

Erich Maria Remarque, Im Westen nichts Neues, translated by T.S.

M 6 **Trenches at Ypres,** 1917

M 7 **Battleground at Ypres,** 1917

spout: send out a liquid in a stream with great force

shell fragment: part of a granade

Tasks

1. Describe the photos (M1, M2) and explain why many people were enthusiastic about war.
2. Explain why it was so difficult for each side to attack and capture the enemy's position (M4).
3. a) Describe the photos (M6, M7) and read the text (M5) carefully.
   b) Imagine you are a soldier in the trenches. An attack is just over and many of your comrades are hurt or dead. Write a letter to your parents about your experiences in France.

effort: a group activity organized to achieve sth.
turnip: a round root vegetable
dough: a mixture of flour, water, etc. that is made into bread

The War at Home

World War I – the First Total War

Once the war began, the countries involved mobilized their entire populations and economic resources to achieve victory on the battlefield. The term "home front", which was used for the first time during World War I, perfectly expressed this new concept of a war in which the civilian population behind the lines was directly involved in the war *effort*. Governments forced men to enlist in the army and took control of important industries. Women found themselves doing jobs that they would never have dreamed of doing before the war: They drove ambulances, took jobs in arms factories and on buses and trains. During the war women gained more confidence in their abilities and began to challenge traditional ideas about female behaviour and roles in society. In 1918 they gained the right to vote in Britain and a year later in Germany.

M 1 Women Producing Grenades
Photo, 1917

Shortages in Germany

As soon as the war started the British navy blockaded all German ports. This cut off supplies of raw materials and food to Germany. Expecting a short war, the German economy was not prepared for a long war on two fronts. Stocks of supplies were low and soon they had to be rationed. In 1917 the daily food ration sank to one-third of the peace time ration. The meat supply collapsed completely and was finally limited to nineteen grams a day. When the bread ration had to be reduced, hunger strikes broke out. The winter of 1916/17 was called the "turnip winter", because *turnip* sirup was used as a substitute for coffee and jam; turnips were added to meat and bread *dough*. Children were asked to collect all sorts of things to be recycled. The shortages in food and raw materials were to play an important part in Germany's decision to end the war in 1918.

M 2 "Selling Potatoes on the Alexanderplatz"
Photo, 1917

M 3 Economic Situation in Germany

British secret agents in Germany reported to the Foreign Office in September 1918:

"In addition to other hardships, the German public is threatened this winter an almost complete lack of lights of every description: electric light, gas, lamp oil and candles. The lack of soap and washing powder makes personal cleanliness impossible and helps the spread of disease. Medicines are difficult to *obtain* [...]. In the industrial district of Westphalia many of the women have hardly any clothing and are going about in a thin blouse and skirt, barelegged with wooden shoes."

The Foreign Office, The Economic Situation in Germany and Austria-Hungary, 1914–1918, Confidential Report no. 11025, September 1918.

M 4 A Strike in Berlin 1918

Towards the end of the war protests in Germany increased. The paper "Vorwärts" of the Social Democratic Party reported on a workers' strike meeting in Berlin on 29 January 1918:

"The meeting formulated the following demands:

- The speedy bringing about of peace [...].
- Better food supplies [...].
- The complete restoration of the right of assembly as well as the right of free discussion [...].
- An end to military control of industries.
- The immediate *release* of all persons convicted or arrested for political action.
- The right to vote in the Prussian parliament for all men and women over 20 years old."

Josh Brooman, Germany 1918–45, Longman, Harlow 1996, p. 9.

M 5 Women Urged to Quit Home for Factory

A British report from 1915:

"March 18.
The Government has issued an urgent appeal to the women of Britain to serve their country by signing on for war work. The aim is to get as many women as possible doing vital jobs so that men can be freed for fighting. Women are desperately needed in trade, industry, agriculture and above all in armaments, where thousands could be employed immediately making shells.
The Government is now setting up a Register of Women for War Service. Any woman, trained or untrained, can sign on at her local Labour Exchange. The move has been warmly welcomed by leaders of the women's movement including Emmeline Pankhurst who said: 'Women are only *anxious* to be recruited.'
During her recent visit to France she had seen many jobs previously done by men now being done by women, including bank telling and cabdriving. Another official of the Women's Social and Political Union, Mrs Dacre Fox, said: We believe women can be employed in almost any capacity of intellectual or physical work."
Mrs Fawcett, president of the National Union of Women's Suffrage Societies, said it would raise the standard for women in both work and wages. 'This war has really had a good effect in bringing men and women together and making them *rely upon mutual* friendship and cooperation.'"

Chronicle of the 20th Century, Dorling Kindersley Ltd, London 1995, p. 200.

M 6 "Home front": A Coalwoman
Photo, during First World War

to obtain: to get
release: the act of setting free
anxious: wanting sth. very much
to rely upon: to depend on sb./sth.
mutual: shared by two or more people

Tasks

1. How did the war affect the life of people at home? Analyse the sources to find answers.
2. Make a mindmap with the term "home front" as a starting point.

Towards Allied Victory – The USA Enters the War

M 1 **"Destroy this Mad Brute"**
US poster, 1917

1917 – an Epochal Year

1917 was a year of change with the tide turning against Germany. Communist Russia left the war, but the USA decided to join it against Germany. The US had never before been an ally in European wars, and had remained neutral in 1914. Many Americans were of German *descent* and approved of the policy of "isolation". When the war began, President Woodrow Wilson said, "We have to be neutral. Otherwise our mixed population would *wage* war on each other." But at the same time, many Americans, including Wilson, wanted the Allies to win the war. They preferred democratic governments to the old-fashioned rule of the monarchies in Germany and Austria. American business interests realized that big profits could be made by trading with the Allies, and when they were asked to supply raw materials, food and weapons they agreed. Payment was arranged in the form of generous loans which had to be repaid after the war. But what would happen if the Allies lost the war?

M 2 **"US Troops at War"**
US troops in France, 1917

However, the USA became the arsenal of Great Britain and France and thousands of ships sailed across the Atlantic. This did not seem neutral to the Germans and they used submarines (U-boats) to sink all merchant ships bringing supplies to Britain. The sinking of the passenger ship "Lusitania" in 1915 – over 1000 people including 128 Americans died – caused some anti-German feeling in the States.

The German emperor ordered the U-boat warfare to be cut back, but two years later the Germans returned to unrestricted submarine warfare. Believing that Britain could be brought to her knees in six months, they declared that any ship sailing to Britain would be attacked. The German U-boats were very successful, but the sinking of neutral ships bringing supplies to Britain greatly *angered* the USA. On 2 April 1917 President Wilson asked Congress to declare war on Germany. "The world must be made safe for democracy," he announced, and four days later the USA entered the war.

The American decision to *interfere* in European matters and the Communist *seizure of power* in Russia had far-reaching consequences for the history of the 20th century and thus 1917 is called an "epochal year".

descent: a person's family origins, ancestry
to wage: to begin and continue a war, a battle, etc.
to anger: to make sb. angry
to interfere: to get involved in a situation that does not concern you
seizure of power: act of suddenly taking control of a country, esp. by force

M 3 **"Irishmen Avenge the Lusitania"**
British poster, 1915

M 4 **"Hero's Death on the High Sea"**
German postcard, about 1915

M 5 The Fourteen Points

President Woodrow Wilson, 8 January 1918:

"We entered this war because violations of right had *occurred* […] and made the life of our own people impossible unless they were corrected and the world made secure once and for all against their *recurrence.* What we demand in this war, therefore, is […] that the world be made fit and safe to live in […] The program of the world's peace, therefore, is our program; and that program, the only possible program, as we see it, is this:

1. No more secret treaties
2. Free *access* to the sea at all times
3. No restrictions on trade between countries
4. Disarmament by all countries
5. Colonies to have a say in their own future
6. Russia to be free of German troops and to choose her own system of government
7. Belgium to be evacuated and *restored* as an independent country
8. Alsace-Lorraine to go back to France […]

10. The peoples of the Austro-Hungarian Empire to be free
11. *Self-determination* for the peoples in the Balkans […]

14. A League of Nations should be set up to settle *disputes.*"

Adapted from: Wolfgang J. Mommsen, Imperialismus, Hamburg 1977, S. 262 ff., translated by T. S.

occur: to happen
recurrence: when sth. that has happened before happens again
access: the right to enter a place, use sth., see someone, etc
restore: to make sth. return to its former state or condition
self-determination: the right of the people in a country to choose their own government
dispute: a serious argument or disagreement

Tasks

1. Explain the message of the three propaganda posters (M1, M3, M4).
2. Wilson's Fourteen Points have been summarized in the following principles:
   a. safeguards (against war) for the future
   b. no discrimination against any nation
   c. no occupation of foreign territory
   d. self-determination of the peoples
   e. free trade

   Discuss with your partner in which points these principles can be seen.

The End of the War

Allied Superiority

The support of the USA was a huge *boost* to Allied morale when it was badly needed. The economic and military strength of America encouraged the Allies in their hope of victory in 1918. The US navy was *crucial* in helping the British break the submarine blockade, and in the summer of 1918, the fresh and well-equipped American troops played a decisive role on land. After the German spring offensive was halted the Allies began counter-attacks in August 1918 and forced the Germans to withdraw their demoralized troops to a specially constructed area of defences known as the Hindenburg Line. By October 1918, an American army of over 1,750,000 soldiers was in France. German commander General Ludendorff finally asked his government to ask the Allies for an *armistice* before the fighting reached Germany itself.

Revolution in Germany - The End of Monarchy

In Berlin, political leaders saw that the situation was hopeless. Bulgaria and Turkey had asked for peace and the Austro-Hungarian Empire was falling apart. An epidemic of *influenza* had added to the problems of the starving German people. Over 1700 Berliners died in one day. A naval *mutiny* in Kiel and revolutionary uprisings in Munich began. On 9 November, a republic was proclaimed, marking the end of the monarchy. The situation was so grave that Emperor William abdicated and fled to exile in the Netherlands. On 11 November, the armistice was agreed and signed in a railway carriage at Compiègne. After four long years the First World War was over. It has been called the "*primordial* catastrophe of the twentieth century" and was the largest global conflict yet seen, leading to the deaths of millions and the *devastation* of parts of Western Europe. Three great empires - the Austro-Hungarian, the Russian and the Ottoman - had collapsed. New boundaries were drawn and America became a world power. Europe's dominance in the world was destroyed, and the war's political, economic, and social consequences were felt throughout the century. The "war to end all wars" caused widespread *disillusionment* and produced burdens that finally *culminated* in the even worse disaster of World War II.

boost: sth. that helps or encourages sb.
crucial: extremely important, decisive
armistice: a formal agreement during a war to stop fighting and discuss making peace
influenza: an infectious disease
mutiny: the act of refusing to obey the orders of sb. in authority, especially by soldiers or sailors
primordial: existing at the beginning of time or the beginning of the Earth
devastation: destruction
disillusionment: having no ideals and becoming disappointed or bitter because of this
to culminate: to bring to a climax

M 1 "End of the Great War"
Crowds of people celebrating the signing of the armistice by Germany on 11 November 1918 in London

M 2 The "Stab in the Back" Legend

a) Diary notes of Colonel von Thaer, who attended a meeting of the German Supreme Command on 1 October 1918:

"As we were gathered together, (General) Ludendorff stood up in our presence, his face was *pale* and filled with deep worry, but his head was still held high [...]. He said *roughly* the following: It was his duty to tell us that our military condition was terribly serious. Any day now, our Western Front could be breached. He had had to report this to His Majesty the Kaiser recently [...] that the Supreme Army Command and the German Army were at an end; the war could no longer be won, but rather an unavoidable and conclusive defeat awaited. [...] Therefore, the Supreme Army Command demanded of His Majesty the Kaiser and of the Chancellor that a proposal for the bringing about of peace be made to President Wilson of America without *delay*, for bringing about an armistice on the basis of his Fourteen Points."

The World War I Document Archive, on the server of the Brigham Young University Library

b) The German Chief of Staff Paul von Hindenburg 1918:

"In spite of the superiority of the enemy in men and material, we could have brought the struggle to a favourable conclusion if determined and *unanimous* co-operation had existed between the army and those at home. The German army was stabbed in the back. It is plain enough on whom the blame lies."

Adapted from: Michaelis, Herbert / Schraepler, Ernst, Ursachen und Folgen. Vom deutschen Zusammenbruch 1918 und 1945 bis zur staatlichen Neuordnung Deutschlands in der Gegenwart, Berlin, S. 7 f., translated by T. S.

M 3

143G Countries	Total Mobilized	Killed & Died	Wounded	Prisoners & Missing	Total Casualties	Casualties % of Mobilized
Allied Powers (Without: Japan, Romania, Belgium, Greece, Portugal)						
Russia	12,000,000	1,700,000	4,950,000	2,500,000	9,150,000	76.3
France	8,410,000	1,357,800	4,266,000	537,000	6,160,800	76.3
British Empire	8,904,467	908,371	2,090,212	191,652	3,190,235	35.8
Italy	5,615,000	650,000	947,000	600,000	2,197,00	39.1
United States	4,355,000	126,000	234,300	4,500	364,800	8.2
Serbia	707,343	126,000	133,148	152,958	331,106	46,8
Montenegro	50,000	3,000	10,000	7,000	20,000	40.0
Total	42,188,810	5,152,115	12,831,004	4,121,090	22,104,209	52.3
Central Powers						
Germany	11,000,000	1,773,700	4,216,058	1,152,800	7,142,558	64.9
Austria-Hungary	7,800,000	1,200,000	3,620,000	2,200,000	7,020,000	90.0
Turkey	2,850,000	325,000	400,000	250,000	975,000	34.2
Bulgaria	1,200,000	87,500	152,390	27,029	266,919	22.2
Total	22,850,000	3,386,200	8,388,448	3,629,829	15,404,477	67.4
Grand Total	**65,038,810**	**8,538,315**	**21,219,452**	**7,750,919**	**37,508,686**	**57.6**

German Supreme Command: a group of officers or officials who give orders
pale: having a skin colour that is very white
roughly (adv.): saying sth. without giving exact details or information
delay: a period of time sb. has to wait
unanimous: a unanimous decision, vote, agreement, etc is one in which all the people involved agree

Tasks

1. Summarize the text from Thaer in two sentences (M2a).
2. Why did the general ask for an armistice based on Wilson's Fourteen Points?
3. Comment on Hindenburg's point of view. List possible reasons why Germany lost the war (M2b).
4. Study the table on casualties in the First World War (M3). What would have been the likely outcome if all of your class had volunteered to fight in the war?
5. It was called "The Great War" and certainly there has never been anything like it in history. Take notes on aspects that made this war so extraordinary.
6. Looking back: Look at the introductory pages of this chapter again and explain the context and message of each source.

abolition of serfdom: Reforms of the 18th and 19th centuries which freed the peasants from serfdom and hereditary subservience. The reforms also ended the manorial system.

absolutism: (lat. absolutus: loose, unlimited) Form of government in which a monarch rules as sovereign with unlimited authority. The monarch is responsible only to God, derives his authority from God ("king by the grace of God") and demands complete obedience from his subjects. Absolutism was the prevailing system of government in Europe from the 16th to the 18th centuries, and is the term given to the same era ("the Age of Absolutism"). The French king Louis XIV is considered the leading example of this type of government. He centralized monarchical power by bringing the politically independent nobility under his control and rescinding the right of the estates to approve taxation. He extended his power through a standing army, a professional bureaucracy and the economic system of mercantilism.

bourgeoisie (English: middle class): A diverse concept which includes the Third Estate during the Age of Absolutism as well as middle social groups in the Age of Industrialization. The concept is further defined when speaking of "grand" or "petite bourgeois" or "educated and propertied" classes. In Marxism it is the bourgeoisie which exploits the proletariat. Today we speak of social groups, as a class society no longer exists.

capitalism: Economic system in which capital is invested in business to earn profit. Supply and demand determine the price of wares, the state does not take any role in the system. To Marxists capitalism is a system of profit-oriented property which exploits the workers and leads to their impoverishment. Productive capital is the central force which includes all means of production such as machines and factories. They belong to private persons – entrepreneurs or capitalists – who oppose the workers or proletariat. According to Marx only class warfare can end this exploitation.

Central Powers (also Dual Alliance): In World War I the allies German Empire and Austria-Hungary, later joined by the Ottoman Empire and Bulgaria.

code civil: A civil set of laws written for Napoleon (1804), based on the principles of the French Revolution (personal freedom, legal equality, separation of church and state). The code (also "Code Napoleon") had great influence on later European laws.

Committee of Public Safety, The: A governing organ of the French Convention and an instrument of terror during the Jacobin dictatorship. The committee consisted of twelve executive commissars. Its leading member was Robespierre.

Confederation of the Rhine: In 1806 sixteen imperial princes declared their withdrawal from the Holy Roman Empire and founded the Confederation of the Rhine under the protection of Napoleon. The Habsburg Franz II gave up the imperial crown of the Holy Roman Empire and became Emperor of Austria instead. After Napoleon's Russian campaign was lost, the Confederation of the Rhine quickly dissolved.

Congress of Vienna: Conference of European rulers and statesmen (1814-15) to determine the political reordering of Europe after the fall of Napoleon. Chairman was the Austrian foreign minister Prince Metternich, who directed the main negotiations. The participants of the Congress of Vienna based their decisions on the principles of legitimacy and restoration.

constitution: The political order of a state which defines the form of government, the use of power and the function of political organs. A democratic constitution is written by a constituent, or national, assembly and is ratified by the voters directly or by their elected representatives in parliament. It is based on the principles of the separation of powers and the right of the people to take part in political decisions.

constitutional monarchy: Form of government in which the monarch is bound by a constitution, which guarantees the participation of a parliament in making the laws.

entrepreneur: Someone who runs a business and is its legal representative is called an entrepreneur. This is also the case with master craftsmen, distributors and business owners in the pre-industrial age. During the Industrial Revolution entrepreneurs, as the leaders of industrial branches, became more important, because they influenced the economy and determined the fates of large parts of the population. Originally, the entrepreneur was the investor of capital ("capitalist") and thus bore the greatest risk in his business. Later capital investment and management of the company were often divided. Joint-stock companies (for example, public limited companies or corporations), in which capital is owned by stockholders, are formed, and the company is managed by employed executives.

estates: Social groups which differ from each other in origin, profession, education and rights. In the Middle Ages there were three different estates: the clergy, the nobility, and the burghers and farmers. After the French Revolution and the reforms of the 19th century the system of estates disappeared. In the 19th century workers came to be called "the fourth estate". (In GB and USA "the fourth estate" refers to the press.) A corporative state is one in which the representatives of certain estates take part in governing.

Estates-General: Assembly of the representatives of the three estates (clergy, nobility, burghers and farmers) in France with the right to approve taxation.

freedom of trade: In pre-industrial times price and production in trades were controlled by trade guilds. During the 19th century guild controls were abolished, and freedom of trade was introduced. Anyone could open a business selling any product.

German Confederation: Loose confederation of thirty-five principalities and four free cities (as well as territory ruled by three foreign states) founded at the Congress of Vienna in 1815. Its only governing organ was the Diet in Frankfurt am Main, where delegates met under the chairmanship of Austria. It was destroyed by Austro-Prussian rivalry in 1866.

German Customs Union: Association of eighteen German states founded under Prussian leadership in 1834. Eventually all German states (except Austria) joined. Its goal was to create a German economic bloc without customs barriers or duties among the member states.

human rights: Opinion rooted in the Enlightenment, in which every person has inalienable rights which the state must preserve and protect. These include equality, personal inviolability, the right to own property, freedom of opinion, freedom of religion, the right to resist oppression. These rights were first formulated in the American Declaration of Independence (1776), taken up in the French constitution of 1791 and in many constitutions since then.

imperialism: The efforts of a state to extend its authority to other countries and peoples. Power is extended through conquest or economic control due to economic superiority. During the Age of Imperialism (1880-1914) the Great Powers established colonial empires and divided the world into spheres of influence.

Industrial Revolution: Decisive economic and social change, starting with industrialization in England around 1760. By 1840 it spread to Germany and later all over the world. It required the use of machinery, which led to new industrial production processes (mass production, division of labour, factories). In its early phase it is connected with social impoverishment, at the same time class differences developed because of the social problems of workers (the Social Question).

Kulturkampf: Conflict led by Bismarck between the Prussian state and the Catholic church, 1871-78.

labour movement: The Industrial Revolution created social problems which made the workers feel a sense of community. They developed class consciousness and organized workers' political parties and trade unions to represent their interests at the end of the 19th century.

liberalism: Political movement with roots in the Enlightenment which came to prominence in the 19th century. It states the right of the individual to develop freely without state control. It demands religious freedom, freedom of opinion, guaranteed human rights and participation in political decisions. Economic liberalism demands a free market without state controls or customs barriers.

Marxism: Theory of scientific socialism founded in the 19th century by Karl Marx and Friedrich Engels. Its main tenet is "historical materialism", which calls for a socialistic society following social and economic development (class warfare, communism). Marx also criticizes capitalist means of production and their effect on society (capitalism) in "A Critique of Political Economy" (Capital, vol. 1).

National Assembly: Elected parliament of a country, especially one which writes a constitution, for example, the French National Assembly of 1789-92 or the Frankfurt National Assembly of 1848-49.

nationalism: Usually negative concept for exaggerated national feelings and attaching too much importance to one's own nation.

North German Confederation: Confederation of Prussia and all states north of the Main, created by Bismarck in 1867. The executive power lay in the Federal Council of the allied governments, whose president was the king of Prussia. Bismarck was the chancellor. Legislative power lay with the Federal Council and the Diet, which was elected directly according to universal male suffrage. This constitution was the basis of the Imperial Constitution of 1871.

parliament: A freely elected popular assembly in a democratic state. It is the supreme organ for the laws and checks the power of the executive (separation of powers).

pauperism: (lat. pauper = poor) Term formulated around 1840 for the continuing poverty of large groups of people. Because of this mass poverty people were unable to earn even a meagre living and had to depend on charity.

political parties: Organized associations of citizens with similar political ideas to influence the state. Modern political parties developed at the beginning of the 19th century as loose associations of prominent personalities. The socialist parties were formed by the labour movement as a new type of mass party, which also was found among Catholic or religious parties (such as the Centre Party). Parties received important political functions as parliamentarianism established itself securely in the 20th century.

popular sovereignty: Unlike the sovereignty of a monarch, popular sovereignty rests in the hands of the people. Therefore, the election of a government by the people is the expression of popular sovereignty. Next to the separation of powers, popular sovereignty is the hallmark of the modern democratic state. The theoretician of popular sovereignty in modern times was J.J. Rousseau, who explained it in his work, "The Social Contract".

proletariat: In ancient Rome the lowest strata of the population, without property. In the 19th century it is defined by Marxism as the class of dependent wage labourers in capitalism. According to Marx the proletarian has only his work to sell and therefore depends on the bourgeoisie which owns the means of production and exploits him. Only class warfare and the "proletarian revolution" can end this oppression.

reaction: Term for the political attempts to turn back all progressive developments begun during the French Revolution. In Germany this is especially the time from 1819-30 and 1850-58. An anti-progressive attitude which defends outdated conditions is called "reactionary".

restoration: Attempts to bring back earlier conditions. The concept refers to the era between 1815 and 1848 when statesmen tried to return to the political principles which prevailed before the French Revolution.

revolution: A violent overthrow of the political order, which leads to thorough political and social changes. It is supported by large sections of the population – unlike a coup d'état or a Putsch, in which only a new group of political leaders takes power. Typical examples are the French Revolution in 1789 and the Russian Revolution in 1917.

secularization: Making church goods worldly property. In France a far-reaching secularization occurred during the French Revolution. In Germany this occurred after 1803 and later.

separation of powers: Division of governmental power into law-giving (legislative), law-fulfilling (executive) and law-judging (judicative) branches. The principle stems from the Enlightenment and is to prevent the abuse of governmental power. Constitutional organs independent from one another, such as parliament, the government and courts, result from this principle.

social laws: In general all the laws passed to secure the social well-being of citizens. In Imperial Germany the social laws refer to the legal measures passed by Bismarck to ease problems caused by age, illness and disability.

Social Question, The: Term for the unresolved social problems of labourers following the Industrial Revolution in the 19th century. Among them were: poverty because of low wages and high unemployment, extremely long working hours, unreasonable working conditions, unfit living conditions, heavy labour for women and children. The lack of security in case of illness, disability, labour accidents or old age made the conditions even worse. Attempts to solve the Social Question came from individual factory owners, the Church, and after 1883 from the government, with its social laws. The workers themselves founded trade unions, political parties and various self-help organizations to protect their interests and further their goals.

socialism: A political movement begun in the 19th century to change society in order to achieve social equality and justice. In Marxism this is the transitional phase between capitalism and communism. After the end of the 19th century moderate and radical socialist groups tried to realize different goals from reform of the capitalist system to overthrow of the existing social order (class warfare).

Socialist Law: A law introduced by Bismarck to combat Social Democracy. It forbade all Social Democratic, socialistic or communistic organizations, assemblies and publications and threatened to ban "agitators" from a district. The goal was the destruction of Social Democratic organizations and trade unions; however, the Social Democratic Party remained in the Diet. The law proved a political failure, as Social Democracy continued to grow even after the law was revoked in 1890.

steam engine: Steam was used at the end of the 17th century to pump water out of coal mines. James Watt invented a machine for use in industry in 1769. Water and manpower were replaced by steam, making industrialization possible.

strike: A plan for a large number of labourers to refuse to work in order to get higher wages or better working conditions from their employer(s). In the 19th century industrial strikes led to the founding of trade unions; the strike became one of the most important means to emphasize union demands. In Germany prior to 1918 strikes were illegal and punished by law. Today the right to strike is recognized in many countries and has become an important part of democratic thinking.

student society (German: Burschenschaft): Student fraternity movement founded first in Jena in 1815 which quickly extended to all German universities. The movement demanded university reform as well as national unity in Germany and proclaimed its liberal goals at the Wartburg Festival in 1817. The Carlsbad Decrees in 1820 made the student societies illegal, but the movement continued in secret. After the founding of the German Empire in 1871 conservative groups had a dominant role in the movement.

terror (lat. = frighten): Violent form of political conflict to cut off all resistance by frightening people. It can be introduced by the state (state terrorism) or by extreme organizations to overthrow the political or social order. Typical examples are the Terror of the Jacobins during the French Revolution from 1793-94 or terror under the regimes of fascism, National Socialism and communism.

three-class-electoral system: Electoral system for the Prussian House of Deputies valid from 1849 to 1918. Voters in each electoral district were divided into three classes, each of which paid one-third of the taxes in the district. Each class chose electors who then voted for deputies (indirect election). The principle of the system was that those voters who paid the highest taxes should have the most prominent voice in parliamentary decision-making.

trade unions: Organizations of workers to protect their economic interests. In England workers organized at the end of the 18th century; in Germany various local unions were established after 1848. After 1890 (when the Socialist Law was revoked) the unions became large mass organizations.

War of Secession: American civil war caused by the controversy between the northern and southern states on the question of slavery. Armed conflict began in 1861 with the withdrawal (secession) of the southern states from the Union and ended in 1865 with the victory of the northern states.

women's rights movement: Organized struggle of women for political and social equality. The movement began during the French Revolution and grew during the Industrial Revolution. Its main demands aimed at attaining full political citizenship for women, as well as entrance to all professions, trades and educational institutions. In 1865 a national German women's association was founded, in 1897 an international group followed.

(to) abandon: to desert, to leave alone
(to) abdicate: to give up a position as king or queen, to give up the throne
(to) abhor: to hate sth.
(to) abolish: to officially end a law
abolition: the ending of a law, system or institution
abominable: extremely unpleasant and disgusting
(to) accept: to agree with sth.
access: the right to enter a place, use sth., see someone etc.
(to) acquire: to buy sth., to get sth.
acquisition: (here) the act of getting land and power
(to) administer: to manage and organize the affairs of a country
(to) ally (with): to join forces with
alms: charity, gifts
ambassador: an official or diplomat who represents his country in a foreign one
(to) amend: to change
(to) anger: to make sb. angry
animosity: hostility, hatred
(to) annex: to add a territory to another state
annexation: to take control, occupy
(to) annihilate: to kill sb., esp. an enemy or opponent
(to be) answerable: to be responsible for
anvil: heavy iron block on which metal is hammered into certain shapes
anxious: wanting sth. very much
apologist: a person who tries to explain and defend sth.
(to) appall: to horrify, to shock
appropriate: correct or suitable for a particular time, situation, or purpose
arbitrary: not seeming to be based on reason, system or plan and sometimes seeming unfair
ardently: intensely
armaments: weapons and military equipment
armistice: a formal agreement during a war to stop fighting and discuss making peace
armour: covering (usually metal) to protect the body from weapons
arsonist: sb. who sets things on fire
(to) assassinate: to kill (mostly for political reasons)
asserting: behaving in a confident and determined way
assessment: an opinion or judgement about sb./sth.
attributes: features
(to) audit: to listen to
Augean stables: in Greek mythology a task assigned to Hercules. King Augeas had the largest herd of cattle in Greece and kept it in stables which had never been cleaned. Hercules had to clean them in one day.
avarice: greed, extreme desire for wealth
(to) avert: to prevent

(to) backfire: to have the opposite effect
banquet: large, formal dinner
(to) become acquainted with: to get to know
(to) befit sth.: to be suitable for sth.
beloved: dear
benediction of God: blessing, approval of God
(to) bequeath (formal): to give sb. property
(to) bestow: to give
(to) bid sth. cease: to ask sth. to stop
blast furnace: a large structure like an oven in which iron ore is melted in order to take out the metal
blessing: sth. that is good or helpful
blight: plant fungus
bloodshed: people losing blood
blueprint: draft, model
(to) blur: sth. that is blurred cannot be seen clearly anymore
body: assembly, group
bone of contention: reason for a conflict
boost: sth. that helps or encourages sb.
bourgeois (adj.) / *bourgeoisie* (n.): middle class
branch: a special section or department
(to) breed (bred, bred): to mate, to couple
brisk: busy
(to) broadcast: (here) to throw by hand
burden: heavy task and responsibility

campaign: a series of attacks and battles in a war
capability: the ability or qualities necessary to do sth.
capacity: the ability to understand
cart: a vehicle pulled by a horse for carrying loads
casualties: killed, wounded or missing soldiers
(to) cavil: to complain about
chain: a series of connected metal rings
charcoal: coal made from burnt wood
(to) cite: to quote
(to) coalesce: to unite
(to) compensate: to provide sth. good in order to balance a loss
compensation: payment
(to) compose: to make up
comprehensive: broad, thorough
(to) conceive: to form an idea, plan etc. in your mind; to imagine
concise: clear and short, in a few words
conclusion: decision
(to) conduct: to organize a particular activity
(to) confiscate: to officially take away sb.'s possessions
conquest: the act of taking control of a country or a city
conscripts: men required to do military service, draftees
consent: agreement
considerable: great in importance
consideration: the act of thinking carefully about sth.
(to) consolidate: to make strong or stable
conspiracy: a group planning and acting in secret
constituent assembly: group which writes a constitution
constitution: a written set of laws governing the country
contemplation: the act of thinking deeply about sth.
contemporary: a person who lives at the time in question
contention: belief
(to) contribute: to give sth., esp. money or goods
(to) convey: to make ideas or feelings known to sb.
conviction: a strong opinion or belief
core: most important, central
coronation: ceremony in which a king or queen is crowned
corpse: dead body
cottage industry: people working at home
coup d'état: a sudden, illegal and often violent change of government
cowardice: lack of courage
credit: borrowed money
crucial: extremely important, decisive
cruel: causing suffering
(to) culminate: to bring to a climax
curiosity: strong desire to know about sth.

debt: sum of money that somebody owes
decade: period of ten years
(to) deceive oneself: to refuse to admit to yourself that sth. unpleasant is true
(to) deceive sb.: to make sb. believe sth. which is not true

(to) decipher: to succeed in finding the meaning of sth. that is hidden
decisiveness: ability to decide
delay: a period of time sb. has to wait
deliberately: willingly, according to a plan
demagogic: leading the people in a false direction; using emotion, not reason, to persuade people
demagogue: a leader who misleads the common people
(to) denounce: to criticize
dependency: area or country contolled by another
(to) deport: to send away to a foreign country by force
depravity: the state of being morally bad
descent: a person's family origins, ancestry
despotic: using great power, often in a cruel way
devastation: destruction
diligence: working hard
directing: pointing, leading
disabililty: not being able to use body or mind fully
(to) disband: (here) to send away
disillusionment: having no ideals and becoming disappointed or bitter because of this
disobedient: refusing to obey
dispute: a serious argument or disagreement
dissolution, of decomposition: falling apart, rotting
(to) distinguish: to recognize the difference between two things
donation: sth. that is given as charity
(to be) doomed: to be certain to fail
dough: a mixture of flour, water, etc. that is made into bread
draft: plan, version
dues: charges, money you owe sb.
dwelling: living

effort: a group activity organized to achieve sth.
emulation: competition
encirclement: being surrounded
encouragement: the act of giving support or hope to sb.
engineering works/factory: a factory that produces machines, etc.
ensuing: happening as the result of another event
enthusiastically (adv.): with spirit, excited by
entirely: totally, completely
entrails: the organs inside the body of a person or an animal
envoy: diplomat who represents his country, (here) at the Confederation in Frankfurt
equal: each vote counts the same
(to) escalate: to grow larger and more dangerous
ethnic: having a common cultural background (customs, language, history, etc.)
(to) evaluate: to judge how good, useful, or successful sth. is
(to) exaggerate: to overstate, overemphasize
(to) exceed: to be greater than …
executive: leading
(to) exploit: to use sth. in order to gain as much from it as possible
external apparatus: outside machinery

faithful: loyal
fallow: not used for growing crops
famine: little or no food for a long time
(to) feel obliged: to think sth. is necessary or must be done
ferocious: very aggressive and violent
fertilizer: substance added to soil to make plants grow
fine: a sum of money that must be paid as punishment
(to) flog: to punish somebody by hitting him with a whip or stick
fluttered: nervous and confused
(to) foment: to create trouble or violence
foresight: ability to see sth. clearly before it happens
formidable: sth. impressive or powerful, because it is very difficult/ complicated
fortress: building or place made stronger and protected against attack
fortune: success
fugitive: escapee, sb. who flees

geneticist: a scientist who studies genetics
genocide: the murder of a whole race or people
gentry: the high social class in the country
German Supreme Command: a group of officers or officials who give orders
(to) "germanize": to make someone more German
(to) give vent to: to express a feeling, esp. anger, strongly
glorification: extreme praise
governess: woman employed in a private home to train and teach children
(to) grasp: to understand sth. completely
groundnuts: peanuts
guardian: protecting
gulp: swallowing sth. all at once
gutter: edge of street carrying water and waste

hard coal: coal found in the ground
harmful: causing damage or injury to sb./sth.
harsh: cruel and severe
hath: has
(to) haunt: if sth. scary keeps coming to your mind
(to) have a preference: to like sth.
headache: pain in the head
heathen: not a Christian
heathen folly: the fact of doing sth. stupid because of not being a Christian
heavy harness: horses have harnesses to pull a heavy load
hegemony: being the first among countries, domination of others; dominance of one state or power over others
highwayman: a robber
(to) heighten: to increase
hence: for this reason
heraldry: the study of the coats of arms and of old families
humanity: the quality of being as kind as possible to people
(to be) humiliated: to lose pride, to seem foolish

(to) ignite: to start to burn
immaturity: the state of not being fully developed
impact: powerful effect
impetus: sth. that encourages a process to move more quickly
improvement: something made better
in face of: regarding
in flagrante delicto: while doing sth. bad
in spite of: without considering
incompatible: not acceptable or possible together
indispensable: absolutely necessary
(to) indulge: to enjoy, to give in to
infallibility: not being able to make a mistake
inferior: lower in rank, opp.: superior
(to) inflict: to make sb. suffer sth. unpleasant
influential: having influence and power
influenza: an infectious disease
inhabitants: people living in a place
inherited: passed from parent to child
innumerable: uncountable
inquiry: (BE enquiry) official process to find out sth.

insane: mentally ill
insolent: extremely rude
intelligible: clear to understand
intended: planned
interest: money you have to pay when you have borrowed money
interfere: to get involved in a situation that does not concern you
interrelated: closely connected and affecting each other
intervention: getting involved in order to help
intimation: stating sth. in an indirect way
invention: production of sth. new that has not existed before
(to) invoke: to call on, to refer to

(to) join: to unite
joint stock company: a company that is owned by all the people who have shares in it

laborious (adj.): taking a lot of time and effort
latitude: (here) liberty
legacy: a situation that exists now because of actions in the past
(to) levy: to use official authority to collect payments

(to) maintain: to keep sth. in good condition by checking and repairing it regularly
malnutrition: poor condition of health caused by lack of food
masters: leaders (ironical)
means: method
(to) mediate: to help others solve a problem
mercenary: a soldier who will fight for anybody for money
merchant clothier: a person who sells clothes or cloth
merely: only, just
meticulousness: paying attention to details
midst: middle
militia: citizen's army
(to) mobilize: to assemble troops at the start of a military action
modest: not talking much about your abilities
(to) modify: to change sth. slightly
monotonous: one-sidedly, boring
mortality: the number of deaths in a period of time
mutiny: the act of refusing to obey the orders of sb. in authority, especially by soldiers or sailors
mutual: shared by two or more people

NAACP: National Association for the Advancement of Coloured People
national assembly: group which writes a constitution
necessity: the fact that sth. must happen
nightmare: bad dream
nought: nothing

obedience: the act of doing what you are told to do
obsolete: no longer used because sth. new has been invented
obstacle: sth. that hinders you
(to) obtain: to get
occasion: a particular time when sth. happens
(to) occur: to happen
old maids: women who did not marry
oligarchy of sovereigns: a small group of rulers
on account of: because of
opportune: suitable, at the right time
option: something you can choose to have or do

pace: the speed at which sb. walks, moves, runs etc.
Palatinate: (German) Pfalz
pale: having a skin colour that is very white
pamphlet: (here) a leaflet containing a political message
(to) perish: to die
pernicious: harmful
perpetual: never-ending
(to) persecute: to treat somebody in a cruel or unfair way
persecution: extremely bad treatment of sb.
(to) persuade: to convince
petition: an official document asking for sth. to be done
pigtail: hair braided together, symbolizing authority
plant: factory
(to) plead: to ask urgently
(to) postpone: to put off
powder keg: small barrel of gunpowder
preliminary: coming before
preoccupation: thinking about sth. for a long time
presumption: overstepping proper behaviour
(to) prevail: to be accepted, esp. after a struggle
primordial: existing at the beginning of time or the beginning of the Earth
principality: a country ruled by a prince

procedure: the way sth. is done
(to) prohibit: to forbid, to ban
(to) promote: to help sth. to grow
(to) propose: to suggest
prosperity: wealth, success
providence: God's control of people's lives
punctuality: always being on time
pursuit: the act of looking for or trying to find sth.
(to) put store upon: to value

(to) quadruple: to multiply by four

(to) rage: to continue in a violent way
range: limits
(to) raze sth.: to destroy, to flatten
(to) reap: to cut and collect a crop from a field
recent: that happened or began only a short time ago
reckless: irresponsible, careless
(to) recoil: to pull back from sth.
recollection: memories
(to) reconcile: to bring into agreement
reconciliation: end to a quarrel and start of a good relationship again
record: written document
recurrence: when something that has happened before happens again
redress: payment for sth. wrong that has happened to people
reinsurance: buying insurance for an already made insurance policy
(to) release: to set free
relocation: moving to a new place
(to) rely upon: to depend on sb./sth.
reminder: sth. that makes you remember
(to) renounce: to state publicly that you no longer have a particular belief or position
reparations: payment for wartime expenses or losses (paid by the loser to the winner)
(to) repeal: if you repeal sth., it is no longer valid
(to) reply: to answer
resembling: similar to
resistance: opposition
resolutions: parliamentary decisions
(to) resolve: determine, to decide firmly
responsibility: a duty to take care of so that you may be blamed if sth. goes wrong
(to) restore: to make sth. return to its former state or condition
restraint: a rule that limits or controls what people can do
revenue: the money a government receives from taxes

ridiculous: laughable, silly
roughly: saying sth. without giving exact details or information

(to) safeguard: to protect sb. from loss
sansculottes: (French) people not wearing fashionable clothing
(to) sap one's strength: to weaken oneself
(to) saturate: to fill to the maximum capacity
scourge: a thing that causes trouble or suffering
seamless: with no spaces between one part and the next
seizure of power: act of suddenly taking control of a country, esp. by force
self-determination: the right of the people in a country to choose their own government
severity: the state of being extremely serious
share: part
shares: units of equal value sold by a company to raise money
shell fragment: part of a granade
shelling: shooting by big guns
shortcoming: a fault in a plan or system
shuttle: a wooden stick that pulls the thread from left to right
significance: the importance of sth., esp. when it has an effect on the future
Silesia: (German) Schlesien
skilful: good at doing sth.
(to) slight: to treat sb. rudely
slogan: a short phrase used by a political party
sloth: laziness
social companion: person employed to live or travel with another
sovereign: having independent power
spark: a piece flying out of a fire
spectre: ghost
sphere of interest: area a power declares interest in
(to) spout: send out a liquid in a stream with great force
spring: (here) source or origin of sth.
spur: (here) motivation
(to) squander: not using sth. in a sensible way
stagecoach: a large carriage pulled by horses for carrying people
staggering: hard to believe
stalemate: situation in which neither side can win or make any progress
(to) stall: to stop sth. from happening until a later date
standing army: army on permanent duty
status quo: things as they are at the moment
(to) stir up: to make people feel strong emotions
stock exchange: a place where shares in companies are bought and sold
striking: clear
stunning: surprising
(to) stunt: to keep sth. from growing
(to) subdue: to bring somebody under control by using force; to conquer
subject: person who was born in a country that has a king or queen
(to) submit: to give, to give in to sth.
subsidies: money the state gives people for investment
successor: person who follows another in an office
(to) succumb: to submit, to surrender
(to) sue: to make a legal claim
(to) suffer hardship: to have really bad times
suffrage: the right to vote in political elections
sullen: dark and unpleasant
(to) summon: to arrange an official meeting
superior: better, more powerful
superstition: the belief that particular events bring good or bad luck
supply: an amount of sth. that is provided or available
(to) suppose: to imagine
(to) surrender: to give up sth. when you are forced to
(to be) surrendered: (here) to be without any right or hope
(to) survive: to live on

(to) take a toll: to pay a high price
(to) take into account: to consider particular facts when making a decision
(to) tender: to offer
the latter: the last named, (here) parliamentary rule
the slain: the people who were killed
threatened: dangerous
(to) thresh: to separate grain from the rest of the plant
throng: crowd
trade union: organization of workers to represent their interests, improve working conditions, etc.
treason: the crime of trying to destroy one's country or government or helping its enemies
(to) tremble: to shake from fear or cold
trenches: a long deep hole dug in the ground
(to) trigger sth.: to make sth. happen suddenly
trust: a group of companies working together to reduce competition, control prices, etc.
turnip: a round root vegetable

ultimately: finally
unalienable: sth. that cannot be taken away from you
unanimous: a unanimous decision, vote, agreement, etc. is one in which all the people involved agree
unbearable: not acceptable
undisputed: sth. that cannot be questioned
unique: there is only one of it
unjustly: unfairly
unmerciful: not willing to forgive
unprecedented: that has never been before
upheavals: uprisings
upstate: in the northern part of a state
urgency: need to deal with quickly
urgently: that needs to be dealt with or happen immediately
usurper: a person who takes sb.'s position illegally
(to) utilize: to use
utterly: completely

vaccination: medicine that is given to immunize a person or animal
vassal: servant, sb. who depends on sb. else
(to) venerate: to have or show a lot of respect for sb.
violations: not respecting sth.
virtue: high moral standards
vital: living

wage: to begin and continue a war, a battle, etc.
war of attrition: wearing the other side down by killing so many men that they could not be replaced
war of succession: war over who will be the next king
well-secured: guaranteed
wicked: evil, bad
(to) winnow: to blow air through grain in order to remove its outer covering
witness: a person who sees sth. happen

ye breed: (that) you can produce
yoke: situation that restricts people's freedom

abdication 86, 140
abolitionists 34
absolutism see monarchy, absolute
academies 20
ADAV, Allgemeiner Deutscher Arbeiterverein (General Association of German Workers) 74–75
Africa 34, 116–122, 124–125
agriculture 11, 56–57
alliance system 110–111, 122–123
Allies, allied forces see Entente
America (see also USA) 20, 24, 26–27, 41
American Indians s. Native Americans
Anglican Church, Anglicans 18
aristocracy 8
armistice 140–141
Asia 116
Austria, Austro-Hungarian Empire 42, 51, 53, 80, 82, 86, 88, 92, 96, 99, 104, 110–111, 122, 130, 132–133, 138, 140

Baden 50, 92
balance of power 14–15, 80, 122
Balkan 110, 130
bankruptcy 38
Bastille 38, 44
Battle
- of Aboukir 48
- of Gettysburg 35
- of Jena and Auerstedt 51
- of Leipzig (Battle of the Nations) 53, 84
- of Marengo 48
- of the Marne 132–133
- of Sedan 100
- at the River Somme 133
- of Tannenberg 133
- of Trafalgar 48, 51
- of Verdun 133
- of Waterloo 53
- of Ypres 133, 135

Bavaria 50
Bebel, August 105, 108
Belgium 80
Bell, Alexander 67
Berlin 63, 86–87, 92, 110, 118, 140
Berlin Conference 118
Bill of Rights 18–19, 29, 41
Bismarck, Otto Eduard Leopold von 76, 96–102, 104–105, 110–113, 116, 120, 122
Blum, Robert 92
Bonaparte, Jérôme 51
Bonaparte, Joseph 52
Bonaparte, Napoleon see Napoleon
Bordeaux 100
Boston Massacre 26
bourgeoisie 74
Brandenburg 86
Britain see England
Bülow, Bernhard von 117, 120
Burschenschaften s. student societies

Canada 26
capitalism 74
caricatures 90–91
Carlsbad Decrees 84–85
Catherine II of Russia 21
Catholicism, Catholics 10–11, 18, 48, 76, 100, 104–105
censorship 49, 84–86
Centre Party 104
chancellor 102, 120
Charles I of England 18
Charles II of England 18
children 72–73
China 132
Churchill, Winston Leonard Spencer 71
civil rights 18, 34–35, 40, 86
Civil Rights Act 35
civil war 18, 24, 34–35, 44, 125
clergy 8, 10–11, 40, 42
Code Napoleon (Code Civil) 49, 51, 53
Colbert, Jean Baptiste 9, 12–13
colonialism, colonies 12, 25, 118, 120–122, 124–126
colonists 26, 32
Columbus, Christoph 32
communism, communists 74–75, 138
Communist League 74
Communist Revolution see October Revolution
compensation 80
concordat 48
Confederation of the Rhine 50
Congress (USA) 28–29, 33–34
Congress of Berlin 110
Congress of Vienna 80–82
conservatism, conservatives 86, 92, 96
constitution 19–20, 25, 27, 29, 38, 40, 42, 86, 88, 96, 102
Continental Congress 26
Cordeliers 44
Cromwell, Oliver 18
Customs Union (Zollverein) 82

Danton, Georges-Jacques 44
Davis, Jefferson 34
Declaration of Independence 27–28
Declaration of the Rights of Man and the Citizen 40–41
democracy 74, 80, 92
Denmark 80, 98, 106
Diderot, Denis 20
Disraeli, Benjamin 71, 101
Dohm, Hedwig 108–109
Dolchstoßlegende (myth of the stab in the back) 141
Douglass, Frederick 34
Dresden 63
Dual Alliance 110
Dutch Republic see Holland

Edict of Nantes 8, 10
Edison, Thomas Alva 67
Egypt 48
Elba 53
elections 28, 35, 86, 88, 102, 112, 136
Elizabeth I of England 24
Emancipation Proclamation 35
emigration, emigrants 24, 93
Encyclopaedia 20
Engels, Friedrich 74–75
England 12, 15, 18–19, 24–29, 34, 40, 48, 50, 52, 56, 58, 62–63, 74, 80, 82, 85–86, 98, 110–111, 116–117, 122, 130, 132, 136, 138, 140
Enlightenment 20–21, 38
Entente 132, 140
estates (see also Estates General and Third Estate) 8, 10–11
Estates General 8, 10, 38
exploitation 74

factories 12–13, 34, 60, 67, 72–73
feudalism 92
Fourteen Points Plan 141
France 8, 12–15, 18, 20, 26–27, 38, 40–43, 48–49, 80, 82, 86, 96, 106, 110–111, 122, 130, 132, 138
Frankfurt am Main 80, 88
Frankfurt Parliament 88–89, 92
Franz Ferdinand, Archduke of Austria 130–131
Frederick II of Prussia 21
Frederick William IV of Prussia 86–92, 96
French Revolution 38–51, 80
Fronde 8
frontier 31

Gagern, Heinrich von 88–89
genocide 120
gentry 18
German Confederation 80, 82, 84–85, 96–98
German Empire 100–102
Germany 14, 42, 50, 62–63, 66–67, 69, 74, 91, 106, 110–111, 116–117, 120, 131–133, 136–137–141
Girondists 44
Glorious Revolution 18
Göttingen Seven 85
Gouges, Olympe de 41
Great Britain see England
Great Fear 38
Greece 82
Gründerzeit 100
guerilla warfare 52

Habsburg 14, 51, 80
Hambach Festival 85
Hamburg 52, 63, 112
Hanover 85, 98
Hardenberg, Karl August von 51
Hargreaves, James 60
Harkort, Friedrich 62
hegemony 14, 50, 80, 96, 102
Henry IV of France 8
Henry VIII of England 18
Herero uprising 118, 120–121
Hindenburg, Paul von 133, 141
Hohenzollern 100
Holland 13–14, 19, 27, 80
Holstein 98
Holy Roman Empire 14, 51, 80
Huguenots 8, 10
human rights 88

immigrants 25
imperialism 116, 124–126, 130
independence 26–27
Indians see Native Americans
Industrial Revolution, industrialization 56–57, 59–63, 66–67, 69, 71–73, 106
industry 56, 60
- chemical industry 66–67
- electrical industry 66–67
- textile industry 73
inventions 56–57, 67, 133
Ireland 82
Italy 82, 86, 92, 104, 110–111, 132

Jacobins 44
James I of England 18–19
Japan 116, 122, 132
Jefferson, Thomas 26–28
Jews 51
John of England 18
Joseph II of Austria 21
July Crisis 130

Kant, Immanuel 21
Ketteler, Wilhelm Emmanuel Freiherr von 76
King, Martin Luther 35
Kolping, Adolph 76
Kotzebue, August von 84
Krupp 67, 69, 72, 75
Kulturkampf (struggle between church and state 1872–1878) 104–105

Lange, Helena 108
Lassalle, Ferdinand 74
legitimacy 80
Leipzig 63
Lenin (Vladimir Ilyich Ulyanov) 133
Leo XIII 104
levée en masse 44
liberalism, liberals 84–85, 86, 96, 99
Liebknecht, Wilhelm 108
light bulb 67
Lincoln, Abraham 34–35
Liselotte of the Palatinate 14
List, Friedrich 82
living conditions 72–73
Locke, John 21
Louis XIII of France 8
Louis XIV of France 8–17
Louis XVI of France 27, 38, 42–43
Louis Philippe, the Citizen King of France 82, 86
Ludendorff, Erich 140–141
Lüderitz, Adolf 120

Magna Charta Libertatum 18
Malthus, Thomas 56
Manifesto of the Communist Party 75
maps 30–31
Marat, Jean Paul 44
Marseillaise 44
Marx, Karl 74–75
Massachusetts 24
Mayflower 24–25
Mazarin, Jules Cardinal 8
mediatization 50
mercantilism 12
merchants 13
Metternich, Klemens Wenzel Fürst von 80–82, 84, 86
militarism 107
military reform 96
militia 26
Minutemen 26
Moltke, Helmuth von 133
monarchy 18, 42, 48, 140
- absolute monarchy 8, 18, 41, 85
- parliamentary monarchy 19
Montesquieu, Charles-Louis de Secondat 20–21, 28, 42
monuments 112–113
Moroccan Crises 122
Munich 140

Nama 118, 120–121
Napoleon I Bonaparte, Emperor of the French 48–53, 80, 84
Napoleon III of France 100
National Assembly 38–44, 86, 88, 91–92, 100, 108
National Guard 38
nationalism, nationalists 99–100, 104, 106, 130
Native Americans 24–26, 32–33
Nelson, Horatio 48
Netherlands 14
Nobel, Alfred 69
nobility 8, 10–11, 40, 50
North German Confederation 97–98, 102

October Revolution 133
Otto, Louise 108–109
Ottoman Empire 110, 130, 140

Paine, Thomas 26–27
paintings 16–17
Paris 38–39, 42, 44, 48, 53, 86, 96, 100, 132
Paris Commune 38
parliament 8, 18–19, 26, 28, 38, 40, 43, 77, 86, 92, 97, 99, 102
patriotic federations 44
patriotism 41, 122, 132
Peace
- of Brest-Litowsk 133
- of Campo Formio 48
- of Lunéville 48
Pennsylvania 25
Peters, Carl 126–127
Pilgrim Fathers 32
Pius IX 104
Poland 51, 80, 82, 98, 106
pollution 69
pope 48, 77, 104
population 58
Portugal 52
Prague 92
Preliminary Parliament 88
propaganda 132
Protestantism, Protestants 8, 10, 18, 24, 50, 76, 104
Prussia 21, 42, 50–51, 53, 62, 80, 82, 86, 88, 92, 96, 99–100, 102, 104, 106, 109
Prussian reforms 51
Puritanism, Puritans 18, 24–25

railway 62–64, 66, 118–120, 124
Raleigh, Sir Walter 24
Rastatt 92
reaction 92
Realpolitik 98
Reformation 84
reforms 42
Reichstag 77, 102, 104, 109
religion 18, 24
relocation 33
reparations 98, 133
republic 18, 20, 40, 110
restoration 80
reunion chambers 14
revolution 38, 40, 42, 49–50, 100, 133, 140
- Revolution of 1848 74, 86–89, 91–93, 96
Rhodes, Cecil 116–117
Rhodesia 117
Richelieu, Armand-Jean du Plessis Cardinal 8
Rights of Man and the Citizen 40–41

Robespierre, Maximilien de 44–45, 48
Rousseau, Jean-Jacques 20–21, 40, 44
Ruhr area 62–63, 65
rump parliament 92
Russia 21, 48, 50, 52–53, 80, 82, 96, 98, 110–111, 122, 130, 132–133, 140

Saint-Just, Louis Antoine de 42
Sand, Carl Ludwig 84
sansculottes 42
Sarajevo 130–131
Saxony 51, 92
Schleswig 89, 106
Schlieffen, Alfred Graf von 130, 132–133
school 49, 68, 108–109, 124
science 20
scramble for Africa 116, 122
SDAP, Sozialdemokratische Arbeiterpartei (Social Democratic Worker's Party) 75
secularisation 50
settlers see colonists
Seven Years War see war
Siegfried Line 133
Siemens 67
Silesian weavers 75
slavery, slaves 25, 34–35
social contract 40
Social Democrats see SPD
social laws 77
socialism, socialists 110
Socialist Law 77, 105
solidarity 80
Southwest Africa 118, 120–121
sovereignty 88
Spain 27, 52, 100
Spanish Netherlands see Netherlands
SPD, Sozialdemokratische Partei Deutschlands (Social Democratic Party of Germany) 75, 77, 105, 108–109, 112, 137
spinning jenny 60
St. Helena 53
Stalin (Josef Vissarionovich Dzhugashvili) 71
standing army 14, 96
statistics 71
steam engine 56, 62, 70
Stein, Heinrich Friedrich Karl vom und zum 51
Stephenson, George 62
Strasbourg 14
strike 74
Stuart 18
student societies (Burschenschaften) 84
submarines 138–140
Sudan 122
suffrage 35, 102, 108–109, 136
Sweden 80

tanks 133
taxes 8, 10–13, 18, 26, 38
telephone 67
territories 80
terror 44–45
Third Estate 8, 10–11, 38
Third Republic 100
Thirty Years War see war
three-class voting system 86, 102
Thyssen 67
Tories 18
trade 12–13, 52
trade unions 76
train see railway
Treaty
- of Frankfurt 100
- of Paris 27
- of Prague 98
- Reinsurance Treaty 111, 122
trench warfare 133–135
Triple Alliance 110
Trotha, Lothar von 120–121
trusts 67
Tuileries 42
Turkey 132

universities 20, 84–85, 108–109
unrest, uprising 8, 75, 82, 84–85, 120–121, 140
urbanization 56
USA 27–29, 31–35, 58, 92, 116, 132, 138–140

Versailles 9, 11–12, 39, 100–101
Victoria of the United Kingdom 85, 89
Vienna 80–81, 86, 92
Virginia 24
Voltaire (François Marie Arouet) 40

War(s)
- Austro-Prussian War 98
- Franco-Prussian War 98, 100
- French and Indian War 26
- German-Danish War 98
- of Independence 26, 38
- of Liberation 52–53, 84
- of the Spanish Succession 14
- Seven Years War 26
- Thirty Years War 24
- World War I 120, 124, 130–141
- World War II 140
Wartburg Festival 84
Washington, George 26–27, 29
Watt, James 62
Westphalia 51
Wichern, Johann Hinrich 76
William of Orange 18–19
William I, German Emperor 96–98, 100, 105
William II, German Emperor 102, 105, 112, 120, 122, 133, 140
Wilson, Woodrow 138–139, 141
women 25, 34–35, 41, 61, 108–109, 136–137
Women's Rights Convention 35
working class 60–61, 72–75, 107
working conditions 60–61, 72–73
world power 140
World War I see War
World Wide Web (www) 126
Württemberg 50, 92

Zetkin, Clara 108

akg-images, Berlin: Schutzumschlag, 6 o.li. + u., 7 o. + u., 14 M1, 16 M1, 20 M1, 22 u., 23 o.li., 26 M1 + M2, 34 M1, 37 (3), 39 M3–M5, 48 M1 (E. Lessing), 49 M2 (VISIOARS), 49 M3, 52 M1, 54 u., 74 M1, 75 M2, 76 M1, 78 o.li., 80 M1 + M2, 81 M3, 82 M1, 84 M1, 92 M1, 93 M3, 94 o.li. + u., 96 M1 + M2, 98 M1 + M2, 100 M2, 108 M2, 109 M3, 121 M5, 126 M2, 127 M3, 130 M2
Archiv der sozialen Demokratie der Friedrich-Ebert-Stiftung, Bonn: 54 o.lo.
Art Institut of Chicago: 72 M2

Baumgärtner, U., Puchheim: 60 M1
Bibliothèque Nationale du France, Paris: 40 M1, 41 M2
Bildarchiv Preußischer Kulturbesitz, Berlin: 11 M2, 21 M2, 36 (2), 51 M1 + M2, 78 o.re., 87 M3 + M4, 88 M1, 89 M2, 94 o.re., 104 M1 + M2, 105 M4, 106 M2 (H.-J. Bratsch), 106 M3, 110 M2, 116 M1, 119 M4 (D. Katz), 122 M1 + M2, 128 o.Mi., 128 o.re. (D. Katz), 136 M1
Bismarck Museum, Friedrichsruh/ Carstensen, Hamburg: 101 M3
Braunschweigisches Landesmuseum: 78 u.
Bridgeman Art Library, London: 12 M1, 34 M3 (Privatsammlung), 42 M1 (Giraudon), 46 M1 + M2, 86 M1 (Giraudon)
British Library, London: 18 M1 + M2
British Museum, London: 19 M3

Cabinet des Estampes, Straßburg: 106 M1
Colorado Historiacal Society, Denver: 33 M1
Corbis, Düsseldorf: 22 o. (Bettmann)
Creatic Team Friedel & Bertsch, Heilbronn: 85 M3

Deutsches Historisches Museum, Berlin: 76 M2, 139 M4
Deutsches Museum, München: 60 M2

Germanisches Nationalmuseum, Nürnberg: 84 M2

Heinemann Publishers, Oxford: 54 o.re. (R. Stewart)
Historisches Archiv Krupp, Essen: 66 M1, 67 M2, 69 M7

Karl Ernst Osthaus-Museum, Hagen: 62 M1
Keystone Pressedienst, Hamburg: 138 M2
Kinkelin, Worms: 12 M2
Köhler-Kaeß, J., Flintbeck: 126 M1

Lichtbildwerkstätte Alpenland, Wien: 53 M2

Mannesmann Demag, Duisburg: 63 M2
Mary Evans Picture Library, London: 34 M2, 61 M3, 68 M4–M6, 128 u.li.
Mauritius-images, Mittenwald: 102 M2
Musées de la Ville, Paris: 10 M1, 44 M1

Nebert, D., Schleswig: 113 M3

Österreichische Nationalbibliothek, Wien: 100 M1

Picture Alliance, Frankfurt/M.: 140 M2 (dpa/PA)

Roger Viollet, Paris: 44 M2

Shelburne Museum, VT: 23 o.re.
Staatsarchiv, Bremen: 124 M1
Staatsarchiv, Windhuk: 115 u.
Straube Verlag, Erlangen: 128 o.li., 138 M1
SV Bilderdienst, München: 108 M1, 128 u.re

Topham Picturepoint, TopFoto.co.uk, Edenbridge: 135 M6 + M7, 137 M6

ullstein bild, Berlin: 35 M4, 67 M3, 90 M1 (Archiv Gerstenberg), 92 M2 (Archiv Gerstenberg), 97 M4, 112 M2 (Kujath), 120 M2, 132 M1, 133 M3, 136 M2, 139 M5 (histopics)

Verkehrsmuseum, Nürnberg: 63 M4
© VG Bild-Kunst, Bonn 2007: 128 o.Mi.

alle übrigen Schaubilder und Karten: Westermann Kartographie/ Technisch Graphische Abteilung, Braunschweig